South Afri
As/And Inter

Cross / Cultures

Readings in the Post/Colonial Literatures in English

38

Series Editors:

| Gordon Collier (Giessen) | Hena Maes-Jelinek (Liège) | Geoffrey Davis (Aachen) |

Amsterdam - Atlanta, GA 1999

South African Theatre
As/And Intervention

—— ℘ ℜ ——

Edited by

Marcia Blumberg and Dennis Walder

∞ The paper on which this book is printed meets the requirements of "ISO 9706:1994, Information and documentation - Paper for documents - Requirements for permanence".

ISBN: 90-420-0547-5 (bound)
©Editions Rodopi B.V., Amsterdam - Atlanta, GA 1999
Printed in The Netherlands

Table of Contents

❦

Valley Song *and Beyond*

Performing Race, Gender, and Sexuality

Theatre in/and Education

Theatre Festivals

Interviews

Acknowledgements

CꙄ

We wish first of all to thank all our contributors, many of whom had to interrupt pressing engagements as theatre practitioners as well as academics in order to attend the Open University South African Theatre Conference in London from which the essays here are drawn, as well as to give interviews and revise their material for the final book.

We would also like to thank the Open University Arts Faculty Research Committee for funds to assist in setting up the conference in 1996, including airfares and accommodation for guest speakers and playwrights from South Africa. Rebecca Dawson, of the Centre of English Studies, University of London, earned our gratitude for her very willing assistance throughout.

Ruphin Coudyzer's name is well-known to anybody wishing to represent South African Theatre work by photographic illustration: he has been particularly helpful in enabling us to find appropriate slides and photos, and generous in permission.

Finally, we owe thanks to Geoffrey Davis for his commitment to the project from the start; and an enormous thank-you to Cheryl–Anne O'Toole, Literature Department Secretary at the Open University, for working well over the odds to assist us in preparing hard copy and disks.

MARCIA BLUMBERG AND DENNIS WALDER

Illustrations

CR

Cover:

William Kentridge and the Handspring Puppet Company, *Faustus in Africa* (Dawid Minnaar, Basil Jones and Lesley Fong, April 1995)

Plates following page 124:

1. Mark Fleishman and Jenny Reznek, *Medea* (Jay Pather and Bo Petersen, January 1996)
2. Andrew Buckland, *The Ugly Noo Noo* (Andrew Buckland, July 1988)
3. Athol Fugard, *Boesman and Lena* (Bill Currie and Nomhle Nkonyeni, July 1993)
4. Athol Fugard, *Valley Song* (Esmeralda Bihl and Athol Fugard, July 1995)
5. Junction Avenue Theatre Company, *Sophiatown* (Ramolao Makhene, Siphiwe Khumalo, Arthur Molepo and Patrick Shai, February 1986)
6. Junction Avenue Theatre Company, *Tooth and Nail* (Megan Kruskal and Daphne Hlomuka, July 1989)
7. Gcina Mhlophe, *Have You Seen Zandile?* (Thoko Ntshinga and Gcina Mhlophe, 1986)
8. *Madam & Eve* (cartoon, *Mail & Guardian*, June 14, 1996, page 30)
9. William Kentridge and the Handspring Puppet Company, *Faustus in Africa* (Adrian Kohler and Basil Jones, April 1995)
10. Fatima Dike, *So What's New?* (Doris Sihula, Nomsa Xaba, Motshabi Tyelele, and Petunia Maboa, 1990)
11. Gcina Mhlophe and Janet Suzman, *The Good Woman of Sharkville* (Pamela Nomvete, June 1996)

(all photos by Ruphin Coudyzer; cartoon © Harry Dugmore)

Introduction

౭ Marcia Blumberg and Dennis Walder

The project

SOUTH AFRICAN THEATRE is renowned for its combination of protest and
innovation. Works by playwrights and theatre practitioners as varied as
Athol Fugard, Gcina Mhlophe, Barney Simon, John Kani, Mbongeni Ngema,
and Fatima Dike, as well as groups such as Serpent Players, Workshop 71, and
Handspring Puppet Company, have excited audiences and critics at home and
abroad by engaging with the immediate issues of apartheid through collaborative
techniques which have crossed race and class boundaries, thereby challenging not
just the conventions of mainstream Western theatre, but also the very laws of the
country. However, now that those laws, if not also the underlying structures, have
been dismantled, and a democratically elected, multiracial state is emerging,
where is this extraordinary cultural form going? Will its historic contribution to
world theatre cease? Or how will that contribution change?

The Open University Conference "South African Theatre As/And Intervention"
(London, 30–31 August 1996) was part of a project attempting to address these
questions. Two years into the post-election period, the conference signalled an important transitional moment in the country's history, while providing a space for
new and familiar players in South African theatre studies from around the world
to respond to or anticipate the altered conditions of the country at that moment.
The broad focus of the title enabled a wide range of approach and method; and
contributions examined strategies of 'intervention' among audiences, theatres, established and fledgling writers, canonical and new texts, familiar and innovative
critical perspectives. As at other times of political and social uncertainty and transformation, there was a striking focus upon identity and the body as sites of race,
gender and class questioning.

While many South African playtexts have been published, the few books that
analyze South African theatre – such as Martin Orkin's *Drama and the South African*

State (1991) and *Theatre and Change in South Africa*, edited by Geoffrey V. Davis and Anne Fuchs (published in 1996 from essays gathered in 1992) – speak from the apartheid and interregnum periods. This book, however, arises out of the immediate post-election period, with the aim of exploring the notion that theatre continues to 'intervene' in a country that may seem to have changed irrevocably since April 1994, and yet in which the material conditions of the majority remain the same. Commenting on the long-awaited census results released on 20 October 1998, President Mandela said the statistics showed a society in which the lines between rich and poor were the historical lines of a racially divided society. The census included pertinent facts: more than a quarter of the total population of 40.5 million earn R500 (about £50) or less a month; more than ten million men and over eleven million women have received no education. It was, said Mandela, a "clarion call" to all South Africans to "re-dedicate ourselves to the historic mission of a generation charged with transforming South African society."[1]

This historic mission is shared by the contributors to our volume. One of the most striking aspects of South African cultural life in recent decades has been the extent to which one area of cultural practice – theatre – has more than any other testified to the present condition of the country, now poised between its colonial past and a newly decolonized future. It has been a testimony evident not only in the written, or printed and published, medium in which plays are commonly made available; but also, and often more effectively, in the performed or theatrical medium in which plays are first communicated. Critical attention has long focused on South African theatre as writing (insofar as interest has been shown in theatre – as opposed to novels and poetry – at all); while there has been a massive increase in the range and depth of performance arts. So the Open University Theatre Conference included the performance of a play (*Glass House* by Fatima Dike) in a newly revised and unpublished form; and performed readings from their work by playwrights Reza de Wet and Sue Pam–Grant. This was also a conscious attempt on our part to acknowledge the contribution of women to theatre in South Africa.

The interaction between text, production and audience is always a central feature of drama, although in Western cultures, in which literature has long been dominated by print, this interaction is often forgotten. In many former colonial societies, however, from Australia to Zimbabwe, the traditional, communal and ritual origins of drama are closer at hand and more familiar, and so are also drawn on, sometimes in preference to, or simply at the same time as, more recent, imported conceptions of drama. In South Africa, the hybrid or syncretic nature of

---

[1] Ryan Cresswell, "Harsh facts of a land still divided," *The Star* (October 20, 1998): 1 [Tonight].

theatre has been apparent since at least the time of Herbert Dhlomo (1903–56), the first important modern South African dramatist, and a believer in drama which addresses the present by means of the past, involving a merging of indigenous and imported approaches, to create national regeneration.[2] Whether or not this is realizable today remains an open question.

In any case, to the Conference organizers it seemed of the utmost importance to ensure that contributors from South Africa played as much of a role as contributors from abroad, if not more so, despite the setting in London; and to that end we invited playwrights, performers and producers, as well as academics, teachers and critics from within South Africa first – with the result that they predominated on the day. This was also one reason for adding to this volume interviews with South African theatre-workers from before as well as after the Conference itself (in one case, over a year later). On the other hand, a certain distance – in geographical, cultural, and/or linguistic terms – has undeniable advantages, and some of our more distant contributors (distant both literally and in terms of specialist knowledge or experience) provided very welcome new perspectives or 'interventions' within the debates – interventions which helped rescue us from the parochialism or special pleading which too often mars discussion among South Africans, at home or abroad.

This is not to claim that what follows is either objective or complete. What we provide here is a range of responses and positions, within the overall project of encouraging new thinking about the factors shaping theatre culture in a society still struggling to realize basic freedoms. New awareness does not necessarily follow from even radical change: it has to be created. In that sense, the conference itself was attempting a kind of intervention, while recognizing that we are part of an ongoing process of renewal and reconciliation: many of the contributors had been on different sides of the divide separating those for and against the cultural boycott, for example. It was taken for granted that, on the model of the negotiations which helped bring about change in the country, we should be willing to address each other as participants in dialogue and exchange, without forgetting the past, but looking to the future. These sentiments will be familiar to anyone who knows about the Truth and Reconciliation Commission, referred to in several papers and providing an important part of our context. The complex and troubling sense in which the Commission may be considered to have been a form of historic intervention within South African realities suggests one important version of the viability of 'intervention' as an instance of sociopolitical and cultural process. The term

---

[2] Martin Orkin, *Drama and the South African State* (Manchester: Manchester UP, 1991): 22–51.

itself is, of course, not transparent, and it is worth considering how it has come into play.

Intervention

The Open University Conference was based on the assumption that one useful way of organizing contributions was around the idea of 'intervention.' In its most obvious, everyday sense, to intervene means to 'step in' or interfere in any affair, so as to affect its course or issue. But what is the source of the term 'intervention' as a concept for articulating the meaning and impact of contemporary theatre? Its origin lies in the broadly left-wing, 'committed' theatre which developed in central Europe during the Twenties and Thirties, in the aftermath of the First World War and the Bolshevik Revolution, and which was crushed by the advent of Fascism. A new socialist theatre aesthetic was formulated by theatre practitioners and playwrights such as Erwin Piscator and Bertolt Brecht, which re-emerged after World War Two, influencing politically engaged theatre-work all over the world, notably in South Africa during the Seventies and later.

Of course, from its medieval, allegorical roots, European drama has had its propagandistic or polemic side, attempting to move audiences towards accepting a set of beliefs implying action. The arrival of a kind of theatre that aimed at addressing specific social problems, attempting to change public attitudes towards women, the working classes and sexuality, towards the end of the nineteenth century, with the appearance of the naturalistic drama of Ibsen, Shaw and Hauptmann, marked a crucial new stage in this development. But it was especially the arrival of a committed, anti-fascist, self-styled 'proletarian' theatre practice among the avant-garde in Germany during the Twenties, specifically the radical work of the director Erwin Piscator (1893–1968), which inaugurated a notion of 'engaged' theatre influencing all subsequent attempts to define and create a drama of intervention.

For Piscator, the role of the theatre was *"aktiv in den Gang des Zeitgeschehens einzugreifen."*[3] Like Brecht, whom he influenced, and through whom this approach to theatre developed a lot further, Piscator initiated a theatre practice aimed at altering the consciousness of the spectator through devising a new, anti-naturalist aesthetic using topical, historical and factual material, such as newspaper reports and photographs. The author was relegated to a relatively unimportant position, while a chorus, on stage or in the auditorium, spoke or sang the message to be

---

[3] "to intervene actively in contemporary events"; quoted in Arrigo Subiotto, "Epic Theatre: A Theatre for the Scientific Age," in *Brecht in Perspective*, ed. Graham Bartram & Anthony Waine (London: Longman, 1987): 32.

drawn from the sequences of sketches. The new technology of film was applied to create an effect of visual montage, of interrupted and simultaneous narratives, exemplified by the work of South Africa's Junction Avenue Theatre Company (*The Fantastical History of a Useless Man*, 1976) or the more recent Handspring Puppet Company (*Faustus in Africa*, 1995). Theatrical production was a process involving a fresh look at the means of communication, so as to expose the workings of contemporary society to the audience, thereby altering their awareness and preparing the way for change. The potential for intervention could only be created by creating an awareness of the underlying presuppositions, or ideology, which ensured the continuation of the status quo.

Piscator situated his theatre-work outside the mainstream, established theatre of the time, using both amateur and professional performers and a minimum of props, although Brecht became strongly critical of his work at the massive Berlin *Volksbühne* (People's Theatre), where his first production, *Fahnen* (1924, "Flags"), was a docu-drama by Alfons Paquet about the struggles of immigrant workers in Chicago in the 1880s. Piscator believed in moving the audience: 'epic' to him had to do with scale and a new kind of narrative technology; whereas for Brecht, coolness, detachment and the stimulation of thought were required for an 'epic' effect. The tragedy for both was that their radical, experimental theatre was rejected by their own mass movements and politicians, as well as by the authoritarian regimes that came to power during the Thirties. But their legacy survived, re-emerging for example in the Sixties workshop theatre of Joan Littlewood and John Arden in England, and John McGrath's 7:84 Company in Scotland; while in North America, the anti-Vietnam War movement fuelled the growth of radical theatre groups such as the Yippies' Guerrilla Theatre, and the Pip Simmons Group, who used the techniques of Piscator and Brecht to open out the concept of theatre so as to engage new audiences and to mobilize opinion.

Both Brecht and Piscator shared a view of the theatre as a weapon in the class struggle; and it is in these terms that much dissident or oppositional theatre in South Africa was conceived during the Seventies and Eighties, by intellectual playwrights and producers such as Maishe Maponya, Matsemela Manaka, and Robert Kavanagh – as well as, for a time, the Serpent Players group with Athol Fugard. As mediated by postwar Marxist critics such as Raymond Willams, however, a broader left-wing notion of the politics of theatre also came into play, as was evident in the responses of a growing number of scholars and academic critics such as Martin Orkin, Bhekisizwe Peterson and Ian Steadman within the country, and Marcia Blumberg, Loren Kruger and Dennis Walder outside. To some extent, oppositional, protest or resistance theatre took the place of open dissent during the darkest decades of the apartheid regime, when the liberation movements were banned and dispersed, and censorship was most severe. It may soon be forgotten that, until 1989, left-wing or Marxist publications from *The Communist Manifesto* to Frantz Fanon's *The Wretched of the Earth* were almost entirely unavailable in South Africa, much less the revisionist Marxist writings of Louis Althusser or Fredric Jameson which characterized the discourses of the Left in European or North American metropolitan circles from the late Sixties onwards.

South African oppositional or dissident theatre can be too easily dismissed, now that its role appears to have gone. But not only did such theatre provide a focus for dissent – acknowledged by the regime's many attempts to silence it, although that policy was also reversed at times to show how 'liberal' they were – it also provided the outside world with an alternative view of what was going on in the country, playing a certain if intermittent and undefinable part in the long international struggle against apartheid. From *Sizwe Bansi is Dead* to *Woza Albert!*, from *Survival* to *Sophiatown*, from *Born in the RSA* to *Have You Seen Zandile?*, the range, variety and impact of these plays has been extraordinary, considering the difficult circumstances of their production and reception. The fact that they were accompanied by many less memorable, if often more direct and banal attempts to 'intervene' should not blind us to their achievement.

Nevertheless, the question remains: in what sense and how far does the critical force of the theatre in South Africa as a mode of intervention continue? In the immediate post-election (but not, perhaps, post-colonial) moment, theatre in South Africa seemed in 1996 to be pursuing an escapist, even nostalgic route, as if relieved of what had become a historical burden. Yet, simultaneously, new voices were emerging, and a more complex politics of the theatre, involving feminist and gay initiatives, has become apparent. Important playwrights long absent from the country, such as Zakes Mda, had returned, to argue for a "theatre of development" on the model of Augusto Boal. Mda, who was unable to attend the conference, has argued against what he calls "protest theatre" on the grounds that it addressed the oppressor, not the oppressed – that plays such as Fugard's *Boesman and Lena* (1970) lacked a "spirit of defiance"; whereas the so-called "theatre of resistance," typified by Maponya's *Umongikazi/The Nurse* (1983), "crossed barriers, was seen at weddings and funerals" – although, ironically, as it became better known it "moved away from the people" and, like other radical work, ended up an item of white liberal and black middle-class consumption.[4]

---

[4] Zakes Mda, "Introduction: An Overview of Theatre in South Africa," in Zakes Mda, *Four Plays* (Florida Hills, S.A.: Vivlia, 1996): xi–xxiv.

The point is, as Piscator and Brecht long ago recognized, the value and extent of intervention depend on the immediate theatrical and cultural context, itself an aspect of historical change and process. What, then, was our immediate context?

Post-election theatre

Many practitioners and critics at the time of the conference considered South African theatre to be in the doldrums. Prior to the 1994 elections, theatre-in-education projects had assumed heightened relevance, especially through the contributions of playwrights such as Fatima Dike and Gcina Mhlophe to voter education; while the immediate post-election period offered revivals of significant anti-apartheid plays, as well as productions of drama by overseas playwrights, many of whom had previously supported the cultural boycott and had then decided to lift the ban on the production of their work. By 1998 the number of new local productions had markedly increased, as had the range of contemporary theatre on South African stages. It is worth offering a brief account.

In a 1995 survey, Mark Gevisser cited Barney Simon's argument that the "collapse of theatre is the result of a crisis in faith. [People] don't want to feel or to be challenged like they used to. And theatre has difficulty surviving in such a climate"; according to Pierre van Pletzen, "If people sense that a play is about angst and soul-searching, they'll run a mile [...] The sense that we are getting from our patrons is: 'We are free, so let's enjoy life again'."[5] Gevisser expressed disappointment in the post-election theatre scene: "Thinking back across 1994, it is hard to think of a brilliant new script that came out of this country [...] If there is a crisis in South African theatre, perhaps it lies there."[6] A temporary halt in the output of new texts was not surprising, given the monumental changes in the offing: uncertainty, and the fear of large-scale violence, exacerbated by a spate of bombings just before the election, diminished in the wake of amazement at the 'miracle' of peaceful voting and a largely trouble-free transition.

The relatively bloodless political transformation from apartheid into a new democratic system brought about jubilation and juridical reform while adding to a profound sense of cultural and national flux. Every aspect of South African life was affected, and of course theatre was no exception. But theatre for and by whom? According to what agenda? In which location and language(s)? With what audience/actor dynamic?

[5] Mark Gevisser, "South African Theatre: A Crisis in Faith," *Mail and Guardian* 10.51 (5 January 1995): 30.
[6] Gevisser, "South African Theatre: A Crisis in Faith," 33.

One obvious parameter is provided by funding. Funding for the arts has (perhaps understandably) been relegated to a less important status than that designated for health, roads, housing, and education; moreover, funding bodies have been reconstituted, while new agendas for the arts emerge. According to Temple Hauptfleisch, "The publication of the White Paper on Arts and Culture [1996] confirmed the fears of many, particularly in terms of the future role of the Performing Arts Councils, which [are] being replaced by a National Arts Council."[7] With institutional funds less freely available for theatre, attempts to explore the commercial potential of the arts have been gaining ground. Ties to the business community have developed in different directions: while more professional marketing approaches have been made in the hope of partial sponsorship or support for individual productions, corporate employers have proved a lucrative source of work for actors involved in specific projects, exploring such vital issues as sexual harassment, domestic and other violence, and HIV/AIDS awareness. Probably the most 'profitable' area concerns the enhancement of the corporate image and the promotion of new products. The proliferation of non-governmental organizations has also facilitated community arts ventures. The slow establishment of new community centres, alongside the fostering of existing venues, has added to the physical spaces and facilities where education and the arts can jointly thrive. Problems and needs differ markedly in rural areas and in the cities; although, according to Maishe Maponya in 1995, "The glaring truth is that there is still no properly built theatre structure in any black township, and community centres in rural areas are almost non-existent."[8]

It is a mistake to argue, as many have done since 1994, that the demise of apartheid created a void in obvious subject-matter for South African theatre to address, since what could be more pertinent than the material conditions for the majority of South Africans? – conditions which have remained the same or have even deteriorated, as the 1998 Census has confirmed. Athol Fugard has emphasized his relief at being released from the obligation of creating "relevant theatre"; yet he has, at other times, also acknowledged the continuing effects of oppression from the apartheid legacy, and the continuing abundance of stories and scenarios that can be represented on the stage. In an interview in September 1998, he explained the focus of his new work: "My voice has certainly become very personal,

---

[7] Temple Hauptfleisch, *Theatre and Society in South Africa: Reflections in a Fractured Mirror* (Pretoria: J.L. van Schaik, 1997): 163.

[8] Maishe Maponya, "New challenges facing theatre practitioners in the new South Africa," in *Writing South Africa: Literature, Apartheid, and Democracy, 1970–1995*, ed. Derek Attridge & Rosemary Jolly (Cambridge: Cambridge UP, 1998): 255.

and that might in fact be the tone for what remains of my work."[9] Yet the personal is both individual and interpellated within communities; moreover, it is always political in the sense that every text is also inextricably part of a context, and language is never neutral. An interventionary dynamic assumes a greater self-awareness towards involvement in any of the activities relating to theatre: production, marketing, writing, acting, and critical evaluation.

Where, then, do we stand? Without contradicting productions and readings of contemporary South African theatre which previously employed neo-Marxist and liberatory approaches, with their emphases on the race/class nexus, we see more attention at last being paid to gender, subjectivity, and the differentials of marginality. Critics such as Yvonne Banning, Marcia Blumberg, and Miki Flockemann have focused on the complexity of gender issues as they impinge upon the axes of race and class in interregnum and post-election theatre. Feminist agendas, particularly in the field of theatre, have met with a mixed reception in South Africa, notwithstanding excellent analyses in the fields of sociology, cultural and women's studies. Of course, there can be no automatic assumption that women will embrace feminist positions. A conference panel discussion chaired by the editors with the three invited playwrights revealed profound unease with the term and the perceptions embodied in feminist discourse. The playwrights offered varying assessments of their positioning.

Thus Fatima Dike considered theatre to be

> a male domain. In protest theatre women never had a voice. There was a disregard for African women. We were not part of the flood of 'verbal diarrhoea.' It didn't bother me – I didn't want to be part and parcel of that. Now since this tide has died, I feel it is my time to rise up as a woman writer and be counted.

Resisting the term 'feminist theatre,' Dike nevertheless writes from a particular understanding of the range of positions of black women. Her play *So What's New?* (1990) depicts the triad of a shebeen owner, an aspiring estate agent, and a drug dealer; as former members of a famous singing group, the Chattanooga Sisters, they counter the stereotypes of black women as domestic workers, lowly employees, or housewives. These women resolutely refuse to position themselves as victims; while they confront official structures that marginalize them as black women, they also direct energy into their personal and professional lives, and contend with obstacles within the larger social arena. Dike regards "these women as intellectuals in the university of life and survival; they know how to hassle

---

[9] Quoted in Gerrard Raymond, "A Lesson from Athol," *Stagebill: The Kennedy Center* (September 1998): 21.

around and make things happen."[10] The fourth character, a young black woman, represents youth; her involvement in the struggle emphasizes a voice that demands political awareness and the necessity for change.

For Sue Pam–Grant, the practical exigencies of gender limitations in South African theatre were the main factor:

> I am an actor. There were not enough parts for women actors. I decided to write my own work and work for other women. I went into the streets and interviewed women – that is how I collected material for *Curl Up and Dye*. Here I wanted women characters to be strong, and to have a voice. I don't only write for women, but I want women to have strong powerful roles.

Although neither Dike nor Pam–Grant would entertain the discourses of feminism *per se*, they both focused on women's positions and predicaments in South African society. By contrast, Reza de Wet, the most prolific of the three, objected to the gendered focus of the discussion:

> I never regarded myself as "a woman in South African theatre." I strive to balance the masculine and feminine in myself. I can't divide people by their genitals. I relate to the feminine way of being, which is a way of being in itself – a more intuitive way. I feel in that way I can contribute. Certain archetypes are in there, but the plays are very personal.

When asked about feminist theatre, de Wet answered the question with another: "what does that mean?" She added: "If women become politicized they lose femininity, the abysmal mystery, the allure of writing. Seductive writing is feminine – once politicized it defeats that process for me."

These strong differences in approach foreground the imperative for a gender-sensitive assessment of South African theatre. We argue that feminist concerns constitute an important social issue – evident when careful attention is paid to gendered silences and absences, or lives not explored on stage. In South Africa, politics has long been understood by many critics and practitioners in a limited or narrow sense, despite the fact that in practice its ramifications are all-pervasive – networks of power are effected by positions people occupy according to race, class, gender, cultural difference, and sexuality. Indeed, according to Ramphela Mamphele, who runs the University of Cape Town, "sexism is actually a bigger problem in Africa than racism."[11] To us, awareness is not synonymous with restriction; but de Wet found it "limiting to be described as a woman playwright dealing with and

---

[10] Personal interview, May 1991, Toronto.

[11] Suzanne Daley, "I'll have to ask my Husband," *Weekly Mail and Guardian* (16–22 October 1998): 5.

writing for women," and claimed that she had "never found discrimination against women."

While feminist discourse is being employed and countered, another previously muted set of problematics involving gay and lesbian issues has come to be more widely represented on the stage and in South African society. Rather than merely reflecting societal conditions, new plays and performance-pieces represent and at the same time construct different expressions of desire in South African society. In assessing the post-election theatre scene, Alexandra Zavis commented thus on the trajectory from the past to the present: "When apartheid finally collapsed with joyous and staggering swiftness three years ago, South African drama was set adrift [...] Writers [...] are now moving in new directions, finding new inspiration. Local theatre is experiencing a rebirth."[12] In addition to the imperative for more sensitive critical approaches to old and new material, the former rigid categorizations of generic marking may be avoided. Freeing ourselves from the expectations generated by South African theatre's strong association with eurocentric and Western forms provides the potential for new and creative combinations of artistic media. For example, music-drama has become a category offered at the National Arts Festival in Grahamstown. Physical theatre, which combines movement/dance with some verbal component, transcends the specificities of the eleven official languages, while it allows for a cross-fertilization of cultural practices.

According to South African critic Sifiso Maseko, "The word going around is that theatre is dead. What has really died, however, is protest theatre [...] The good news is that street theatre [...] revives the tradition of taking theatre to the people."[13] Street theatre can take forms other than the advertised performances of theatrical troupes. The American academic Jan Cohen–Cruz has recorded her attempts to follow up Peter Larlham's argument that "funerals of anti-apartheid activists in the townships during the 1970s and 1980s [...] were the most compelling instances of anti-apartheid street performance, as well as the least widely known."[14] On her visit to South Africa in 1997, Cohen–Cruz searched unsuccessfully for someone to record and analyze the "unwritten history of anti-apartheid street theatre." Funerals were "occasions to build energy and strengthen resolve during the period of resistance; the Truth and Reconciliation Commission

---

[12] Alexandra Zavis, "South Africa's Post Apartheid," *Electronic Associated Press* (16 August 1997).

[13] Sifiso Maseko, "Theatre to the people," *Electronic Mail and Guardian* (2 October 1997).

[14] Jan Cohen–Cruz, "Notes Toward an Unwritten History of Anti-Apartheid Street Performance," in *Radical Street Performance*. ed. Jan Cohen–Cruz (London: Routledge, 1998): 283.

hearings currently are a means of remembering the dead."[15] While offering the opportunity to mourn and bury the dead, funerals could be seen as interventionary vehicles for the performance of protest, through the celebration of lives lived in a particular sociopolitical context. In the very public light of day, these mass gatherings operated as a constant reminder of the worthiness of the cause, while providing tangible evidence of anti-apartheid resistance.

But a new sociopolitical, cultural phenomenon has emerged, with even more striking consequences. From the outset of its establishment in 1996, the TRC's restorative justice model has created disagreement about the efficacy of granting amnesty: especially to people who have committed heinous crimes and then come forward and promise to tell the truth, apparently to avoid punishment. Some feel that the commission has aborted the process of the law; many have reacted with cynicism, even derision. Yet others consider that truth and reconciliation are the most vital and urgent processes in the rebuilding of a democratic nation. Could any system satisfy the historic needs? Or fully solve the problems, or provide compensation for the horrors? Adam Small denounced the TRC as "useless – it wastes hard-earned money to listen to a bunch of crooks. Only literature can perform the miracle of reconciliation."[16] The Truth Commission's work has continued, despite the criticisms, disappointments and sense of betrayal for those whose painful remembering brought little new information, much less remorse from the perpetrators. This national drama has been performed in villages and towns throughout the country, and has reached many homes through television coverage, its proceedings disseminated to millions of spectators.

Theatrical productions (as well as other literary genres) have touched on the complex processes of reconciliation. Two examples demonstrate vastly different approaches and areas of concern. Thus, in late 1998, Fatima Dike completed the first draft of her play *R.I.dP* [sic] (Raped in Detention/Rest in Peace), written in honour of all those women raped in detention who were never able to divulge their stories to the TRC; in voicing their silences, her play explores the prevalent but not publicly acknowledged incidence of sexual assault on black women in prison, various responses to injustice, and role models for dealing with trauma. Dike integrates TRC witness narratives with characters' stories in order to focus on the plight of black women in the turbulent Nineties. Then there is the collaborative effort by artist and film-maker William Kentridge, writer Jane Taylor, and Handspring Trust puppeteers Basil Jones and Adrian Kohler, which has resulted in a

---

[15] Cohen–Cruz, "Notes Toward an Unwritten History of Anti-Apartheid Street Performance," 286.

[16] Quoted in Antjie Krog, *Country of My Skull* (Johannesburg: Random House, 1998): 18.

remarkable theatrical production positioning a literary intertext within the TRC process, by inserting Pa and Ma Ubu as protagonists: their *Ubu and the Truth Commission* (1997) is a multimedia theatrical production that acknowledges while it disrupts generic, cultural, political, artistic, and historical categories, to occupy a liminal space and time. Employing actors for the pro-apartheid Afrikaner Pa Ubu and the black Ma Ubu, and a variety of puppets as choral voice, perpetrator accomplices, and, most importantly, witnesses, this theatre may be said to intervene in the sense that it raises questions, refuses solutions, and insists on spectatorial confrontation with a disturbing range of fictional and historical events from the past and present.

Much of the new, post-election theatre is showcased at festivals – some of the dynamics of which are discussed in the penultimate section of this book. The Standard Bank National Arts Festival held annually in Grahamstown since 1974 as "a conscious effort at promoting English theatre and culture"[17] has provided a range of theatre more representative in the post-election period, now that the Festival Committee includes men and women across the previous racial divide. This has ensured a more varied programme, and the participation of some artists who in apartheid times refused to be associated with what they considered an elitist, exclusionary body. Billed as the second-largest festival in the world (after its model, the massive Edinburgh Festival), this event has by virtue of the effects of the earlier cultural boycott featured mainly indigenous theatre. Unlike its Edinburgh counterpart – which heavily emphasizes international participation – the National Arts Festival has an explicitly national agenda, and features what is new on stages throughout South Africa at the same time as it offers remountings of earlier plays, as well as some local productions of texts by 'international' playwrights.

Comparing some aspects of the 1996 main festival with that of 1997 suggests the shape of South African theatre during this period of flux. In 1996, nine Main festival productions featured four plays by North American playwrights, two productions of classics that were school set works, and a few new South African theatre pieces. Ronnie Govender's *1949* constituted a performance of storytelling from Cato Manor during that period, while *Good Woman of Sharkville*, adapted and directed by Janet Suzman with Gcina Mhlophe's textual collaboration, reworked Brecht's *Good Person of Sechuan* with a cast of black characters in a township locale. If the Govender stories afforded some insights into the Asian community, the reworked Brecht, with its happily singing "Sharkville" inhabitants, realized the township situation in a strangely un-Brechtian way. Pieter–Dirk Uys filled the

---

[17] Hauptfleisch, *Theatre and Society in South Africa*, 124:

largest Festival theatre with a new satire, *Truth Omissions*. His usual brilliantly conceived characters (such as Evita Bezuidenhout) and his performances of various political figures, updated to include current events, drew laughter from capacity audiences. Andrew Buckland's *Human Race*, a mime-play in which he appeared with a group of actors, demonstrated his creativity and the potential of the expanding genre of physical theatre; while Deon Opperman's epic five-hour Afrikaans saga, *Donkerland*, historicized the Afrikaners' plight by focusing on a single family and succeeding generations over the past 150 years. Opperman's use of multiple role-playing created resonances between personal events in different historical periods to evoke a complex network of representations: of the independent trekker, the Boer War underdog, the apartheid aggressor, and the dispossessed, uncertain Afrikaner.

The 1997 Festival reflected a more varied, mostly indigenous programme of plays: dealing with reconciliation (*The Dead Wait*, *Ubu and the Truth Commission*), African rituals (*iMumboJumbo*), boys' private schooling (*Old Boys*), black women prisoners (*The Game*), a black singing group (*Homegirls*), comedy/physical theatre (*I Do (times 22)*), and a stylized period piece by Yukio Mishima (*Madame de Sade*). Deon Opperman's *Die Skandaal* ("The Scandal"), which combined aspects of *School for Scandal* and *The Country Wife* in a contemporary South African setting, drew full houses, non-stop laughter, and disapproval from those who felt that his efforts were wasted on a "silly play" instead of another Afrikaner saga. But, as with Anthony Akerman's *Old Boys*, *Ubu and the Truth Commission*, and Greig Coetzee's Fringe show, *White Men With Weapons*, Opperman's play explored an important new theme: the crisis in masculinity. When the superiority associated with whiteness and Afrikanerdom, the previous 'givens' of power networks, are challenged, we can talk of a dynamic of intervention. Moreover, the flowering of gay literature highlights the instability of gender role perceptions in this period.

At the same time, figures released by the Festival Office reflect a disturbing, if easily explicable, trend. Ticket sales have steadily decreased – on the Main Festival from 1996 (64,508) and 1997 (53,685) to 1998 (47,277); and on the Fringe from 1996 (120,253) and 1997 (105,522) to 1998 (87,096). While factors such as the fall in the value of the rand, competing sports events, and film and theatre festivals such as those in Oudtshoorn, Johannesburg, Pretoria, Durban and Hermanus, exacerbate the effect of high prices, the question remains, as we write, whether events such as the bumper two-week 25th-anniversary festival planned for 1999 will reverse the trend. The figures tell only part of the story, since certain high-profile artists or events are booked out, while others, especially Fringe events, struggle to find audiences even if they receive good reviews. On the other hand, the fledgling Klein Karoo Nasionale Kunstefees ("Little Karoo National Arts Festival") has since its inception in 1995 gone from strength to strength, with total numbers of productions in the Main and Fringe sections increasing steadily: 1995 (97); 1996 (145); 1997 (262). Does this contrast in figures mean that the festival of Afrikaans theatre draws an increasing number of Afrikaner spectators from all over the country in a bid to support 'their' festival as they try to reverse the erosion of Afrikaans influence in government, media, and commercial situations in favour of English – in fact, the only one of the official languages that is widely used? The 1998 figures recorded a further increase in ticket sales, and the new Afrikaans festival has gained a significant space in the South African theatre circuit.

Many productions have also made their mark internationally. Athol Fugard's *Valley Song* (1995) was acclaimed in South Africa and received mostly favourable reviews in productions in London, New York, Toronto, and Sydney. His 1997 autobiographical play, *The Captain's Tiger*, has received mixed reviews to date from South African critics; its run in the United States began in 1998 with a South African cast and has continued with Fugard and two American actors. The musical *Kat and the Kings* (Peterson and Kramer) played on the 1996 National Arts Festival Fringe to full houses, followed by an invitation to London which resulted in an expanded version with a new female character and more lavish theatricality. After two sold-out runs at the Tricycle Theatre in London, it transferred for a six-month run on the West End, prior to a world tour. David Kramer and Taliep Peterson wrote *Kat*, like its predecessor *District Six* (1987), to recover the cultural history of the Cape Coloureds, whose removal from District Six and dispersal by apartheid laws to various parts of Cape Town meant the destruction of a community. Temple Hauptfleisch expresses incredulity at the "box-office success of unusual proportions [...] despite [...] a rather mediocre production of a very flawed text and dubious premise,"[18] but *District Six* at least provided the opportunity for spectators who had lived in the locale before it was razed to the ground to meet each other. The repetition of these spontaneous meetings has meant the informal reunion of many members of the community after decades of lost or disrupted connections – enacting a local intervention absent from overseas productions. An international audience will read these productions quite differently. While most British reviewers of *Kat and the Kings* lauded the infectious energy of the cast and the 'feel-good' quality of the event, many have also pointed to a somewhat rose-tinted nostalgia for long-departed times, questioning the use of cheerfully singing and dancing people to represent an era when oppression was also widespread. The sexist, racist

---

[18] Hauptfleisch, *Theatre and Society in South Africa*, 67.

milieu of the Fifties is exposed as a given, but never countered, except perhaps in the final scene, when some of the characters find life in South Africa intolerable and emigrate to Canada.

A one-man tour-de-force about army life, Greig Coetzee's *White Men With Weapons* not only achieved sell-out success at the 1996 and 1997 National Arts festivals but also played to acclaim at the "Woza Afrika: After Apartheid" festival at Lincoln Center, New York, in the summer of 1997. *Ubu and the Truth Commission* premiered in Germany, toured through Europe, and played in New York, Washington, and Los Angeles in September 1998. Another 1997 Fringe sell-out production, *Silk Ties,* was invited to a festival in Toronto, where Gina Shmukler employed singing, mime, words, accents, physical gesture and dynamic energy-levels to engage the spectators in a scary and poignant story confronting the effects of crime through the complex relationship between a black domestic worker and her beloved white charge. Andrew Buckland has been acclaimed for his solo mime/physical theatre performances at many recent Edinburgh Fringe Festivals. His specifically South African shows, such as *The Ugly Noo Noo*, have been followed in the post-election period by performance pieces based on more general, global concerns – such as food (*Feedback*) and water (*The Water Juggler*, retitled for its February 1999 Market Theatre run *The Well Being*).

Visits by these South Africans and others to international venues have set in motion a new, post-cultural-boycott, two-way process. South African theatre is seen on international stages as an opportunity to have 'outsider' input. The reception of a theatre event by a non-South African audience aids the playwright and the director in understanding what 'translates' successfully. South African artists also see new plays and productions abroad, meet other actors, directors and playwrights, and so are enabled to expand their horizons before returning to their homeland, where they may share their increased expertise. But to what end?

In post-election South Africa, the sharing of skills and the harnessing of new talent point towards one very significant area for the continuation of theatre-making. The establishment of theatre laboratories and specific theatre training facilities in the townships has made a significant, interventionary impact. For example: the Market Theatre Laboratory has workshopped vibrant fringe theatre pieces such as *Bunju* (1996) and *Gomorrah* (1997), with young actors constructing narratives based on their own experiences. A new initiative is the Barney Simon Young Directors' festival, spanning two months of new plays for which, in 1998 at least, audiences arrived in good numbers.[19] The main Market's winter 1998 sea-

---

[19] Matthew Krouse, "Bashing it out at the Market," *Weekly Mail and Guardian* (October 9–15, 1998): 14.

son of award-winning new plays from abroad (such as Patrick Marber's *Closer* and Paula Vogel's *How I Learned to Drive*) reportedly drew substantial, new, young audiences. Late 1998 saw the opening of the Cape Town Theatre Laboratory, run by Royston Stoffels and Warrick Grier, modeled on the successful Market Laboratory. Veteran Market theatre practitioners John Kani and Vanessa Cooke provided initial guidance. Another venture that has grown enormously is the Studio project run by Janet Buckland, who has auditioned groups from Grahamstown and elsewhere in the Eastern Cape; once she has chosen a number of productions she continues to facilitate their work and follow their development. The New Africa Theatre Association, founded by the late Mavis Taylor in Cape Town, each year offers courses in theatre practice and history for twenty school-leavers from the age of eighteen. In 1998 Fatima Dike was appointed their creative writer, a task including work on a play with the aim of performance at community venues.

This evidence of the multifaceted nature of post-election South African theatre provides a potent corrective to earlier expressions of gloom and despair. Diverse sites for the operation of an interventionary dynamic by practitioners and critics are becoming available to ensure an ongoing engagement with historical process and cultural change.

New freedoms, new theatres

The idea of location has become increasingly important in discourses concerning colonial and post-colonial cultural activity. Our conference was held in London: partly because of support and a site offered to the Open University's Post-Colonial Literatures Research Group by London University's Centre for English Studies; but mainly because we considered London a convenient location for participants from both within and outside South Africa. The declining fortunes of the rand and local institutional problems have made it difficult for South African theatre-people, critics and practitioners, to travel. But we assumed that no conference on South African theatre today would be worthwhile without a strong South African presence; and, in particular, we felt that the considerable expense of bringing playwrights from South Africa was a vital element in ensuring the credibility of any project aiming to register the realities of theatre in the post-boycott era, while testing the "As/And" potential of the idea of "Intervention." In choosing the conference rubric, we deliberately constructed the opportunity for a wide range of possible responses to the idea, which materialized in a variety of approaches and thematic concerns. These, perhaps inevitably, proved the continuing validity of a broadly 'interventionist' conception of theatre in South Africa.

The interplay of national and international reactions to, and understandings of, the situation and force of South African theatre today was a notable feature of proceedings: which made the appearance, for example, of so many papers on Athol Fugard's work, early and more recent, a surprising testimony to the lasting and widespread effect of this playwright – whether viewed critically or sympathetically, in terms of production, text, or reception. But, as this suggests, our agenda was to a large degree determined by our contributors; and the section headings represent no more than our attempt to indicate what emerged as their main foci of interest. The final section consists of four interviews with practitioners of South African theatre to highlight perspectives of a more practical, non-academic nature. These dialogues with playwrights and directors, some of whom were able to participate in the conference, offer, in and of themselves, vastly differing interpretations of what theatre means and their particular roles within the South African theatre scene.

Asking Ian Steadman to provide the "Keynote Address" was, of course, not a chance matter. At the time Dean of Arts and Professor of Drama at the University of the Witwatersrand, and one of the most experienced and informed commentators upon indigenous drama from within the country, Steadman has shown a critical self-awareness which we thought would strike the right note from the start. Long connection with the US academy means that he has listened attentively to the influential Black American critique of literary and cultural formations there – influential also in South Africa, upon the Black Consciousness Movement of the Seventies and Eighties, as upon the many playwrights, poets and self-styled cultural workers who were caught up in its oppositional stance.

Steadman's account of 'race' and 'nation' as terms frequently (and often unthinkingly) deployed in the discussion of theatre aims to encourage continued critical vigilance towards the conceptual language characteristic of approaches to African or black theatre. As he says,

> To insist on a rejection of Western aesthetics and influences in the name of an imagined African or black aesthetic [...] is to forget the fundamental point of the intertextuality of theatre in any society [...] We understand Soyinka differently by knowing Euripides, just as we understand Euripides differently by knowing Soyinka.

This is not to deny the "salience of race" (or class); rather, it is to try and intervene in critical debate in order to defamiliarize cultural texts as one historicizes them. If, as Steadman argues, the war against racism and nationalism of the last five decades in South Africa has been won (or, at least, "the major battle"), we must not then abandon our critical vigilance, or "we lose the war against fundamentalism, against essentialism, and [therefore once again] against nationalism and racism."

Interventionist criticism and scholarship, in other words, are as necessary as ever; what this involves now is a scrutiny of our own, revisionist critiques of recent years – whether we are performers, writers, directors, critics or academics, or some combination of these roles.

In the first section, "Physical Theatre," articles address a significant and newly developing form in South African theatre that transcends, or at least bypasses, language. David Alcock's call to "define a new performance aesthetic" that neither limits nor contains is amplified by an analysis of a number of individuals and companies committed to work marked by innovative generic crossings and rich possibilites for audience-accessibility in the South African multilingual context. He views physical theatre as an interventionary vehicle, a way of questioning and challenging accepted social and political structures, thereby inflecting Banning's opening cautionary observation that an innovative form may not "escape the old binocular vision of cultural difference." For Yvonne Banning, responses to Jazzart's *Medea* (1994) reveal how one production may inadvertently perpetuate gendered and ethnic stereotypes if its foregrounding of formal innovation leaves troubling cultural and ideological issues unattended. Yet, by positioning the arguments of local critics, Banning clarifies the interventionary potential of reception.

In "Early Fugard," Errol Durbach and Robert Leyshon review, from specifically literary and directorial perspectives, plays by Athol Fugard first performed in the late Sixties and mid-Seventies. Durbach espouses a liberal-humanist reading of *Boesman and Lena*, arguing that the exposure of apartheid injustice is not synonymous with an acceptance of the status quo. While his declaration that "any ideological reading of the text will necessarily delimit its complexity and push it towards either/or formulations of propaganda" demonstrates a certain antagonism towards what he classifies as liberal–left or neo-Marxist readings, this position is strongly countered in articles by Colleran and Walder, who demand that any reading acknowledges its political implications at the same time as it analyzes aesthetic and production issues. According to Leyshon, to direct "*is* to intervene," as his production of *The Island* in Barbados in 1994 revealed to him, " a metropolitan European" who had much to learn from his actors and his audiences about cultural collision and the immediacies of history.

"*Valley Song* and Beyond" focuses on Athol Fugard's first post-election play. Four different approaches to the play mark the degree of continuing interest in Fugard's theatre, while showing the possibilities for critical interaction when a single play receives the attention afforded by these analyses. Kristina Stanley's paper argues for an interventionary theatre in South Africa to fulfil the role of reconciliation. Reading *with* Fugard, Stanley deems his text powerful in its construction of a young coloured woman, Veronica, as a subversive force intervening in the discourse of two older men. She resists her grandfather's assumption that she would follow in the footsteps of her grandmother, a gendered, racialized subjugation that Veronica refuses to perpetuate; she also challenges the white Author's injunction to curtail her grandiose dreams and his imposition of "practical realities" by her decision to leave the Valley and make a new life. For Toby Silverman Zinman, *Valley Song* raises aspects of home, which Veronica evokes in "offensively simple" songs; her "conspicuous lack of talent and poetry posits failure," thereby rendering problematic the construction of Veronica as a metaphor for the new country. Citing the powerful tension of otherness and ambiguity enacted in Fugard's early plays such as *The Blood Knot*, Zinman finds the "arrival of unearned hope" in *Valley Song* "preachy and saccharine."

Dennis Walder's article centres on questions: those that he asks of himself as a critic, and other questions about the role of theatre – in this instance, *Valley Song*. His most significant question marks a deep analysis of the political effects of language and texts in the context of past and present, notwithstanding authorial sincerity or intentions: "how far is the space Fugard creates for the voices of others an illusion, and to that degree an attempt (unconscious of course) to maintain white hegemony?" Walder considers *Valley Song* in terms of the continuum of voice: instead of Fugard breaking the silence or speaking for others as in earlier plays, here he *provides space* for his character, Veronica, to speak for herself – a differently situated voice from that of Gcina Mhlophe's character, Zandile. Jeanne Colleran's comparison of *Valley Song* with Jon Robin Baitz's *A Fair Country* juxtaposes contemporary plays set in South Africa, written by a local and an American playwright. Analyzing these domestic dramas of cultural and generational struggle infused with politics, she employs intercultural criteria to "investigate how the depiction of the place and history of South Africa grounds a larger discussion of the idea of liberalism," which also "forces a re-evaluation of plays termed postcolonial." *A Fair Country* "mourns the loss of liberalism," while *Valley Song* "reinscribes liberalism" by eliding the historical and political ramifications of issues that the election has not rectified: poverty, dispossession, and loss.

"Performing Race, Gender, and Sexuality" harks back to Ian Steadman's insistence upon the need to view essentialist structures critically and historically, as Anne Fuchs discusses notions of fragmentation and syncretism in the work of one of South Africa's best-known and most successful workshop theatre groups, The Junction Avenue Theatre Company. Viewing their work in terms both of "the body politic and the 'speaking body' in performance," Fuchs takes a detailed look at their productions from *The Fantastical History of a Useless Man* (1976) onwards, suggesting an increasing "displacement" of the white male dominant figure as their work proceeded towards the final appearance of the "body of change" in the country – a change signalled by a crisis among the devisors themselves, as they return, in the Nineties, to their earlier successes, *Sophiatown* and *Marabi*, while one of their most talented members, William Kentridge, joins forces with the Handpsring Puppeteers to find a new way of operating in the "post-apartheid space."

Fuchs questions the gender stereotyping of Junction Avenue, while admiring their syncretic use of storytelling forms. According to Marcia Blumberg, it is precisely in this "performative form" – individual and sometimes collective – that Gcina Mhlophe and the women from her story-telling group, Zanendaba, "offer a recuperative practice directed at oral history and South African culture," thereby providing empowerment for "the en-gendering of voice in South Africa." Citing Miki Flockemann's admiration for Mhlophe's *Have You Seen Zandile?* as a sort of "counter-discourse" to "protest theatre," Blumberg also finds its characteristic dynamic countering Fugard's *The Road to Mecca* (1985) and *Playland* (1992), which, she argues, depict attitudes and mind-sets "reminiscent of the Sixties." Mhlophe's work, however, offers a positioning of race, class and gender attitudes metonymic of new possibilities, new dreams, as the oppressive structures of the past and their accompanying silences break down.

One example, from present and increasingly visible theatrical activity, of the new possibilities signalled by South African theatre is evident in the growing body of gay and lesbian writing and performance. As Michael Arthur shows, in a detailed account (based on interviews) of the recent, innovative work of Peter Hayes, Pogiso Mogwera and Jay Pather, 'intervention' in attitudes towards homosexuality in drama classrooms and arts laboratories as well as in the theatre may be stronger on mission than on achievement. For many others involved even peripherally with theatre in today's South Africa, day-to-day economic realities loom very large and determine what can be done; nevertheless, this example of gay theatre manages to occupy a space between the promises of the new society and its remarkably open constitution on the one hand, and the realities of the present on the other. As such, it must not be ignored, or marginalized yet again.

"Theatre in/and Education" offers different approaches to this vital but usually ignored component of South African theatre. Michael Carklin explores possibilities for transforming the classroom from "a sinister place" synonymous with danger and, for the majority of scholars, an inferior learning experience. He envisages a new education system in which access to the information highway opens up international communication, while the new constitution guarantees an openness towards previously taboo topics. Carklin considers theatrical intervention an invaluable aspect of a new curriculum – both "learning about drama and theatre" and, even more necessary, "learning *through* drama and theatre." As an example, he examines the complex four-step project initiated by DramAidE in the Eastern Cape. Hazel Barnes's account of her production of *Desire*, a play by the anthropologist David Lan about reconciliation after the Zimbabwean independence struggle, demonstrates the complex interaction of students and spectators in KwaZulu–Natal confronted with sensitive issues of violence, religion and gender in the immediately post-election period.

In contrast to Carklin's account of a programme for AIDS education with an informed team of practitioners, Bernth Lindfors's exposé of South African theatre practitioner and self-styled "Broadway Star" Mbongeni Ngema's lack of consultation and gross negligence during the *Sarafina 2* fiasco demonstrates the failure of theatre as an interventionary, educational vehicle. Ngema's handling of the 1995 sequel to *Sarafina!*, which was meant to replace the liberation struggle with the struggle against AIDS, neither appealed as a theatre production nor fulfilled the role promised by its rationale.

The potential of theatre in the public realm has been better realized by the growth of a festival culture within South Africa. It is now possible for young practitioners to spend the whole year moving from one festival to another – many of them extremely small-scale but grassroots activities. As Annette Combrinck suggests in the last subsection before the Interviews, "Theatre Festivals," the two largest festivals – the oldest, at Grahamstown, and its more recent competitor, at Oudshoorn – are contributing to a resurgence in theatrical activity which, to many contributors and commentators at least, represents an "interventionary structure" in the making. On the other hand, as Eckhard Breitinger points out after a close look at the rewriting of classic European plays by local playwrights for festival production, despite the interest and power of the results (especially in Kentridge and Handspring's *Faust* and *Woyzeck*), adaptations such as Suzman's and Mhlophe's *Good Woman of Sharkville* also highlight the limitations of looking abroad. The hybrid or syncretic venture does not in itself promise successful intervention.

Nevertheless, in conclusion, what this collection proposes is multiple possibilities for interventionist theatre, broadly defined, within the transitional state; leading to engagement, empowerment, and a re-siting of marginalized identities.

———— ℘ ℭ ————

Keynote Address ℭ

"When you see an African..."
Race, Nationalism and Theatre Reconsidered

℘ Ian Steadman

what does Africa mean to the world? When you see an African what does it mean to a white man?[1]

But black philosophy must be rejected, for its defense depends on the essentially racist presuppositions of the white philosophy whose antithesis it is. Ethnocentrism – which is an unimaginative attitude to one's own culture – is in danger of falling into racism, which is an absurd attitude to the color of someone else's skin.[2]

RACE AND NATION are seductive concepts which have been frequently harnessed in South African scholarship. Thinking about cultural expression in terms defined by notions of race and nationalism produces a convenient shorthand for recording history. Complex patterns can be reduced to apparently unambiguous trace-lines. Similarities and oppositions can be defined in relation not to the specificities of cultural artefacts, but to their assumed location on the trace-lines. Such efforts to chart the multiple layers of cultural expression have produced contradictions in South African theatre scholarship, particularly in scholarship which purports to be interventionist in the struggle against apartheid. In attempting to intervene, some of these efforts have become complicit with the very discourse which they sought to subvert.[3] This paper suggests the need for critical vigilance in regard to notions of race and nationalism, particularly as scholarship moves from a focus on apartheid to a focus on the legacy of apartheid.

---

[1] Chinua Achebe, interview, in Kwame Anthony Appiah, *In My Father's House: Africa in the Philosophy of Culture* (New York: Oxford UP, 1992): 73.

[2] Appiah, *In My Father's House*, 92.

[3] I do not exempt myself from the charge of complicity in this regard. Some of my early analyses of South African theatre took for granted the existence of separate categories such as 'English language' 'Black' and 'Afrikaans-language' theatre.

What I suggest here is that because apartheid provided such an easy moral target (who could not agree with the *content* of material which opposes apartheid?), and because the battle against apartheid has, to all intents and purposes, been won and resistance has turned to celebration, it is *precisely* now that our critical vigilance against apartheid discourse must be sharpened. Yesterday's soldiers have become today's members of parliament and yesterday's critics have become today's controllers of cultural institutions. A war has been waged against racism and nationalism for five decades, and the major battle has been fought and won. But if we abandon critical vigilance at this crucial moment, we lose the war against fundamentalism, against essentialism, and against nationalism and racism.

Africa in the theatre

Many scholarly assessments of the cultural significance of South African theatre in the last quarter of the century have drawn attention to the prominence of the theme of apartheid and the struggle against apartheid, while attempting to make visible the work of African artists who were rendered invisible during the years of grand apartheid. In this scholarship, "Africa" has featured prominently. The ways in which the continent has been conceived produce a number of contradictions, both in the theatre and in scholarship on the theatre.

The epigraphs above point the way into the discussion. As Appiah has shown, Achebe's statement assumes that an African identity is produced by the gaze of the European.[4] On one side of the divide is Africa and on the other is the European – specifically, the white male. It is a short step from this assumption to the conclusion that the expression 'African' means 'black.' The conflation of 'African' and 'black' experience has been a feature of commentary on South African theatre, and of creative work in the theatre, for decades. These ideas provided important stimuli for experimental creative work in theatre during the years of contest and struggle against apartheid. They also provided important formulae for innovative and challenging creative work during the years of consolidation of that struggle. But as theatre work moved from the formulaic to the dogmatic, these same ideas came to provide the flypaper on which have perished many promising themes, plots, forms, methods and styles in South African theatre.

Africa in 'the black aesthetic'

Let us start with a brief look at one aspect of the theme: how race thinking has featured in (sometimes passionate) debates between African–American scholars

---

[4] Appiah, *In My Father's House*, 71.

about a 'black aesthetic,' and how those debates have changed since 1968. The debates in the American academy about these issues are useful for my purposes because of the important influence of the American Black Arts Movement on South Africa's Black Consciousness Movement in the Seventies, and because of the similar ways in which subsequent critical reflection on these two movements has produced a critique of the notion of a 'black aesthetic' in both contexts. Henry Louis Gates, Jr. has been quite clear about how race features in his voluminous work on African–American literature:

> "Race" as a meaningful criterion within the biological sciences has long been recognized to be a fiction. When we speak of the "white race" or the "black race," the "Jewish race" or the "Aryan race," we speak in misnomers, biologically, and in metaphors, more generally.[5]

Having made this much clear, he demonstrates that he nevertheless views race as a deep reservoir in the landscape of African–American memory and cultural expression. Race features for him as a *trope* in American literature. His concern is not only with how black people are figures *in* literature, but how they *figure* literature of their own.[6] But for Gates, when race is used as an expression of an essence, as was done by Negritude, then "we yield too much, such as the basis of a shared humanity."[7]

What does he mean by this? What foundation for a "shared humanity" does he seek? For the answer, we can refer to a recently published essay where he does not need to *seek* a space in American cultural life for the voice of the black artist; does not have to *assert* the importance of the black voice; and does not have to *invoke* the 'blackness' of art in order to authenticate the position of the African–American artist. Suggesting that the influence of African–Americans on social life in America is found less in electoral politics that in the cultural arena, he argues that

> For all that African–Americans have been shunted to the margins of national politics, they've resurfaced in the cultural mainstream. There is a sort of logic to this. Disaffection, alienation, opposition: this is the very air that most artists and intellectuals breathe. Yet even to speak of the cultural mainstreaming of black America can be misleading. The point isn't that there are black artists and intellectuals who matter; it's that so many of the artists and intellectuals who matter are black. It's not that the cultural cutting edge has been influenced by black creativity; it's that black creativity, it so often seems today, *is* the cultural cutting edge.[8]

---

[5] Henry Louis Gates, Jr., *Loose Canons: Notes on the Culture Wars* (New York: Oxford UP, 1992): 48.

[6] Gates, *Loose Canons*, 56.

[7] Gates, *Loose Canons*, 66.

[8] Henry Louis Gates, Jr., & Cornel West, *The Future of the Race* (New York: Alfred A. Knopf, 1996): 38–39.

This is no wishful thinking. The veracity of this can be demonstrated with reference to the prominence of African–American artists in modern dance, music (both classical and contemporary), poetry, fiction, fine arts and film. Gates says:

> Assigning a date to this upsurge in creativity is an exercise in arbitrariness, but the year 1987 will do as well as any. That was when August Wilson's *Fences* premiered on Broadway and Toni Morrison published *Beloved*. Both would receive Pulitzer prizes. In that same year, PBS aired Henry Hampton's *Eyes on the Prize*, the six-part civil rights era documentary, Cornell scholar Martin Bernal published *Black Athena*, a controversial, revisionist history of the African origins of classical Greek civilization...[9]

– and he could extend the list of examples. Who could deny the prominence in the 'culture industry' of, for example, 'rap'? Or the impact of Alice Walker, Gloria Naylor, Spike Lee ... the list is extensive.

The point about all of this, to put it with no subtlety, is that for Gates there is now less of a *need* than there was in 1968 to stake out a territorial claim for an exclusivist black aesthetic. This is an opinion likely to be scorned in some quarters, of course. Joyce Ann Joyce, for example, urges African–American artists, writers and critics to "look within, to self and community" in order "to shape a characteristically Black art and to mould healthy African–American minds" against the "serpent's bite" of what she calls "Euro-American criteria of art" and "artistic criteria established by the European and American white hegemony."[10] Joyce has more than once demonstrated her rejection of Gates's views,[11] and Gates is unlikely to persuade her and other race thinkers like her, despite attempts to do so.[12]

Gates's words must be understood as coming at the end of a long period during which the debate about black aesthetics has polarized the African–American academy.[13] He represents one side of the debate, and Joyce's is only one of many voices

---

[9] Gates & West, *The Future of the Race*, 41.

[10] Joyce Ann Joyce, *Warriors, Conjurers and Priests: Defining African-Centered Literary Criticism* (Chicago: Third World Press, 1994): 3.

[11] Joyce *Warriors, Conjurers and Priests: Defining African-Centered Literary Criticism* (Chicago: Third World Press, 1994): 289–97; "The Black Canon: Reconstructing Black American Literary Criticism," *New Literary History* 18.2 (1987): 335–44; and (somewhat hysterically) "'Who the Cap Fit': Unconsciousness and Unconscionableness in the Criticism of Houston A. Baker, Jr. and Henry Louis Gates, Jr.," *New Literary History* 18.2 (1987): 371–84.

[12] Henry Louis Gates, Jr., "'What's Love Got To Do With It?': Critical Theory, Integrity, and the Black Idiom," *New Literary History* 18.2 (1987): 345–62.

[13] The prominent features of the same debate with specific regard to theatre go back to W.E.B. DuBois, "The Drama among Black Folk," *The Crisis* (August 1916): 11–14, and Alain Locke, "Steps toward the Negro Theatre," *The Crisis* (December 1922): 66–68. Samuel A. Hay has traced in some detail the main features of this early form of the debate: Hay, *African–American Theatre: A Historical and Critical Analysis* (New York: Cambridge UP, 1994).

recently raised from the opposing side.[14] The opposing viewpoints have been presented with varying degrees of sophistication, and I do not want to trivialize the
debate by concentrating too much on Joyce's views. Nevertheless, her argument
with Gates does draw in broad outline the specific terms of the race thinking
which is my focus, and it is worth pursuing her arguments to some extent. Because
the debate has a long history, with articulate voices in both camps, in order to understand Gates's view it is worth tracing the outline of at least one moment in that
history. The 'moment' of 1968 represents the cultural ferment of a whole generation, but the year was a significant one. One of the prominent voices which anticipated Joyce was that of Larry Neal:

> Black Art is the aesthetic and spiritual sister of the Black Power concept. As such, it
> envisions an art that speaks directly to the needs and aspirations of Black America. In
> order to perform this task, the Black Arts Movement proposes a radical reordering of
> the western cultural aesthetic. It proposes a separate symbolism, mythology, critique,
> and iconology. The Black Arts and the Black Power concept both relate broadly to the
> Afro-American's desire for self-determination and nationhood. Both concepts are na-
> tionalistic. One is concerned with the relationship between art and politics; the other
> with the art of politics.[15]

Neal's arguments here reflect the militancy of black artists at the time both in
South Africa and in the USA. Implicit in his call for a re-evaluation of "the Western
aesthetic" (which has "run its course"), he goes on to say, is "the need to develop a
'black aesthetic'"; further, that "The motive behind the Black aesthetic is the destruction of the white thing, the destruction of white ideas, and white ways of
looking at the world."[16]

These two views, held three decades apart by Neal and Gates, provide us with
one perspective on the theme of race and nation as it has been used in literature
and theatre. Gates's point is that, although the political and cultural aspirations of
African–Americans are by no means satisfied, the cultural expression of those aspirations has moved encouragingly away from the notions of race and nation as
essences. Since 1968 the essentialism of Neal, and of much of the literature and
drama of African–Americans, has been replaced by the more nuanced explorations
of artists who, as Gates might say, now articulate their view of a shared humanity,
and do so not by any means through abandoning race, but by theorizing the rela-

---

[14] One of her soul-mates is Molefi Asante. His own ethnocentric habits can be discerned in
just one reference from his work: "The African American's approach to language is principally
lyrical [...] The closer a person moves to the white community psychologically, the further he
moves from the lyrical approach to language" (Asante, *Afrocentricity* [Trenton NJ: African World
Press, 1986]: 43–44) – an observation which might surprise scholars of William Blake.

[15] Larry Neal, "The Black Arts Movement," *Drama Review* 12.4 (1968): 29.

[16] Neal, "The Black Arts Movement," 30.

tionship of race to experience quite differently. The notion of a "shared humanity" is perhaps an oversimplification by Gates. It certainly will be rejected as sentimental in some quarters. But Gates's opponents are guilty of their own kind of sentimentality, and few of them can match his theoretical sophistication. Joyce, for example, argues that "Traditional Euro-American literary tools fall short of unearthing the total craft"[17] of the African–American novel, and that what is needed is "Afrocentricity," "African-centredness." She invokes as authorities the controversial work of people like Cheikh Anta Diop, "considered by many as the father of African-centred thought,"[18] Martin Bernal, and Yosef ben–Jochannan, without reference to the abundant criticism that has been levelled at their work.[19] African–American artists and scholars who fail to embrace her crude form of racist essentialism, who are "unable to place Blackness and/or Africa at the center of their critical praxis," are accused by her of "Black self-hatred."[20] These ideas are taken by Joyce to great heights of sentimentality on the one hand,[21] and to absurdity on the other.[22] Despite her excesses, her work is useful as an indication of the kind of essentialist view of black aesthetics against which Gates has stood. And Joyce provides a useful definition of that view:

> the Black aesthetic is the critical process that transforms an African-centred philosophical outlook into art in which African history and culture become essential elements of theme, structure, mythology and language. Thus, the practitioners of the Black Aesthetic are inherently African-centred.[23]

This is precisely the sentiment which drove Black Consciousness theatre in South Africa. At the very time that Larry Neal was asserting the values of a black aesthetic in the USA, Steve Biko was formulating the programme of Black Consciousness in South Africa. In voices directly parallel to those represented in America by Amiri Baraka (at that time still LeRoi Jones), Ed Bullins, Ben Caldwell,

---

[17] Joyce, *Warriors, Conjurers and Priests*, 1.

[18] Joyce, *Warriors, Conjurers and Priests*, 7.

[19] See, for example, Frank M. Snowden, Jr., "Bernal's 'Blacks', Herodotus, and other Classical Evidence," *Arethusa* (Special Issue, 1989): 283–93, on some of the errors in the work of Bernal and Diop. It is interesting that Gates, in his own mention of Bernal's work in the important year of 1987, quoted in my text, takes care at least to refer to the controversial nature of his work, while Joyce is effusive on the claims but silent on the controversy.

[20] Joyce, *Warriors, Conjurers and Priests*, 6.

[21] "Although many Africans have not survived, those who have are real human beings who understand what it means to be human, to suffer. This cry of the human being is the dominant theme in African and African-American literature"; Joyce, *Warriors, Conjurers and Priests*, 24.

[22] She is not above saying, for example, that "deconstruction emerges as the most pernicious poststructuralist project in that it can be used to deny the entire history of African-American literary criticism as well as the experiences undergirding that criticism" (Joyce, *Warriors, Conjurers and Priests*, 24–25)

[23] Joyce, *Warriors, Conjurers and Priests*, 27.

Jimmie Garrett, William Mackey, Sonia Sanchez and Ron Milner, black artists and intellectuals in South Africa, following the line given by Biko, asserted the need for a militant "cultural struggle" in the programme of political consciousness-raising among black people. In the years bridging the Sixties and the Seventies, the political heat was similar in both countries, giving rise to formulaic theatre which essentialized race and nation in the quest for political and psychological liberation.

The significance of this militant Black-Consciousness theatre as a cultural 'weapon' against apartheid in South Africa has been extensively documented and will no doubt be subject to much further documentation and argument. But much of the documentation has been tainted by the sometimes conscious, sometimes unconscious *patronage* by scholars of the work of black artists. Concerned, during the repressive Seventies and Eighties, to draw attention to important work which was severely hampered by censorship, scholars focused on describing the cultural significance of the new work and advertising its merits without detailed interrogation of it. Thus assertions by artists and scholars of the importance of the black artistic voice were largely unaccompanied by detailed analyses either of individual works or of the larger implications of the essentialism inscribed in the notion of a black aesthetic. Perhaps partly because of this, the subsequent historical trajectory of black theatre has been somewhat different in South Africa, taking far longer to shed formulae which lasted barely a few years in the USA but which were still driving some of the work in South Africa as late as the Nineties.[24]

We should note just how quickly the 1968 formula for black theatre was abandoned in the USA. Observers like Joyce appear still to be clinging to the passionate militancy of the period, long after even its chief spokespersons had moved on. She still invokes Larry Neal's "seminal essay" of 1968[25] without a mention of Neal's fairly radically changing his position within a very short space of time. In 1976, in a profound departure from his 1968 sentiments, he proclaimed that the black artist needed to be receptive to the "accumulated weight of the world's aesthetic, intellectual, and historical experience" and that "Literature can indeed make excellent propaganda, but through propaganda alone the black writer can

---

[24] Long after formulaic didactic theatre was abandoned in the USA and more nuanced work became the norm, in South Africa the politics of race and nation continued to drive the work of many black theatre practitioners. Mbongeni Ngema's spectacular commercial successes should not blind the observer to the sometimes naive political didacticism which still drives his plays. And the annual Grahamstown Festivals still produce emulations of the earlier didactic plays of the Seventies. See, for example, Ian Steadman, "Theatre Beyond Apartheid," *Research in African Literatures* 22.3 (1991): 77–90.

[25] Joyce, *Warriors, Conjurers and Priests*, 25, referring to Neal, "The Black Arts Movement."

never perform the highest function of his art: that of revealing to man his most enduring human possibilities and limitations."[26]

Neal's critical opinions do not, in themselves, signify a change from the essentialist black aesthetics of 1968 to the more imaginative pluralism of a later generation. Along with the evaporation of the specific focus of the black arts movement of the Sixties came the demise of journals which had championed the cause. *Black Dialogue, Journal of Black Poetry, Liberator,* and *Black World* all collapsed within a decade. The death-knell was sounded for *Black World,* the most significant of these journals, when the black-theatre champion of 1968, now known as Amiri Baraka, published in its July 1975 issue his essay "'Why I changed my ideology'."[27] By the middle of the Seventies, the passion of 1968 in the Black Arts Movement was virtually unrecognizable. Indeed, the movement came under attack for its earlier excesses[28] and its omissions.[29] The excesses are still underwritten by Joyce in the Nineties as she remains defiant, searching for a return, perhaps, to the moment of 1968 and its stereotyping of black and white culture. The paradox in this is that Joyce says: "The stereotyping of African–American art and its critics has been the single most prohibiting factor influencing the reception and progression of African–American literature."[30]

And it has been the opposing stereotypical view of race expressed by Joyce and her colleagues – a view that in one respect involves being "seduced by the rhetoric of ancestral purity"[31] – that has been a factor militating against the development of the more nuanced work sought by Gates.

To understand how such stereotypical views have impacted on thinking in and about theatre in South Africa, we need to focus a little more specifically on the relationship between race and nation.

---

[26] Larry Neal, "The Black Contribution to American Letters, Part II: The Writer as Activist – 1960 and After," in *The Black American Reference Book,* ed. Mabel M. Smythe (Englewood Cliffs NJ: Prentice–Hall, 1976): 783–84.

[27] Amiri Baraka, "'Why I changed my ideology': Black Nationalism and Socialist Revolution," *Black World* 24 (1975): 30.

[28] Nathan Hare, "Division and Confusion: What Happened to The Black Movement," *Black World* 25 (1976): 26.

[29] The main reason for Baraka's departure was his growing awareness that the concentration on race in the movement's critique of American society meant an undervaluing of other important factors like class. In the South African context, the Black Consciousness Movement was subjected to the same critique. For a discussion of some of the implications, see Bhekizizwe Peterson, "'A rain a fall but the dirt it tough': Scholarship on African Theatre in South Africa," *Journal of Southern African Studies* 21.4 (1995): 573–84.

[30] Joyce, *Warriors, Conjurers and Priests,* 32.

[31] Appiah, *In My Father's House,* 61.

Africa in black and white

So far, I have used the notions of race and nation quite loosely, without bothering to articulate exactly how I see the various meanings which can be attributed to them in a discussion like this. This is because my concern has been so far simply to contextualize what can now be argued more closely as a fundamental paradox in the critical assumptions made by Joyce and others. To insist on a rejection of Western aesthetics and influences in the name of an imagined African or black aesthetic, as they do, is to forget the fundamental point of the intertextuality of theatre in any society, and to forget that, while all theatre has a sociohistorical context, it also enjoys an epistemological context. We understand Soyinka differently by knowing Euripides, just as we understand Euripides differently by knowing Soyinka. Black theatre is no better a label than African–American theatre, American theatre, African theatre, or South African theatre. These are all terms which reflect a crude nationalistic view, an extra-artistic notion of rules of order derived from both material social relations and ideological projections of the State. The difference in the label 'black theatre' is that it reflects not a nationalistic image of the politically defined State but a nativistic image of a racially defined essence. That image is then attached to a mythical continental State called Africa,[32] as the result of an unconscious conflation of the expressions 'black' and 'African' apparent in Achebe's words in the epigraph quotation.

The same problem surfaces in relation to the critical work of even the most careful of scholars. Bheki Peterson's study of some of the gaps in South African theatre scholarship reveals one aspect of this. The abstract of his essay summarizes his theme, which is that, in the politics of representation bedevilling the criticism of African theatre, "Representation must be understood as meaning more than the 'reflection' of the historical experiences of black people in dramatic narratives," and what is necessary, it is quite correctly claimed, is a critical look at the "institutional politics" informing both the creation and the reception of performance.[33] But in this phrase, "the historical experiences of *black people* in dramatic narratives" (my emphasis), is betrayed an assumption that "African theatre" reflects the experiences only of *black* people. This is ironic, given the further statement in the abstract that "What is striking about much of the scholarship [on African theatre] is the implicit or explicit salience of race as a political factor." One

---

[32] Or an assumed homogenous Third World. In this kind of argument it is not uncommon to see "Africa" and "the Third World" substituting one for the other. For example: "the most meaningful statements about the nature of Western society must come from the Third World of which Black America is a part"; Neal, "The Black Arts Movement," 39.

[33] Peterson, "'A rain a fall but the dirt it tough'," 573.

wonders how Athol Fugard would read such an exclusion from the field of African theatre of his own works, and of character-creations such as his autobiographical (white) self in *"Master Harold"* ... *and the Boys*, to take but one example.

But, the abstract aside, Peterson's essay accomplishes a great deal in demonstrating the problems associated with the salience of race as a political factor in criticism and scholarship. It does this by deconstructing some of the "analytical closures which characterised materialist studies" of South African performance in the Eighties. First, he provides a detailed interrogation of the assumptions made in the work of a first wave of "revisionist" scholars who helped debunk "eurocentrism" in the critical reception of theatre, but who did so with insufficient analytical rigour. This lack of rigour, according to Peterson, was the result of the writers in question concentrating on race and undervaluing "the social heterogeneity and ideological contradictions that characterised black theatre," resulting in scholarship in which "the content of African theatre is frequently described as 'true,' 'real,' 'authentic' because it 'is the product of Black social experience'." Secondly, Peterson then provides an equally detailed interrogation of the assumptions of a second wave of revisionists who attempted to overcome these shortcomings but who, in the process, were guilty of equivalent lapses in analytical rigour. This was primarily because, through "recourse to normative prescriptions of tenuously defined socialisms," they overstated the importance of class, and undervalued the importance of race.[34]

Central to Peterson's argument is a critique of what he calls "The assumed dichotomy between race and class" in the work of some scholars. He is interested in how both race and class feature in identity formation, and searches for "a greater interest in marking the specific social relations operative within the sphere of performance." He looks for a "move away from positioning stark dichotomies that lead to analytical closures."[35]

In a different context, Paul Gilroy has argued for the importance of interrogating the relationship between race and class.[36] He discusses the "marginalisation of 'race' and racism" in cultural studies and rejects the subsuming of race in a class analysis, arguing that there is instead a need to retain race as an analytic category. He contends that the politics of race in the United Kingdom is "fired by conceptions of national belonging and homogeneity which not only blur the distinction between 'race' and nation but rely on that very ambiguity for their

[34] Peterson, "'A rain a fall but the dirt it tough'," 576–78 passim.
[35] Peterson, "'A rain a fall but the dirt it tough'," 582–83.
[36] Paul Gilroy, *There Ain't no Black in the Union Jack: The Cultural Politics of Race and Nation* (Chicago: U of Chicago P, 1987): 12.

effect."[37] His book tries to "identify the links between the discourses of 'race' and nation."[38]

> Locating "race" and racism in a Gramscian analysis based on hegemony poses the question of class in an acute form. It points to a view of the causality of class as a complex, multi-determined process in which racialization currently plays a key part. The positions of dominant and subordinate groups are ascribed by "race." It assigns and fixes their positions relative to each other and with respect to the basic structures of society, simultaneously legitimating these ascribed positions. Racism plays an active role, articulating political, cultural, and economic elements into a complex and contradictory unity. It ensures, though this need not always be the case, that for contemporary Britain "race is the modality in which class is lived," the medium in which it is appropriated and "fought through."[39]

Both Peterson and Gilroy provide more sophisticated readings of the relationships between aesthetics, race, class, and nationalism than is apparent in the writings of people like Joyce, where the tendency to sentimentalize the role of race is attributable to a simplistic nativism, in which notions of an 'authentic' and 'harmonious' idyllic African existence are so often invoked.

This has been especially the case in recalling oral traditions. Isabel Hofmeyr has discussed this in relation to the 'oral worker life histories' that became prominent in South Africa in the Seventies and Eighties. These works, it was often claimed, were spontaneous, unmediated, and therefore 'authentic' histories. Despite "the manifest degree of mediation in transcription, editing, and printing, these books claim a special authenticity *because* they are based on the spoken word."[40] Perspicaciously critical of the assumption about authenticity, Hofmyer draws attention to the problems of assuming oral testimony to be in any way pure:

> It is largely these sentimental conceptions of orality that have more recently been made to do signal service in the cause of various nationalisms which have almost invariably lighted on orality as the key signifier of cultural authenticity and purity.[41]

She shows how researchers have paid insufficient attention to the influences exerted on those who provide oral testimony – that, far from being pure, their testimony is 'contaminated' by other influences, written and visual, This "wailing for purity" frequently assumes oral history to be uncontaminated, and she warns

---

37 Gilroy, *There Ain't no Black in the Union Jack*, 45.
38 *There Ain't no Black in the Union Jack*, 68.
39 *There Ain't no Black in the Union Jack*, 29–30. The last sentence quotes Stuart Hall in an essay entitled "Race Articulation and Societies Structured in Dominance," in *Sociological Theories: Race and Colonialism* (Paris: UNESCO, 1980).
40 Isabel Hofmeyr, "'Wailing for Purity': Oral Studies in Southern African Studies," *African Studies* 54.2 (1995): 20.
41 Hofmeyr, "'Wailing for Purity'," 21.

against such assumptions of 'purity' and essentialism.[42] Specifically, she suggests that in "instances where southern African scholars have attempted to read oral text as evidence of consciousness [...] there has been a conflation of testimony with experience and a willingness to see narrative *as* reality."[43]

Notions of race, nationalism, and "authentic African experience" are frequently confused in this way. Anthony Appiah describes the problem in relation to what he calls "topologies of nativism":

> It is as well to insist on a point that is neglected almost as often as it has been made, namely that nativism and nationalism (in al their many senses) are different creatures. Certainly, they fit together uneasily for many reasons. A return to traditions, after all, would never be a return to the contemporary nation-state. Nor could it mean, in Africa (where Pan-Africanism is a favourite form of nationalism) a return to an earlier continental unity, since – to insist on the obvious – the continent was not united in the past.[44]

It is the task of the critic and scholar to cut through the mythologizing and nativizing tendencies of the black aesthetic as it is envisaged by Joyce, to defamiliarize the texts and the claims made about them, and to historicize them and show them as products of more than merely a social function. This is by no means to deny the importance of the functional role of theatre. But when Joyce comments that "The primary characteristic of Black art for the African-centred writer and critic is that it be [sic] functional,"[45] what she is doing is closing down important space for the critic and scholar. Quite apart from the fact that her prescription of the function of art in the service of race has negative implications for an analysis of, for example, gender, her view is little more than what Appiah calls an "anthropological reading," the product of a view of texts which considers literature as little more than "a sociological datum" undeserving of a reading *as* literature.[46]

We need to get away from the habit of viewing Africa as unique. We need to think of Africa as being part of our thinking about theatre generally. There was a time when the invocation of Africa provided a useful stimulus for the assertion of alternative models for the construction of a black aesthetic. In 1968 an important new direction was found, allowing both African–Americans and black South Africans the room to forge new styles and create new themes. But even as we discern the functional significance of such developments, we need to be wary of the assumptions that go along with them. When Gates talks about "the mythological and

---

[42] Hofmeyr, "'Wailing for Purity'," 24.
[43] Hofmeyr, "'Wailing for Purity'," 26.
[44] Appiah, *In My Father's House*, 60–61.
[45] Joyce, *Warriors, Conjurers and Priests*, 30.
[46] Appiah, *In My Father's House*, 62.

primitivistic defense of the racial self that was the basis of the literary movement which we call the New Negro, or Harlem, Renaissance,"[47] he throws down a direct challenge to historians who have romanticized the period. Gates by no means scorns the importance of the Harlem Renaissance, but he sees his task as a scholar quite differently from the romanticists. Mudimbe suggests that the thinking in some quarters of the African–American debate about the return of black people to Africa is like the hope for the Promised Land of the Hebrews.[48] The yearning for a Golden Age of culture which celebrates again the achievements of a race is little more than a search for such a Promised Land. The lesson would serve South Africans interested in the history of Sophiatown, or of Black Consciousness theatre, or of worker theatre, which have all been romanticized in a similar fashion. In all cases, the romantic yearning has been understandable but of little use in trying to provide a clear picture of the history of a period of cultural activity.

It is undeniably true that "it does not take any prophetic vision to predict the continued salience of race in South Africa or, more likely, a turn towards fore-grounding ethnic 'modalities' in social struggles."[49] Nevertheless, it is *because* this is so that a focus on a 'black' experience in the theatre must be reinforced by de-tailed interrogation of the cultural artefact in all of its dimensions. As Mudimbe has warned in another context, scholarly investigation is in danger of just com-menting on, rather than unveiling, *la chose du texte*. We need to find ways of "conciliating a critical consciousness with the authority of regional cultural texts" in order to "unveil and describe African experience."[50] The unveiling as well as the act of conciliation are quite advanced in the scholarship of people like Appiah, Gates, and Mudimbe.[51] This is only beginning in South Africa.[52]

——— ℰ ℛ ———

[47] Henry Louis Gates, Jr., "The Trope of a New Negro and the Reconstruction of the Image of the Black," *Representations* 24 (1988): 136.

[48] Valentin Mudimbe, *The Invention of Africa: Gnosis, Philosophy and the Order of Knowledge* (Bloomington & Indianapolis: Indiana UP, 1988): 117.

[49] Peterson, "'A rain a fall but the dirt it tough'," 583.

[50] Mudimbe, *The Invention of Africa*, 183.

[51] Their work has helped to establish a new paradigm in the study of African discourses. See, for example, the round-table discussion in *Research in African Literatures* 27.1 (1996).

[52] The financial assistance of the Centre for Science Development (HSRC, South Africa) to-wards research upon which this paper is based is hereby acknowledged. Opinions expressed and conclusions arrived at are those of the author and are not necessarily to be attributed to the Cen-tre.

Physical Theatre ❧

Speaking Silences
Images of Cultural Difference and Gender in Fleishman and Reznek's *Medea*

ᏒᏒ Yvonne Banning

W HAT DOES IT MEAN TO BE SOUTH AFRICAN? Questions about
identity are a major post-apartheid preoccupation in South Africa.
And South African theatre is, I think, playing its part in this drive to
construct images of a new South African identity in which difference can be celebrated, rather than used (as in the past) to promote division, separation, isolation
and oppression.

In a very real sense, South African energies and aspirations are directed towards a 'rainbow' national identity. We are currently playing out our dreams,
performing our identities, in real time and real spaces – in, for instance, the streets
of Cape Town, where members of the Muslim PAGAD (People Against Gangsterism
And Drugs) confront the gangs of the Cape Flats. In the law courts, the trial of
Magnus Malan and his co-accused enacts a nightmare historical docu-drama of
clandestine terror and public violence. Individual testimonies before the Truth and
Reconciliation Commission speak of such personal agony and institutionalized evil
that a collective rainbow future seems fragile and ephemeral indeed. Even on the
sports fields where the Bafana Bafana and Amabokoboko teams, and four Olympic
athletes, try to materialize this tenuous rainbow dream of national pride and unity
in diversity, sporting encounters are framed by advertising campaigns in the
media as gladiatorial battles, as national wars.

The media, particularly television broadcasting, have discovered for the first
time in South Africa their potency as the constructors of popular reality. Through
the images transmitted onto our screens and through the community radio stations
that have begun to multiply, we are beginning to see and hear multiple images and
voices that speak and materialize an "us." We are, in Augusto Boal's terms, "spect-

actors" of/in our own dramas of cultural and sociopolitical identity.[1] We are both actors and audience. And these representations of our reality provide a heady experience for people more accustomed to the "us and them" representations of apartheid than to seeing ourselves as subjects of our own dramas. It is easy to forget that what we see and hear is still mediated by the powerful interests that control the media; that representation itself has a politics which is not easily visible in television and radio broadcasting. We, too, have a vested interest in the images that will tell us that we are not who we were; and when we need reassurance about this, it is comforting to return to the conventional wisdom that "seeing is believing." Representation is – has to be – reality.

But there is another danger, too: that through our collective habituation to the starker contrasts and oppositions of apartheid's black and white self-portraits, we, as producers and consumers of images, continue to represent the spectrum of difference through the old polarized filters. Years of solidarity politics have eroded our capacity to mark difference positively. We have to work hard to develop rainbow responsiveness as well as to produce rainbow images.

Theatre now in South Africa is a vital part of our education as sociopolitical spect-actors, because theatre, unlike the broadcast media, strives to render the politics of representation visible. It is in the theatre that we can learn something about those commonalties and differences by which actors and audiences, and contending theatrical and social realities, *act upon each other*.

My concern is primarily with representations of cultural and gender difference in theatrical images and how a particular gendering of consciousness in both production and reception diminishes a play's capacity to represent cultural difference in terms which might affect 'rainbow' popular cultural consciousness. I am, therefore, interested in the relationship between culture and gender, and between the production and reception of theatrical images.

I have chosen to analyze a recent production, *Medea*, which was first performed in late 1994, in Cape Town. It was subsequently presented at the 1995 National Arts Festival in Grahamstown and then at the Market Theatre in Johannesburg early in 1996. It was created by Mark Fleishman and Jenny Reznek, choreographed by Alfred Hinkel, and performed by three professional actors and the Jazzart Dance Company. It attracted considerable critical attention, which enables me to refer to some reviewers' responses as indicators of its reception by local audiences. I shall also touch briefly on the way in which the production constructs a highly specific identity for its audiences.

---

[1] Augusto Boal, *Games for Actors and Non-Actors*, tr. Adrian Jackson (London: Routledge, 1992): 245.

The production enacts the mythical story of Medea and Jason. It offers power-ful visual images of two cultures, Greek and Colchian, and the ways in which these interact, both in Medea herself and in the political relationship between the two countries. Part of the process of the reconstruction and development of South African identity involves re-examining our history as a strategy for transforming the ways in which we construct a present and a future different from the past. *Medea* engages in this, both in its subject-matter and in its aesthetics. Greek and Colchian relations are presented as a metaphor for South Africa's own history of colonizing encounters, in an innovative theatrical style which goes some way to-wards this transformatory goal.

The first image I want to explore is that of the Colchians. Immediately prior to the appearance of the Colchians on stage we have seen Jason's arrival in Colchis – his first entrance into the dramatic action. The encounter between Greek and Col-chians is framed as an act of territorial colonization. Jason descends by parachute from the flies as a literal *deus ex machina*. His first act is to plant his flag in the sandy beach of Colchis. The Colchians gather and dance for him. The dance is a crucial representation of Colchian culture. The questions I have about this scene are: through whose eyes are we seeing? Why is the audience positioned in this way? What possibilities are there for resisting such positioning? All these are, I think, questions about *theatricality* – about interrogating the limits of theatrical representation on its own to shift cultural consciousness.

The first self-evident point to be made is that here the indigenous people, the Colchians, are presented as an *alien* culture, the exotic and erotic 'Other' to the dominant norm represented by Jason. The theatrical language of the dance – its sensuous use of the body and its emphasis on the body's pelvic and buttock areas; the visibility of its musculature and surface planes – "innocent nakedness" as one reviewer saw it[2] – the circular spatial patterning around Jason and the vocabulary of animal-like gesture and so on: this language constructs Colchian physicality as sexual and animal, and thus as not, and less than, human. In contrast to Jason's relative physical inexpressiveness, the concealment of his body surfaces and his sexuality within his modern urban dress, and other semiotic cultural contrasts, the Colchians offer an appealing visual and auditory, romantic stereotype of a naive ('primitive') pre-industrial pastoral community, a kind of composite tribalism. Colchis is generically African, all "Afro beads [...] the hides and feathers of [...] babbling barbarians" according to one reviewer,[3] the cultural 'Other' to Europe.

---

[2] Hazel Friedman, "Two minds meet in *Medea,*" *Weekly Mail and Guardian* (February 3–10, 1996).

[3] Andrea Bristowe, "Beating the Wrong Drum," *The Star* (February 1, 1996).

Significantly, although sexual difference is marked among the Colchians, there is no social differentiation among them. The Colchian dance enacts a ritual sexual invitation to Jason by the women, a ritual sexual challenge by the men. Even Medea's identity is subsumed in a communal identity here. Only the king is socially differentiated, and he is even more exotic and unpredictable than his subjects. Colchian utterances are non-linguistic yet rooted in indigenous South African languages; but when the king speaks, later in the scene, the language he uses is Tamil. The cultural eclecticism of the king's image here both materializes and contains his potential power. He is not only Jason's cultural, political and male 'Other'; he is idiosyncratically extreme even in relation to the Colchians' otherness.

By contrast, Jason's identity is marked as a stereotypical norm. He is god-made man, universal (and male). He is contemporary, urban, 'civilized,' individualized, and the centre of attention and power. Jason is our representative as well as Greece's. We see what he sees because he embodies all the characteristics of dominant South African cultural identity against which difference is measured. His culture, his sexual identity, his power, and his pleasure and curiosity as a cultural tourist-cum-invader are ours. Jason provides the stereotypical signs of cultural and political power and, because we recognize these, theatrical pleasure resides in our 'knowing' him. We may not like him, but he is no stranger to us. If we resist our own knowing, we become 'Other,' less human, Colchian. And so we invest Jason with our own cultural knowledge and experience of this dominance. We cannot resist the pleasure of identifying theatrically with it.

Semiotic richness attends the representation of the Colchians because, like Jason, we need multiple signposts that will tell us about the strange, unknown culture we are meeting. Conversely, Jason needs fewer signs for us to read because he is familiar. Thus theatricality is invested in the new, the different, the strange. One of the features noted approvingly by a reviewer was the way this production's theatrical innovativeness constructed "a thrilling theatrical language of passion for a new order."[4] Our pleasure in the theatricality of the images, the innovativeness of the theatrical language which constitutes the production's style, is precisely what seduces us into relinquishing our power to resist our positioning as vicarious Greeks. Denying such identification means giving up not only our cultural dominance, but the pleasure that theatricality itself provides. We have to take theatricality in its own terms, or refuse the whole theatrical experience altogether.

Perhaps here we are saved from such drastic self-denial by the ever-so-light touch of comic hyperbole that is part of the theatrical style of the piece, particu-

---

[4] Robert Greig, "*Medea* creates a thrilling language of passion for a new order," *Sunday Independent* (February 4, 1996): 21.

larly in the big theatrical moments such as Jason's entrance as well as in later images of him. But this partial unmasking of its own theatricality as effect suppresses the more serious underlying manipulation of audience-positioning by the theatrical semiotic. The evocativeness of theatrical representation is partially permeable, though the cultural hegemony that underpins this remains intact and invisible.

In a sense, theatrical innovativeness is always an act of cultural intervention, a striking materialization of a new way of seeing, which is measured by its theatrical effectiveness. But this kind of intervention may reproduce (unintentionally) those structural and political relations it seeks to challenge.

In spite of its bold theatricality, it seems to me that this *Medea* does not escape the old binocular vision of cultural difference that it seeks to replace. This is partly because makers and reviewers (and probably audiences) share a similar history of hegemonic acculturation, though not necessarily similar relations to it. But the persistence of a binocular view is an effect not only of apartheid's "separate and unequal" cultural ideology. It is symptomatic of, and produced by, a more deepseated, pervasive and often invisible ideological construction of identity as very specifically gendered. Cultural dualism is one of the many manifestations that result when human sexuality is gendered in binary and unequal terms as *either* male *or* female and the universal marker of normative human identity is maleness.

The biological essentialism on which such gendering is premised derives from the longest history of political control by men over women. Such control includes domination of the discourses of identity, sexuality and representation. So that meaningful intervention in the theatre requires not only theatrical innovativeness, but intervention at a discursive theatrical level, too.

This *Medea* demonstrates the difficulties of effecting cultural intervention *without* at the same time engaging in *gender* interventions. For the production reproduces and naturalizes (unconsciously, I think) the hegemony of male dominance and fuses it with cultural dominance as one and the same thing. Thus Jason, described as "that testosterone hero" by one woman reviewer,[5] represents a central Greek/male/masculine identity; Medea a marginal, othered Colchian/female/feminine identity. So fused are culture and gender in this construction of identity that there is little space for developing more complex tensions and discontinuities within or between gender and culture.

The final scene is a useful one to analyze, for it reveals the limitations that result from unifying gender and cultural identity in this way. Medea has just taken

---

[5] Adrienne Sichel, "Getting physical with the classics," *The Star* (October 17, 1994) [Tonight].

her children off stage to kill them. She has removed their Greek clothing (school-boy grey shorts and white shirts) to reveal their Colchian identity beneath (loin-cloths and their visible body planes). She returns, dressed for the first time in a long scarlet dress and her Colchian head-dress, her Greek wig removed to reveal her shaved and leopard-spotted hair. Her image syncretizes for the first time her Greek and Colchian cultural affiliations into something new and different. She crosses the central space and climbs up the far right back wall to a small square aperture some two thirds of the way up, crouching there in silence and immobil-ity. The Greek chorus, androgynous in belted raincoats and black boots, erupts through the metal roller door in the centre of the back wall. Jason bursts in, howling for revenge. He cannot reach Medea. Images of civil disorder and strife fill the stage. Medea's nurse, a silent witness so far, cuts across the chaos with mocking laughter. Jason kills her. He discovers the children's abandoned clothes and realizes their significance. He howls out his pain, repeating Medea's name. As the closing music begins, Jason sinks to his knees centre-stage, harshly spotlit from above, the children's clothes clutched against his chest. The crown is lowered onto his head. Empty space stretches around him. Medea watches in silence and still-ness from her small high square frame as the music swells triumphantly and the lights fade to blackout. The tragedy has played itself out to closure.

What kind of tragedy is this? Whose is it? This ending demonstrates explicitly that the production is not framed (in spite of its title) as a play about Medea. Medea's tragedy is displaced and silenced by Jason's – she is, as one reviewer noted, a "feminist footnote to the better known story of Jason."[6] Medea's combined cultural and gendered othering culminates in marginalization, silence and immo-bility. Her intercultural journeys (a recurring thematic image in the production) end in the familiar gendered patterning of central male and dispossessed, almost invisible, silent female. Cultural identity cannot displace the more formidable power of gendering, which underpins it.

Medea's gendered sexuality encompasses and represents all those forces which threaten the sociopolitical, cultural, and psychological status quo. She is the ar-chetypal female barbarian of socialized mankind's nightmares, all those uncon-trollable, uncontainable transgressive elements that threaten to overwhelm "us" (and I use the pronoun with some irony). She is, finally, not human, because she is not *man*. Further, she must be less than man, or whatever dark powers she pos-sesses may triumph. Many reviewers remarked on her animal-like qualities (women reviewers among them) – for instance, "a preying [sic] mantis who has

---

[6] Justin Pearce, "*Medea*'s angry resonant noise," *Weekly Mail and Guardian* (October 28–November 3, 1994).

devoured her mate";[7] and "a venomously spring-coiled animal."[8] When her female sexuality combines with her cultural and political otherness, she represents a
disruptive power so great that she must be displaced from the centre of even her
own story. She has to be the ultimate outsider. She cannot be explained away, and
she will not speak. The Nurse laughs at a Greek man and pays for it with her life.
The price of expressing an othered sexual/cultural identity is death or exile.

Where Colchian identity is feminized, Greek identity is exclusively male-gen-
dered. There are no female Greeks in the play. Thus Medea is not only culturally
marginal in Greece; she is also sexually unique. She represents multiple othering.
By the end of the play she is the visible image of female silence, an afterglow left
on the retina, a visible sign of speaking absence. Her identity is marked only in her
destructive effects on Jason and, by extension, on the civilized world of Greek men.
Tragic closure is effected only by her withdrawal from the dramatic action.

For me, then, the central tragedy in this final scene is (over)shadowed by another tragedy which exists in the silence and absences around Jason. But this
tragedy went unremarked by reviewers, female and male. Nevertheless, *I* saw it, or
made it out of the images and the shadows surrounding the central theatrical focus
– and perhaps I was not the only one in the audience who did.

Perhaps intervention is at its most intimate and effective in such speaking silences and visible absences in the theatrical performance of identity. It may be that
it is in such silence and absence that perceptions of difference have space to grow,
multiply, and finally materialize. Speaking the silences and materializing the absences may be the most important act that theatre-makers and audiences can
engage in together, now, in South Africa.

---

[7] Sichel, "Getting physical with the classics."
[8] Marilyn Jenkins, "A *Medea* for today," *The Citizen* (February 1, 1996).

Somatic Emphasis
in South African Theatre
Intervention in the Body Politic

℀ David Alcock

Text and performance

IT IS READILY ACKNOWLEDGED that theatre is an ephemeral medium and the difficulty of recording theatre performances, particularly those with a high somatic content and less reliant on text, is one of the problems which face academics and theatre historians. Play-texts are usually available for academic study but the text in performance is, in most cases, lost to us. Ian Steadman,[1] Matsemela Manaka and Maishe Maponya have all drawn attention to South African theatre in the Seventies and Eighties as a medium frequently brought to the service of political and social change in the country; much of this theatre operated through the medium of workshopped/improvised physical action rather than refined dramatic texts – art works written with an aim to performance.[2] The text in performance emerges from improvisation, worked out on the rehearsal floor. Plays such as *Egoli* and *The Hungry Earth* as we have them in published form are after

---

[1] This aspect of the study of South African theatre in the Seventies and Eighties is one of the major concerns Steadman addresses in his doctoral dissertation, "Drama and Social Consciousness: Themes in Black Theatre on the Witwatersrand Until 1984" (University of the Witwatersrand, 1985).

[2] This is discussed at length by Manaka in his article "Some Thoughts on Black Theatre: Theatre as a Physical Word," *The English Academy Review* 2 (1984): 33–39. Steadman makes the further observation: "In both these plays [*Imbumba* and *Pula*] Manaka is not so much a *writer* as a *scribe* of the rehearsal process. He treats his actors as creative, not merely *interpretative*, artists" ("Drama and Social Consciousness," 439). The physicality of the performance is reflected in the many stage directions in the script of Maponya's *The Hungry Earth*. Steadman notes: "The text of the play is very short. The present writer [Steadman] experienced great difficulty in trying to encompass in stage directions the very *theatrical* physical dimensions of the action when editing it for publication" (notes, 508).

the fact.[3] They were put together as a means of recording, however inadequately, remarkable performances in South African theatre history. A similar situation can be found with regard to Junction Avenue Theatre Company's production of *Sophiatown*.[4] Susan Pam–Grant prepared the text of *Take the Floor* from little pieces of paper with suggestions from the cast for action and dialogue, changes which occurred in the rehearsal process and which were never committed to paper in the writing prior to rehearsal. The play's form and content as we will now have it as a published text is the result of its evolution through the rehearsal process. These instances raise the question of the process of creating theatre in South Africa.

About a century ago Chekhov expressed his concern for Russian theatre through the mouth of Treplev in Act One of *The Seagull*: "What we need's a new kind of theatre. New forms are what we need, and if we haven't got them we'd be a sight better off with nothing at all."[5] Adrienne Sichel, dance critic for *The Star* in Johannesburg, in an interview about dance and theatre at the recently formed *Dance Umdudo*[6] in the Eastern Cape, drew attention to the growing evidence of speech and dialogue in dance works:

> People were saying "I want to be heard, I don't just want to be seen," "It's not my rhythm, it's my language." In many ways dance at the moment is definitely setting trends for theatre in the country. Drama as we've known it, has died. It's a whole new era.[7]

Theatre in the post-apartheid era in South Africa is having to engage with its existing diversity – an engagement among residual, dominant and emergent forms of theatre expression. There is a strong call from some quarters to define a South African performance aesthetic; a need for closure, concurrence and affirmation which is reflected in the sociopolitical body. Whether such a unified aesthetic can indeed be achieved or is even desirable in the face of the rich diversity of cultural

---

[3] Steadman in his doctoral dissertation draws attention to the attitude of the dramatist (Maishe Maponya) towards the published text of *The Hungry Earth*: "The final published version represents the form of the play during its first international tour. Since then the play has undergone further metamorphosis. The text is, in short, a *basis* for performance. As the tour proceeded, Maponya and his cast improvised further and changed the scope of the play. The text became a shorthand for the continuing process of performance" (406).

[4] This aspect is discussed in the preamble to the published text of *Sophiatown*, "The New South African Theatre": "It is a living theatre often improvised in the sweat of the rehearsal room, relying heavily on physical performance, sound, dance mime and song in a way which is difficult to capture fully on the page. The reduction of these performances to a permanent text should thus be treated with some caution."

[5] Anton Chekhov, *The Seagull* (Oxford: Oxford UP, 1968): 74.

[6] Held at the Rhodes University Theatre in Grahamstown and sponsored by First National Bank and Vita.

[7] Quoted in Lanon Prigge, "An Interview with Adrienne Sichel," *Physical Intelligence* 1 (June 1996): 5.

forms and expression evident in South African theatre performance is open to question.

Cross-cultural performance has developed in South African theatre, where black theatre style/practice in particular has brought its enriching traditions of oral literature, ritual and dance, all with a strong somatic emphasis, to bear on the dominant European forms. Research into this complex area of hybridization or syncretic development is likely to continue and enrich our understanding of South African theatre.[8]

Work in the field of physical theatre (across the spectrum) includes that of Andrew Buckland, Ellis Pearson, Ilse van Hemert, Susan Pam–Grant, the First Physical Theatre Company, Theatre for Africa, and such highly influential productions as *Woza Albert!*, *Asinamali!*, *The Hungry Earth*, *Egoli*, and *You Strike the Woman, You Strike the Rock*, among many others. Such works do not remain in the realm of 'pure dance' or mime, but explore the gamut of expression, both physical and verbal, at their disposal. This includes probing themes specific to our society and the ideologies through which we must live and express ourselves (for example, those governing race, gender, class and sexuality), and it also challenges accepted forms and structures of theatre performance. My paper analyzes the work of a number of South African artists and companies who have embraced an emphasis on physicality, in order to look at physical theatre and the way in which, in its search for new forms and a performance aesthetic, it intervenes in the body politic.

Andrew Buckland

Andrew Buckland's works, particularly *The Ugly Noo Noo*, *Bloodstream*, *Feedback*, *Between the Teeth* and *No Easy Walk*,[9] are rooted in the protest-theatre tradition in South Africa. Buckland feels he has a responsibility to take a stand – not necessarily to preach, but to raise the consciousness of people about the situation in society. In this way he makes a conscious intervention in the body politic, in the politics and social conditions of the country, setting out "to activate people" and thereby provide a means to empowerment.[10]

In his production of *Bloodstream*, the body becomes the metaphor for society as well as the means of expression. The plot deals with the tyranny exerted over the

---

[8] Work in this area is being undertaken by Temple Hauptfleisch, among others. See his articles "Syncretism, Hybridism and Crossover Theatre in a Multicultural Community: Theatre-Making in (a New) South Africa" and "The History of South African Theatre: An Introductory Overview of Major Trends" (unpublished MSS).

[9] I refer here to the unpublished manuscript copies lodged in the Rhodes University Drama Department.

[10] Personal interview with Andrew Buckland in 1996.

organs and cells of the body by the Conscious Intelligence Army (the CIA), put in
place by the Territorial Instinct, which violently protects the power structures that
maintain its fascist dominance of the body – an analogy for what was being per-
petrated in South African society. The final implication of the play is that there is a
need for an effective democracy in which the vote of one person can make a difference. It raises the importance of taking a stand, as an individual, if one wants to
change society.

Buckland is conscious of his role as a performer in theatre. By virtue of the fact
that we exist in society through our bodies, we are of necessity political creatures.
As performers, we are compelled to *make* theatre, and by *doing* things we affect the
structure. We *have* the means, therefore we *must* act. Buckland aligns himself with
physical theatre – where the body and voice become central to the performance –
and considers his theatre to be 'poor theatre' in the Grotowskian sense. In addition,
by applying the techniques of Brecht, particularly alienation and distantiation, he
uses disparity to create humour. Buckland is making a contribution to South African theatre in terms of creating a new form – intervening in the way we make
theatre. One of his concerns lies in the way the body is used in performance –
pushing it both physically and vocally to its limits of expression. This disciplining
of the body is reminiscent of the pioneering spirit of the creators of *Woza Albert!*
However, the performer's imaginative engagement is also tested. Buckland's mime
technique is of European origin but he emphasizes that the action is culture-spe-
cific. The characters and content are distinctively South African. Buckland is
cognizant of the fact that the origins of theatre lie in mimesis. Moreover, mime encourages audience participation: through suggestion, the audience is involved in
'filling in the gaps,' as it were, and in this manner engages imaginatively and
creatively in the performance.

Buckland's theatre does not repudiate textuality, though his concern in *Between
the Teeth* is, to some extent, a questioning of logocentric communication. He has
constructed a witty non-sense text which, when combined with incongruous accompanying gestures, finds meaning which manages to communicate across the
language barrier. This is particularly pertinent in a country where there are eleven
official languages (sign language has been recognized as the twelfth 'language') –
a factor which challenges the accessibility of theatre. Intervention in Buckland's
work, therefore, lies at the level of questioning and challenging accepted social
and political structures but also inspires performer commitment and training in
creating and performing theatre; in particular, physical theatre.

The First Physical Theatre Company

Gary Gordon, artistic director of the First Physical Theatre Company, explains his rationale for doing physical theatre as follows:

> I think that, historically in this country, we have a sense of art with a capital A and that there are only certain kinds of ways that you can perform or make works. I think that physical theatre really changes that   I think that it alters people's perceptions. To be political, you don't always have to be screaming and shouting. In fact, it can often be the hidden agenda and I think that sometimes in our work, it is that.[11]

The First Physical Theatre Company is fast establishing physical theatre as a vibrant performance aesthetic in South Africa. It incorporates traditional contemporary dance forms, mime, drama, text, song, and voice work. The work strives towards 'total theatre.' It is a theatre of ideas, action and images, distinguished by a vibrant somatic emphasis in performance. Its intervention lies in its exploration of a performance aesthetic, of stereotypes of gender and sexuality, as well as the manner in which the physical body is perceived in society. The body itself becomes the site of exploration. In this sense, it can be described as a political theatre.

In an interview, Gordon gives a sense of the company's direction:

> I think that we are trying to communicate what concerns us here and now. We are making a connection, an image construction between what people experience in their lives and what they see on stage. I do believe that we are being political about the arts and about the state and place of the arts in our society. I feel that the arts have a low status in this country, and it is my commitment that they should be uplifted. I believe that will contribute to the healing of our society, and to the bringing together of our society.[12]

The work of the company shows a clear debt to Antonin Artaud, particularly his call to redress the denial of the body in Western society and in the way we make theatre.[13] The educational outreach programme of the company seeks to address physical perceptions within the academic and intellectual arena. In the manner of the agitprop theatre of the Seventies and early Eighties in South Africa, the body becomes central to the mobilization of people as audiences. The body is very often used as a weapon. Physicality, rather than what is verbally expressed, as in dramatic dialogue, drives the message home.

Ian Steadman gives a perceptive example of the effectiveness of poetry in *performance* (physically expressed) as opposed to poetry as *text*. He discusses Ismail's performance poem, "The Clenched Fist":

---

[11] Quoted in Ilona Frege, "An Interview with Gary Gordon, Rhodes University, October 1994," *South African Theatre Journal* 9.2 (September 1995): 99.

[12] Quoted in Patricia Handley, "The First Physical Theatre Co," *ADA* 13 (Cape Town; 1995) 55.

[13] Antonin Artaud, *The Theatre and its Double* (London: John Calder, 1970): 95..

"The Clenched Fist" is deliberately constructed as a simulated ejaculation. Tight skin, throbbing veins containing hot blood pulsating through every nerve in an upraised limb, and the central dynamic movement illustrated by the word "expectancy," all signify an energy and movement which, while somewhat naive in text form, reads differently in performance [...] The text of the poem inscribes performance values which would include movement to simulate the state of expectancy   and the raised and clenched fist which would be the central dramatic emblem on stage would need little clarification. The presentation of the clenched fist in terms of an impending ejaculation similarly contains movement and breathing which will issue forth in a cheer and participatory exclamations from the audience.[14]

It is instructive to relate this to the First Physical Theatre Company's *Shattered Windows* (1989),[15] which explores human consciousness on the edge of despair and which employs just such a violent physicality. A programme note to the work endorses Artaud's commitment to voice/sound, as opposed to speech and dialogue, as part of the performer's physicality:

no-one knows how to scream anymore, particularly actors in a trance no longer know how to cry out, since they do nothing but talk, having forgotten they have a body on stage, they have also lost the use of their throats. Abnormally shrunk, these throats are no longer organs but monstrous, talking abstractions [...] actors now only know how to talk.[16]

Shattered Windows further questions the extent to which members of society can endure brutal assault on the physical body – a pertinent point in a society all but anaesthetized to acts of physical violence through the South African media and at first hand. We are reminded of the photographs of a bullet-riddled man set alight, kneeling at the side of his car, a result of the PAGAD[17] purges of drug barons operating in the Western Cape.

The First Physical Theatre Company further challenges our preconceptions of gender roles in dance and drama. There is no idealization of the female form. Women lift the men, and each other. Men dance together. They *all* sweat, and the audible breath and 'body sounds' are not hidden. Movement vocabulary incorporates the use of performers of age. One performer in *...They were caught waiting...* (1993) was in her late seventies. The movement vocabulary of older bodies is seen to be valid material for exploration. Accepted notions of age, gender and sexuality

---

14 Steadman, "Drama and Social Consciousness," 214–15.

15 Video copies of the work of the First Physical Theatre Company are lodged in the Rhodes University Drama Department.

16 Quoting Artaud, *The Theatre and its Double*, 95.

17 People Against Gangsterism and Drugs. A largely Islamic pressure group operating in the Western Cape at the time of writing.

are challenged at the core of much of the work: as Gary Gordon, in his interview with Ilona Frege, states:

> One of the strongest things that seem to confront people when they see our work, has to do with gender. They see our treatment of women in particular as quite different, although I think it's our treatment of women and men, because as much as women do the supporting and sharing of weight, the carrying, they have another kind of strength and that's what we've been investigating. In the same way you're also allowing men to be sensitive, vulnerable and delicate.[18]

Gordon's strong grounding in both drama and dance informs the work, which explores the threshold between these two forms of theatre.[19] The work of the Company has moved from the arena of dance into what Gordon now prefers to call Dance/Play. In like manner, Lloyd Newson, in his work in London with DV8 Physical Theatre, professes to be moving in a similar direction; for example, in his work *MSM* he seeks to explore the "delicate balance to be struck [...] between the power of the spoken word and the creation of the theatrical image,"[20] where the performance does not exclude the written text but is constructed with a high somatic emphasis. The First Physical Theatre Company does not deny the use of text, but relegates it to just one of the expressive elements to be utilized in the construction of the work. In *...They were caught waiting...*, a recorded interview with the older woman performer is played and intercalated with live performance of text from Samuel Beckett and Derek Jarman. This exploits the coexistence of more than one narrative – those embodied in the verbal texts as well as those of the physically performing bodies.

The somatic vocabulary echoes everyday movement – gestural and gross[21] patterns – as the basis for expression. The performer's physical abilities are stretched to dangerous limits of endurance, risk, and strength. A recent production, *The Passion of Judas* (1996), a work by Juanita Finestone, a member of the company, is concerned with rewriting Judas's story of betrayal, guilt, and absolution. During the performance, one male performer is in a bent kneeling position while two other male performers, one carrying the other, proceed to stand on the kneeling man's back. The tension of the moment caused by our sense of the endurance of the kneeling performer is felt in kinaesthetic sympathy by the audience to

---

[18] Frege, "An Interview with Gary Gordon, Rhodes University, October 1994," 99.

[19] Gary Gordon is Professor of Drama at Rhodes University. He was on the teaching staff of the Laban Centre in London. His work shows the influence of his Laban based training as well as the influence of Lloyd Newson and the DV8 Physical Theatre Company, Pina Bausch and Merce Cunningham.

[20] Quoted in Gary Carter, "In The Plush Hush of the Mainstream," *Dance Theatre Journal* 10.4 (Autumn 1993): 53.

[21] 'Gross' movement is a Laban term indicating overt, larger movements of the body.

the point of being unbearable. The creative process of this work was influenced to some extent by the start of the Truth and Reconciliation Commission in the Eastern Cape: it explores the impact of human beings "telling their story and collapsing under the weight of it" (programme note), as well as other related issues, such as the tension between public and private experience; the process whereby inner motivations become public information; and how individuals in the present desperately seek absolution from their personal stories of crime in the past.

P.J. Sabbagha, who started working with the First Physical Theatre Company and is now based in Johannesburg, offers his perception of the company's work:

> The sense of immediacy derives from a thinking theatre, a feeling theatre, and a wonderful sense of collaboration, of things working together. There is no way you could perform our work without being there in person, committed and focused, and interacting with the vocabulary all the time. As a thinking and moving theatre, it also involves the integration of the whole being and I think that excites the audience as well.[22]

The work therefore intervenes in the expected abilities of the performer. The Deadly Performer (to use Peter Brook's terminology), who has become accustomed to trotting out the text, dressed in gorgeous costumes exhibited under glorious lighting and cradled in expensive sets, must give way to performers who can interact with technique and idea, who can be critical and creative. They are intelligent performers rather than puppets who merely go through the motions.

Wider horizons

Physical theatre permeates the work of Theatre for Africa, which has for many years had one particular aim in mind: intervention in the way we perceive and treat our environment. *Kwamanzi*, *Horn of Sorrow* and the recent *Guardians of Eden* all use storytelling techniques of oral tradition together with dance, mime (a strong influence here from Ellis Pearson) and voice-work, in order to imitate animals, birds and natural sounds. In a sense, these works can be termed environmental protest plays.

In Ilse van Hemert's production of *Uit die Bloute* [*Out of the Blue*], selected works of Eugène Marais are told largely through mime, song, and dance, with vibrant physicality heightening the rich language of the stories. Van Hemert acknowledges her debt to Gordon's work in this piece of theatre; her research into *Die Dans van die Reen* [*The Dance of the Rain*] revealed the San source of Marais' story.[23] It is a

---

[22] Quoted in Handley, "The First Physical Theatre Co," 55.
[23] Barrie Hough, "*Out of the Blue*: A Celebration of Eugène Marais' Love of Life" (interview with Ilse van Hemert), *Vuka* 1.7 (1995): 58–59.

record of a fast-disappearing body of oral stories. The oral tradition found in Afrikaans literature – for example, the television programme *Spies en Plessie*,[24] which was devoted to informal storytelling – is reaffirmed through physical theatre.

Closing questions

The rise of physical theatre poses a number of questions. The 1996 National Arts Festival revealed, with a few notable exceptions, a paucity of significant new dramatic texts. Why was this? Have we lost a generation of well-educated, able and talented writers as a result of the explicit struggle? Without political ideology and overt protest, theatre is now struggling to find its purpose and means of expression. Should there be a shift from protest theatre to theatre which looks at the individual within society, and similar broader issues? Is the traditional process of writing plays being challenged? Does physical theatre and its processes stand as a viable, emergent, generic form of expression which can absorb the diversity of existing styles already in evidence in South African theatre?

Peter Brook, as spokesman for the International Centre for Theatre Research, made an observation which may well be applied to South African theatre:

> The world's theatre has rarely been in so grave a crisis. With few exceptions, it can be divided into two unsatisfactory categories: those theatres that remain faithful to traditions in which they have lost confidence, and those that wish to create a new and revolutionary theatre but have not the skills that this requires.[25]

Physical theatre, a challenging theatre freed from 'literariness,' intervenes as an emergent and powerful mode of expression in South African theatre.[26]

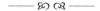

---

[24] This popular programme was called *Spies en Plessie* after the two main contributors, Jan Spies and P.G. du Plessis. They were both academics but became known as humorists. It was on this latter aspect that the programme concentrated – they related ironic, numerous stories and invited other humorists onto the programme to take part.

[25] Quoted in J.C. Trewin, *Peter Brook: A Biography* (London: MacDonald, 1971): 191.

[26] The original delivery of this conference paper was made possible with the assistance of a travel grant from Rhodes University.

Early Fugard ❧

"... No time for apartheid"
Dancing Free of the System in Athol Fugard's *Boesman and Lena*

∽ Errol Durbach

> I think their sense of me is that, even though he makes a lot of noise, he's
> one of those dogs that bark but don't bite.[1]

BARKING DOGS MERELY IRRITATE. It takes a biting dog to intervene.
And even to hazard the concept of "Theatre As/And Intervention" is to
imply a belief that ploughshares can be hammered into swords, that poetry can indeed make something happen, and that theatre can change the situation
as a biting dog in the struggle. Auden's misgiving that poetry makes nothing
happen, or Shaw's patiently evolving Socialism, or even Brecht's commitment to
Verfremdung and the reasoned dialectic must all seem nothing more than counter-
revolutionary irritants to the idea of Theatre as Intervention – just as Athol
Fugard's barking, in recent years, has been vehemently criticized by those who
hold to this model of theatre. His is the "outmoded voice of democratic liberalism"
vainly attempting to "recuperate a political position now severely marginalized."[2]
The L-word, Liberal (usually qualified by "squeamish"), is frequently conjoined
with the E-word, Existential (usually qualified by "stoical" or "altruistic"), and the
H-word, Humanist (usually qualified by "transcendent" or "forgiving"). For a culture in crisis, these non-interventionist barking-dog values bear the activist critics'
censure of axiomatic opprobrium. But if "anybody who takes the risk of writing or
talking about drama in South Africa today must come clean about their position,"[3]

---

[1] Athol Fugard, *Notebooks: 1960–1977*, ed. Mary Benson (London: Faber & Faber, 1983): 391.

[2] Jeanne Colleran, "Athol Fugard and the Problematics of the Liberal Critique," *Modern Drama* 38.3 (1995): 390, 391.

[3] Dennis Walder, "South African Drama and Ideology: The Case of Athol Fugard," in *Altered State? Writing and South Africa*, ed. Elleke Boehmer, Laura Chrisman & Kenneth Parker (Mundel-strup & Sydney: Dangaroo, 1994): 121.

then, as an ex-South African Canadian, I must declare my partiality for the liberal humanism I have enjoyed for the past thirty years as an expatriate: for constitutional forms of change or (in Allister Sparks's term) "negotiated revolution"; for the careful balance between individual and collective rights; for freedom tempered by justice; and for the difficult-to-achieve correlation of human values and political policy. I am bound to declare, with Fugard, that if "the old Liberal Part of South Africa still existed, I'd feel obliged to identify with it";[4] and having made this declaration, I now feel free to argue that Fugard's *Boesman and Lena* is a powerful interventionist play that changes the situation without violating the liberal/ humanist values that shape his politics.

ᘓ

Boesman and Lena has always been a dramatic barometer of the political and the critical weather; and responding to this play has always meant declaring oneself, especially in South Africa, where every utterance and gesture is a sign-system of party-political allegiance. Every relationship in Fugard's play, every action, every word and object resonates politically; and critics, according to their value-systems, will pronounce Fugard more or less politically correct insofar as he conforms to or deviates from their beliefs. Michael Billington, for example, took Fugard severely to task for the apparently reactionary politics of *Boesman and Lena* when it opened in London. "It seems to me not quite enough," he maintained,

> for the white liberal dramatist to offer his coloured contemporaries his pity, his compassion, and his despair. What surely is needed, in the context of South Africa, is an affirmation of the fact that that country's tragedy is man-made and therefore capable of change: in short, some political gesture. The trouble with Mr Fugard's play is that, while deploring the status quo, it also unwittingly helps to reinforce it.[5]

What is needed? What is enough? Critics and scholars have responded in various ways, especially now that the rescinding of the apartheid Acts against which Fugard's drama has been protesting for nearly forty years has altered radically the context of his theatre and the impact of his drama. Interventionist theatre enjoins us to change the present; Fugard's now reads as an injunction to recall the past.[6]

---

4 Dennis Walder, *Athol Fugard* (Basingstoke: Macmillan, 1984): 16.
5 Michael Billington, review of *Boesman and Lena*, *Plays and Players* (September 1971): 49.
6 See Fugard, "Graduation Address, Arts Faculty Graduation, University of the Witwatersrand, 20 March 1990," *Playland [...] and Other Words* (Pretoria: Witwatersrand UP, 1992): 67. He directs his anger at a Cabinet Minister who had declared, in a television broadcast, that the time had come for South Africans to forget the past: "The ease with which he said it left me speechless. It reflected a total insensitivity to, a total lack of awareness of, the damage done, the waste of human lives during the decades of National Party rule."

What critics of the Liberal–left consider to be needed and enough in Fugard's drama is its continuing potential for bearing witness – that resonating idea from Fugard's *Notebooks* that "the truth be told, that I must not bear false witness."[7] Dennis Walder, drawing upon a wide range of political and theological readings from Rousseau to Primo Levi, discovers this crucial act of witnessing in Fugard's projection of "those very ordinary, unheroic, yet particularly human qualities which make for survival under the extreme conditions of colonial and post-colonial oppression with which we are obliged to be familiar."[8]

But none of these resituating strategies is likely to redeem Fugard's post-colonial relevance to the neo-Marxist critics, like Robert Kavanagh, for whom remembering, witnessing, or surviving are merely counter-revolutionary examples of the futility of talking about apartheid instead of changing the situation. The "liberal visionary," they argue, gestures vaguely towards existential assumptions about human nature that are never contextually specified, and endorses survivors who merely accommodate themselves to the circumstances oppressing them.[9] Why continue to remember outrage as unalterable? And what value is there in surviving deprivation by habituating oneself to the status quo? For Martin Orkin, Fugard's politics are ultimately despairing and promote a sympathetic despair in others; against Fugard's liberal angst about his social responsibility to bear witness to the lives of his characters, he sets another familiar passage from the *Notebooks*:

> Boesman and Lena – their predicament, at the level at which it fascinates me, [is] neither political nor social but metaphysical [...] a metaphor of the human condition which revolution or legislation cannot substantially change.[10]

The danger in this liberal–existential discourse, writes Orkin, is that it evokes in audiences and critics alike a corresponding sense of helplessness in the face of any

---

[7] Fugard, *Notebooks*, 166.

[8] Dennis Walder, "Resituating Fugard: South African Drama as Witness," *New Theatre Quarterly* 4 (1992): 343. In this essay, Walder explores the origins of 'bearing witness' in the Christian tradition, its quasi-political reading through Rousseau and Richard Wright to Sartre, and the philosophical/existentialist meanings of Octavio Paz, Primo Levi and Albert Camus. His application of these ideas to Fugard affirms a carefully considered "liberal–left" (343) approach to his plays. See also Brian Crow's "Athol Fugard," in *Post-Colonial English Drama: Commonwealth Drama Since 1960*, ed. Bruce King (New York: St. Martin's, 1992): 150–64, which argues that the injustices of apartheid are not merely revealed in the theatre, but that the actor's embodiment of the idea in creative performance, "the power to be knowingly protean in appearance and identity [...] is a necessary weapon of black struggle" (157). Witnessing, for Crow, is an existential process of self-definition "as one watches others watching oneself and so, circumscribed by gazes, seeing oneself" (158–59).

[9] Hilary Seymour, "*Sizwe Bansi is Dead*: A Study of Artistic Ambivalence," *Race & Class* 21.3 (1980): 273–89.

[10] Fugard, *Notebooks* (July 1968), 168; quoted in Martin Orkin, *Drama and the South African State* (Manchester: Manchester UP, 1991): 147.

alternative to Boesman and Lena's destitution. At best, he argues, Fugard offers a delusive image of recuperative insight into the articulated pain of the oppressed – a visionary hope privileged by his liberal critics, despite the brutal negation of hope by the determing powers of apartheid. At worst, his despair encourages "prevailing racist ideological discursive formations"[11] which, in turn, help to account for the licensing for performance of plays like *Boesman and Lena* by government-dominated agencies. Few writers have been so damned by reception as Fugard by his neo-Marxist critics.

For Dennis Walder, it is vitally significant that Fugard bears witness to a woman singing in her act of self-definition and discovering that even the outcasts of the earth can rediscover value in the self. She dances herself into significance and freedom from oppression, affirming identity through voice and body until the audience itself bears witness to the transforming experience. For Martin Orkin, this argument bears all the marks of the liberal visionary: the location of value in abstractions like 'self,' and the unsubstantiated faith in existential solutions to material deprivation. His reading, in contradistinction, insists on the non-recuperative circularity of the action, on Lena's disillusionment that nothing is finally explained by insight or revelation, and on that couple's unaltering status as victims of economic and ecological disaster. His final vision of the play is as bleak as Dennis Walder's had been affirming, for bearing witness or remembering are clearly both inadequate as dramatic responses to the situation. In a postscript to his book, written in March 1990 and entitled "Look back in anger," he endorses a more prophetic and forward-looking post-colonial drama. Remembering, he contends, must finally give way to plays that "provide a glimpse of and prepare for a democratic South Africa – one freer and more able to tolerate both difference and dialogue than the worlds in which they have until now often had to struggle to claim some space."[12] Michael Billington is even less equivocal: what is needed, he insists, is some political gesture.

Walder or Orkin? Liberal–left or neo-Marxist? Any ideological reading of the text, it seems to me, will necessarily delimit its complexity and push it towards the either/or formulations of propaganda. But if, as Fugard claims, his play was conceived as a palimpsest,[13] then a both/and approach to its significance would have

---

[11] Orkin, *Drama and the South African State*, 147. Orkin's example of such "colonialist and assimilationist discourse" is B.A. Young's review of *Boesman and Lena* for the *Financial Times* (10 July 1971): "What emerges from the racial point of view is that the coloured despise the natives as much as the whites despise the coloureds [...] The moral that I find uncomfortably evident is a different one, that when we try to teach primitive peoples the European way of life they have as much right to our faults as to our virtues."

[12] Orkin, *Drama and the South African State*, 252.

[13] Fugard, *Notebooks*, 169.

to take account of the multi-layered blurring so characteristic of his art. A single
sentence, uttered by an unhoused and ragged woman in the dead of a freezing
night on a desolate mudflat, summons up the revisionist politics of *King Lear* in its
intertextual echoes: "Ja!," says Lena to the dying old Xhosa huddling with her
against the cold, "Hotnot and a Kaffer got no time for apartheid on a night like
this."[14] In the context of a stage action that allies the 'coloured' beggar and the
'black,' with the resonating implications of the racist Afrikanerisms and the one
openly defiant rejection of apartheid in all of Fugard's drama,[15] Lena's remark encompasses every criterion required by Fugard's critics for post-colonial
significance: the remembering of historical events that have reduced the 'coloured'
population to outcasts in their own land, bearing witness as a form of revolution,
the glimpse and preparation of a new democratic impulse in South African relations, and a political gesture that breaks down a 350-year-old system which
reduces one human being to another's rubbish. When the authorities ordered the
burning of the play in Cape schools, it may well have been because they saw it as
an indictment of the damage done to blacks and women, and as a dangerous in-
citement to change.

ℭℛ

Fugard's degraded latter-day Khoi – the Boesman and his *Hotnot meid* – carry with
them into the play the memory of three centuries of racist history. It is a history
that traces the slaughter of an indigenous people, followed by their absorption into
the Afrikaner gene-pool, and then their systematic disinheritance and dispossess-
sion by laws that have disenfranchised them, differentiated them by colour-coding
from other light-skinned South Africans, and designated as criminally "immoral"
any sexual contact between a 'coloured' and a member of the 'White' races.[16]
Boesman and Lena asks us to remember, most specifically, the heinous operation of
the Group Areas Act of 1950, licensing the removal of 'coloureds' from a reconfig-
ured 'white' area. Under its operation, they have been forcibly uprooted from their

---

[14] Athol Fugard, *Boesman and Lena* (London: Oxford UP, 1973): 34. Further page references
are in the text.

[15] Russell Vandenbroucke draws attention to the singularity of Fugard's reference to apartheid; he finds the use of the word ironic and off-hand, a reading consistent with his apolitical
contention that "ultimately *Boesman and Lena* does not focus upon the plight of Coloureds, the effect of the Group Areas Act, or the evils of apartheid"; Vandenbroucke, *Truths the Hand Can
Touch: The Theatre of Athol Fugard* (New York: Theatre Communications Group, 1985): 63, 73.

[16] I have dealt with these issues as they apply to Steve Daniels, the middle-class 'coloured'
stereotype in South African Literature; see Vernon A. February, *Mind Your Colour: The 'Coloured'
Stereotype in South African Literature* (London: Kegan Paul, 1981).

shanty by a bulldozer, their lives reduced to beggary, and their identities even further reduced (as Boesman puts it) to "whiteman's rubbish":

> That's why he's so beneked [fed-up] with us. He can't get rid of his rubbish. He throws it away, we pick it up. Wear it. Sleep in it. Eat it. We're made of it now. His rubbish is people. (32)

He enters the play, carrying his rubbished life on his back and wearing "a faded and torn sports-club blazer" (1) – a reminder of the world of white privilege from which he has been excluded by race and class, but also (in the psychopathology of South African semiotics) an emblem of the sort of status-loaded cast-off which no white man is likely to have passed on to a black.[17] The point, as Fugard's play makes abundantly clear to the distress of his non-South African critics, is that the 'black' – in the programmed operation of systemic apartheid – becomes the 'coloured''s rubbish, and that forms of internal colonialization are endemic at every level of racial demarcation. "Kaffer!" shouts Boesman in contempt of the old Xhosa, his own brown skin privileging him over the other's black skin (17) and licensing his inhumanity towards the even more pathetically disadvantaged. The greater the marginalization, the more brutal the struggle for power and position in the jungle of apartheid. Boesman, unlike the middle-class 'coloureds' in Fugard's other plays, exists in the lower depths of racial and genetic coding, bearing in his very name the generic abuse heaped upon those 'coloureds' whose stature and features suggest a predominance of aboriginal blood. "Too small for a real *Hotnot*," Lena explains to the old Xhosa. "There's something else there. Bushman blood. And wild!" (21). In the downward drift of disempowerment and violence, the *Boesman* male is licensed by the system to visit his wrath and scorn upon the *Hotnot* woman, whose only consolation is to brutalize the *Kaffer*. But, on this bitter night of her rebellion, Lena's revolution begins with a refusal to endorse this hideous paradigm of the racist and totalitarian state.

Each detail of the play contains its own *refusal to forget* the damage done and the waste of human life; and if, as Walder argues, the act of bearing witness is both ideological impulse and theme in *Boesman and Lena*, then *remembering* is another human need resonant with simultaneous existential and political implications. Lena is as desperate to *remember* as she is to *be witnessed*: to dredge up from oblivion the ordering of events that evolve meaning out of chaos and identity out of confusion. *Remembering* means rediscovering your history, resisting the insidiously programmed forgetting that deprives the dispossessed of the memory of

---

[17] We were instructed, as schoolchildren in South Africa, never to part with our distinctive school blazers to black children and to buy any cast-off blazer for an amount not exceeding one shilling.

pristine hope. The horror of Lena's life is summed up in her opening word: "Here?" She lives in an eternal present, cut off from continuity, and disoriented mentally and physically by Boesman's planned confusion – the *dwaal* (aimless wandering; 4) – that keeps her perpetually helpless, lost, and dependent:

LENA	It wasn't always like this. There were better times.
BOESMAN	In your dreams maybe [...] *Now* is the only time in your life.
LENA	No! Now. What's that? I wasn't born today. I want my life. Where is it?
BOESMAN	In the mud, where you are, *Now*. Tomorrow it will be there too, and the next day. (13–14)

The *need to remember* is made physical in Lena's repeated attempts to call up the sequence of their wandering and in her anguished attempts to locate herself in the empty space – each time contradicted and mocked by Boesman, whose politics of calculated disorientation replicates the very system that Fugard's neo-Marxist critics accuse him of endorsing.

"One sticks one's finger into the soil," writes Kierkegaard, "to tell by the smell in what land one is: I stick my finger into existence – it smells of nothing."[18] There is a powerful, intertextual presence in *Boesman and Lena* of a long-established European tradition of existential anxiety, an intermittent loss of memory and certainty that places Fugard in the company of Beckett and, as Craig McLuckie argues,[19] invites comparison with *Waiting for Godot*. But his drama belongs more appropriately to the later tradition of Eastern-bloc absurdity where the existential themes and the political are inseparable, and where abstraction mirrors a specific social reality. In many ways, Boesman and Lena appear to be South African variants of Didi and Gogo, bound (or 'tied') in a nexus of dependency and mutual frustration. But Boesman and Lena, as a conjoined unit, also projects an image of the malfunctioning system in which they are mired: power linked to powerlessness, force to subservience, aggressive violence to persuasive endurance. Fugard calls theirs "a camaraderie of the damned"[20] and, as such, their more appropriate analogue would be a political variant of the Pozzo and Lucky pairing in Godot – that coupling of emaciated strength and bombastic weakness, where the dependency is all one-sided and the desperation to remain associated is manifest in the rope that binds them in an alliance of despair.

[18] Søren Kierkegaard, quoted in J. Hillis Miller, *The Disappearance of God* (Cambridge MA: Belknap Press of Harvard UP, 1963): 9.
[19] Craig W. McLuckie, "Power, Self and Other: The Absurd in *Boesman and Lena*," *Twentieth Century Literature* 39.4 (1993): 423–29.
[20] Fugard, *Notebooks*, 205.

Like Pozzo, Boesman is all fake strength, fake confidence, fake power; he beats
the hell out of Lena, but he dare not allow her the freedom of discovering value
and autonomy in herself. And he dare not concede for an instant his inability to
function without her, or the extraordinary power that she can exercise by simply
denying his control and walking away – "*Wie's die man?* [Who's this man?] And
then I'm gone. Goodbye, darling. I've had enough. S'true's God, that day I'm gone"
(12). So he deliberately leads her on the *dwaal* and abuses her for the bottles that
he himself has broken. But revolution begins in knowing the enemy's anxieties
and, with the insight of one of Ibsen's existential heroines, Lena evaluates the man
who is always there, always waiting for her (8), a mass of insecurity whose fear is
palpable even as he beats her up. "When you stop hitting," she tells him, "it's not
because you're *moeg* [tired] or had enough. You're frightened! *Ja*" (13). Lena, like
Nora, has detected the flaw in the system. She has grasped the woman's power
obscured beneath a culturally conditioned powerlessness, the possibility of sub-
verting force by defying it, and her ability to explode the systems of sexual and
political dominance by asserting her freedom from their operation. "Something's
going to happen," she tells Boesman early in the play (12). And that "something"
is nothing less than the dismantling of apartheid.

⟨⟩

The play begins with an earthbound woman staring upwards and cursing the air-
borne condition to which she visibly aspires – the realm of freedom hovering
above her in the gulls gliding over the mudflats. "Must be a feeling, hey," she
mutters. "Even your shadow so heavy you leave it on the ground" (2). The yearning and the spiritual aspiration are urgent, and the process of the play is Lena's
journey towards a redefinition and an assumption of the free condition, despite her
decision to elect the "camaraderie of the damned" and exercise her autonomy
within its restraints. The play ends as it began, with Lena conjoined to Boesman,
moving back into the emptiness and the dark from which they had emerged. But
this is not the hopeless circularity of the theatre of the absurd.[21] Fugard calls her
departure "a walk beyond the moment of rebellion";[22] but the rebellion has happened, power relationships have been radically realigned, and the Boesman and
Lena dialectic has advanced to the next stage of political challenge. Freedom has
limits, and yearning for bird-flight is a Romantic hankering after impossibility. But

---

[21] See Marcia Blumberg, "Languages of Violence: Fugard's *Boesman and Lena*," in *Violence in
Drama*, ed. James Redmond (Themes in Drama series; Cambridge: Cambridge UP, 1991): 239–49.
[22] Fugard, *Notebooks*, 167.

Lena finds her wings in self-sufficiency, in choosing direction, and in finding a voice. "The noise I make now is going to be new," she tells Boesman; and the "something" that was about to happen at the play's beginning is "still happening," as Lena insists, at its conclusion (44–45).

The catalyst in Lena's bid for freedom, and her way out of the colonializing process, is the living presence of mortality in the even more pathetically dispossessed old Xhosa. She must resist everything he stands for by asserting vitality in the face of death, and humane compassion in the face of anything that denigrates human worth and value. Her immediate response is to establish the sort of community from which she and Boesman have been driven, and which Boesman in his despair is determined to leave forever shattered:

LENA	Do something. Help him
BOESMAN	We got no help.
LENA	I'm not thinking of him.
	[*Boesman stares at her.*]
	It's another person, Boesman. (15)

The help is as much for *her* as for the Xhosa. It will restore human status to non-persons and so rehabilitate the "rubbish" to which apartheid has reduced them all. She offers the old man water, fire, shelter, and food; she tries desperately to communicate with him, the uncomprehending *Outa*. And, moment by moment, she asserts value in the desolate mudflats by rediscovering freedom in those very impulses that Boesman, in his fear, has rejected: connection, reciprocity, and an acknowledgement of a need beyond all immediate personal satisfaction. "I didn't buy *Outa* for happiness" (32), she tells the uncomprehending Boesman, who has secured Lena's share of the cheap wine she has bought in her bid for the old man's company. "This is wine, Lena. That's a *kaffer*," he warns her. "He won't help you forget. You want to sit sober in the world? You know what it looks like then?" (25). But it is not their habitual aid to forgetting that Lena bargains for; and, as Boesman's demands escalate, so Lena and the dying Xhosa are edged ever closer to the Lear-like 'thing itself' that defines them: her fellow-feeling for a *kaffer* – denied a share of their bread and wine, deprived of the shelter of Boesman's crudely constructed hovel and a corner of his worn-out mattress – remains totally incomprehensible to Boesman, and he begins to feel increasingly unsure of himself as Lena's altruism keeps pace with his enforced deprivations:

BOESMAN	You think I care what you do? You want to sit outside and die of cold
	with a *kaffer*, go ahead!
LENA	I'd sit out there with a dog tonight! (26)

In her words there is a resonant, intertextual echo of Cordelia's compassion –

Mine enemy's dog,
Though he had bit me, should have stood that night
Against my fire.
(*King Lear* IV.vii.36)

– and it is against such moral force that Boesman is finally defeated. During Lena's brief absence in search of a few pieces of firewood, he snatches away the blanket that she has thrown over the old man and brutalizes him, only to restore the blanket in hasty trepidation as she returns. Act One ends with Boesman lurking in his shelter, resolutely refusing community and leaving his bread and tea untouched, while Lena shares hers with the old Xhosa as they huddle against the dying fire:

Look at this mug, *Outa* ... old mug, hey. Bitter tea, a piece of bread. Bitter and brown. The bread should have bruises. It's my life. (27)

This is the life to which she demands that the old man bears witness – an ontological, Beckettian demand to be witnessed in the extremity of her distress, both as a woman in an oppressive relationship, and as a 'coloured' within a repressive political system. *Esse est percipi*: to be is to be acknowledged: to be seen and heard – not by the absconding God of the 'coloured' (22), but by eyes that can register outrage and recognize injustice. Lena asks to be affirmed in reciprocal exchange for the human value she had witnessed in the 'Other'; and if she can evoke no more from the old man than the repetition of her name and his unwitting audience to her act of pathetic biography, it is sufficient. In political terms, she has forged a link in the "chain of sympathy"[23] that, in all of Fugard's plays, transforms the camaraderie of the damned into a community of sympathy and strength.

However tenuous, this alliance of bruised and bitter lives in human solidarity is a recurrent image of Fugard's most fervent hope for South Africa – and the most insidious threat, in his drama, to the authoritarian systems dedicated to its destruction. Apartheid – 'apartness' – thrives on carefully instigated hatred, the perpetuation of a system that pits race against race, and the promotion of enmity even between dissidents. In the name of democratic safeguards, it promotes illusions of liberty even as it serves the cynical interests of power and supremacy. Boesman has bought completely into the system. It is implicit in his thought-processes, his physical dissociation in self-absorbed isolation, his racism, and – above all – in his sense of the appalling threat in Lena's reversal of the established order of things. Once a *Hotnot* takes a *Kaffer* under her blanket, the whole fabric of his rubbished world is threatened. Another aspect of the 'something' destined to hap-

---

[23] Fugard, *Notebooks*, 151.

pen on this traumatic night is Boesman's terrified reappraisal of his most tenacious assumptions about freedom and power.

In Panglossian praise of the destitution heaped upon him, Boesman argues that the whiteman's demolition of his *pondok* has actually liberated him from his humiliating 'colouredness,' enabled him to stand upright instead of crawling around like a baboon, and empowered him to free himself from circumstance and necessity: "Listen now," he tells Lena:

> I'm going to use a word. Freedom! *Ja*, I've heard them talk it. Freedom! That's what the whiteman gave us. I've got my feelings too, sister. It was a big one I had when I stood there. That's why I laughed, why I was happy. When we picked up our things and started to walk I wanted to sing. It was Freedom! (30–31)

But it hasn't worked. Lena sees through his delusion, as she sees through all his fakery: he's not free. He's lost. His back bent under the rubble from his smashed *pondok*, his feet straying compulsively down determined paths, Boesman (as he himself admits) almost shits his pants in his fear of freedom (31) and merely re-creates his 'colouredness' in self-loathing. Playing the *Boesman* has been his constant refuge, a mocking stereotype that protects him against the whiteman's world until the perversion of his assumed role enters his soul and countermands all hope of human dignity. "We're not people anymore," he concludes in utter despair. "Freedom's not for us" (38). He will not acknowledge his freedom to be other than whiteman's rubbish or to deny a system accepted as an unalterable destiny. All that remains for Boesman is the absolute freedom of death:

> One day your turn. One day mine. Two more holes somewhere. The earth will get *naar* [nauseous] when they push us in. And then it's finished. The end of Boesman and Lena. That's all it is, tonight or any other night. Two dead *Hotnots* living together. (38)

In his profound shame and despair, Boesman refuses to be witnessed: "*Musa khangela!*," he shouts in Xhosa at the old man. "Don't look!" (38) – as if *to be seen* imposes upon him the responsibility to change the situation through an exemplary act. But the alternative to this demanding and fearful freedom is the even more terrifying form before him: the dead *outa*, whom Boesman attacks with the same violent fury visited upon all incarnations of his self-disgust and fear. "Look at you! Look at your hands!" cries Lena:

> Fists again. When Boesman doesn't understand something, he hits it. You didn't understand him [*pointing to the dead man*] did you? I chose him! A *kaffer*! Then he goes and buggers up everything by dying. So you hit him. And now me.
> 'No, Boesman! I'm not going with you!'
> You want to hit me, don't you? (43)

But he does not hit her. In barely controlled panic, he desists in the face of Lena's challenge and the power she had discovered in herself. She will never again permit him to fabricate causes for brutalizing her or making her the whipping-girl for his own insufficiencies. He admits that it was he who broke the bottles, beating her in a replication of the cosmic injustice under which he suffers. But she knows better. Her power derives from her insight into Boesman's deep dependency on her, which is as close as he ever comes to love, and his desperate need for human contact, which he can express only through aggression:

BOESMAN	Why do I hit you? [*He tries to work it out. He looks at his hands, clenches one and smashes it into the palm of the other.*] Why?
LENA	To keep your life warm? Learn to dance, Boesman. Leave your bruises on the earth.
BOESMAN	[*another blow.*] Why?
LENA	[*Still quietly.*] Maybe you just want to touch me, to know I'm here. Try it the other way. Open your fist, put your hand on me. I'm here. I'm Lena. (36)

Instead of hitting her as a surrogate of his appalling life, he can break the chain of violence and free himself from the systemic evils that impel him to repeat, again and again, the conditions of his own humiliation. His last act of anguished destruction in the play reveals Boesman in all the ambiguity of his bruised humanity and his political perversion. Terrified that Lena will choose to remain on the mudflats rather than follow him, and desperate to evade a solitude worse than death, Boesman, *"with methodical and controlled violence"* (44), begins to demolish the *pondok* he has built out of corrugated iron and assorted bits of rubbish. The *"Hotnot* bulldozer" (44) now performs the same rubbishing inflicted upon him that morning by the whiteman's politics.

So why does Lena not leave Boesman? And why does Fugard refuse his audience the satisfaction of the self-liberating impulse that Ibsen offers at the end of *A Doll's House*? His dénouement more closely resembles Ibsen's *Lady From The Sea*, in which the woman deliberately chooses to stay with the inadequate husband who needs her; and, like Ellida, Fugard's Lady of the Mudflats finally discovers freedom in *choosing to remain* as one of her liberating options – choosing the human connection over that form of freedom which, in Nora's experience, is tragically akin to death. The entire play has been a dramatization of Lena's final revelation – "Tonight it's Freedom for Lena" (44); but the most crucial distinction between her definition of freedom and Nora's is manifest in the gesture that creates very different heroines of self-assertion out of a *Hotnot meid* and a Norwegian housewife. They both *dance* their way into freedom: a tarantella and a *tickey-draai*, a dance of death and a dance of life. Nora's is a complex gesture of existential redefinition, the old self dying that the new may be reborn. But Lena's is a dance that joins her joyously to the world by revealing the political implications within the existential impulse. "Learn to dance," she tells Boesman. This is her most powerful antidote against apartheid.

Dancing, in *Boesman and Lena*, is more than the celebration of life's "Happies" (34) and its sorrows, more than the triumph of existence over the mud. Liberal critics take heart from Lena's affirmation of her *Hotnot* identity, and neo-Marxists deride this assertion of vitality in the context of political degradation; but both schools abstract from the reality of her objectives and the exemplary politics of her dance. Lena dances, joyfully and defiantly, to keep warm in the freezing dead of night – and, by warming herself, to share body-heat with the black man under her blanket:

> [*She stops, breathing heavily, then wipes her forehead with her hand and licks one of her fingers.*]
> Sweat! You see, *Outa*, Sweat. Sit close now, I'm warm. You feel me? (35)

For those who have no time for apartheid on such a night, the politics of a life-affirming reciprocity are the only possible antidote to death by separation. The *Hotnot* begins the dismantling process in a gesture of sustaining alliance with a *Kaffer* – the process that Mr de Klerk was later to define politically as *toenadering* [rapprochement] and that even Boesman, in his bewilderment and distress, recognizes as a symbolic act that loosens the manacles of the system. With dread and uncertainty, he begins his own rehabilitation. He admits to his own complicity in the world's injustice, restrains himself from habitual violence against Lena, and finally puts their wanderings into some semblance of order. Ultimately his remembering explains nothing, but it frees them from the *dwaal* and makes orientation possible.

In her discovery of the freedom to choose, Lena elects to remain – out of her need for human connection, out of compassion for a wretch whose rhetoric of despair makes demands upon our pity, and in the certain knowledge that change is possible for both of them: "I'm alive, Boesman. There's daylights left in me. You still got a chance. Don't lose it" (46). She challenges him to beat her if he dare, confident that his grasp of consequence and their realignment of power will liberate them both from the fist of the system. And if the play ends in a dying fall, it nevertheless offers a glimpse of some recovered future and a tentative hope that those who can dance themselves free *from* intolerable oppression can also dance themselves free *to* effect a necessary change. "Freedom's a long walk," says Boesman in one of his flashes of insight (31) – a phrase that echoes in the title of Nelson Mandela's history of his own long struggle against apartheid, *Long Walk to*

Freedom. Indeed, in his concluding definition of South Africa's new-found freedom, Mandela's hopes for the uncertain future of his country offer an eloquent gloss on Fugard's vision of Boesman and Lena's walking off, once again, into the darkness:

> The truth is that we are not yet free; we have merely achieved the freedom to be free, the right not to be oppressed. We have not taken the final step of our journey, but the first step on a longer and even more difficult road. For to be free is not merely to cast off one's chains, but to live in a way that respects and enhances the freedom of others. The true test of our devotion to freedom is just beginning.[24]

---

[24] Nelson Mandela, *Long Walk to Freedom: The Autobiography* (Boston MA & London: Little, Brown, 1994): 624.

"Laughing in the beginning and listening at the end"
Directing Fugard in Barbados

❧ Robert Leyshon

T HE TRANSLATION OF ANY PLAY from page to stage is a juggling act, a matter of reconciling often conflicting parts into a coherent whole while at the same time retaining valued complexity, or "maintaining the dialec-tic."[1] Although partly, of course, one of the responsibilities of the actor (not to mention that of the set, sound, and lighting designer), it is far more fundamentally the job of the director, and is inescapably concerned with a particular kind of in-tervention: intervention between text and *mise-en-scène*, between *mise-en-scène* and performer, between performer and *mise-en-scène* and audience. To direct, one might almost say, *is* to intervene. In this short paper I want to explore the issue of intervention from a director's point of view, using a production of Fugard, Kani and Ntshona's *The Island* in Barbados in 1994 as the focus of my discussion.

There are a number of reasons for this choice. This was a production of a play[2] that was 'devised' by one white and two black South African men which has at its heart a Greek legend ("not even History!") performed (at a crucial historical mo-ment – March/April 1994) by two young black West Indian men (a Barbadian and a Bahamian) before a Barbadian audience purportedly uninterested in 'serious' theatre, and directed by a white British man very recently arrived in Bar-bados. It was a production, that is, of a play of precise historical specificity and plangency being performed out of its original cultural and historical context, di-rected by someone out of *his* cultural and historical context.

At the start of a seminal essay, Patrice Pavis makes a simple but accurate obser-vation. "For a text to give birth to a performance," he tells us, "is no easy matter":

---

[1] Bernard Beckermann, *Theatrical Representations* (London: Routledge, 1990): 84.

[2] All references to *The Island* are taken from Athol Fugard, John Kani & Winston Ntshona, *Statements: Three Plays* (London: Oxford UP, 1974).

> What the first-night audience sees is already an end-product, for it is too late to observe the preparatory work of the director: the spectators are presented with a gurgling or howling infant, in other words they see a performance which is more or less successful, more or less comprehensible, in which the text is only one of several components, others being the actors, the space, the tempo. It is not possible to deduce from the performance the work that led up to it; *mise en scène*, as we understand it, is the synchronic confrontation of sign-systems, and it is their interaction, not their history, that is offered to the spectator and that produces meaning.[3]

This is something most theatre practitioners know, and sometimes (though by no means always) regret. We present a product, not a process, and unless we decide to emulate Grotowski's para-theatrical experiments and dissolve entirely the distinction between performer and spectator, it is a theatrical given we learn to accept. What follows is an attempt to shift the perspective, to provide a glimpse into a little of the history of a particular production, then to discuss the production itself, or at least a very small part of it. I make no apologies for the fact that it's a very practical account. Like many people who work in theatre, I'm most comfortable dealing with concrete detail, any theory only developing out of the empirical. By the same token, it's also a very personal, not to say confessional, piece. I was taught a salutary lesson by working on this production of *The Island*, one which will be of interest, I hope, to anyone concerned with theatrical interculturalism. While members of the audience may ultimately have enjoyed a "pure theatrical experience" of the kind envisioned by Fugard, what they could not know was that the rehearsal process had been anything but pure. What began joyfully as a meeting of cultures turned into a bitter confrontation, and at its heart was the issue of race. In directing *The Island*, I learned that I wasn't merely out of my cultural/historical context; I was also out of my depth.

I arrived at the Cave Hill Campus of the University of the West Indies in September 1993. As the new specialist in Drama and Theatre Arts in the Department of Literatures in English, I was expected to put on a dramatic production involving students within the next six months. There were absolutely no infrastructural facilities, finances or personnel in place to help me do so, no dramatic work having been seen on campus for many years. So I knew that my first production in Barbados would have to be cheap – I was told my budget would be six hundred Barbadian dollars (about three hundred US$) and it would have to demand minimal resources to stage (we had – still have – no designated theatre space, merely a lecture hall). What the University authorities did not know was that the kind of theatre I actually preferred to make was empty, rigorous, stripped to essentials,

---

[3] Patrice Pavis, *Theatre at the Crossroads of Culture* (London: Routledge, 1994): 24.

Beckettian – in other words, 'poor,' though ideally poor in the strictly aesthetic rather than financial sense of the term. But, unlike my illustrious predecessors, the state-subsidized Grotowski or Peter Brook, whatever production I decided to mount at Cave Hill was going to have to be poor in both (though hopefully not in all) senses.

This realization led fairly rapidly to a consideration of the plays of Athol Fugard. I was familiar with some of his earlier, pre-Serpent Players work, but had long been a passionate admirer of *Sizwe Bansi is Dead* and *The Island*, and had included *Statements* on the new syllabus I was to teach. There were other factors, too, a very practical one being the gender, not to mention the colour, of my Theatre Arts students; in a class of twelve, eight were young black men. Lastly, and I hope understandably, I wanted the first production at Cave Hill Campus for so many years to have maximum impact, to make its presence felt, to have a significance transcending that of a mere course requirement. The forthcoming all-party democratic elections (and above all the name of ex-Robben Island prisoner Nelson Mandela) being constantly in the news at that time, I soon made up my mind that Cave Hill Theatre Workshop's inaugural production would be of *The Island*.

Before I had even discussed my decision with the group, let alone thought of setting up auditions, two of my students came to see me. Gawaine Ward, a Bahamian with some acting experience, and Alan Newton, a Barbadian whose only previous appearance on stage had been as a male stripper, had read *The Island*, were fired up by it, and wanted my help in how to stage it. Would I be prepared to direct them? After a perfunctory audition – their energy and passionate engagement easily outweighed any reservations about their technique – I cast Gawaine as John, Alan as Winston. We then set a performance date and put the production wheels in motion.

"Enthusiasm incredible [...] they have transmitted this to me and I look forward with pleasure to the three weeks ahead. I am very glad I committed myself. It is a positive act – creating hope and meaning."[4] These words aren't from my production journal but from Fugard's *Notebooks*, and were written after his first rehearsal with Serpent Players in July 1963. But they could easily have been mine, so closely did they accord with my exhilaration during initial rehearsals. We did the usual kind of preparatory research, but it felt unusually compelling. We read a lot about the history of apartheid, about conditions on Robben Island,[5] we spent a day at the

---

[4] Athol Fugard, *Notebooks 1960–1977*, ed. Mary Benson (London: Faber & Faber, 1983): 92.
[5] Chiefly in accounts by Moses Dlamini, *Hell-Hole, Robben Island: Reminiscences of a Political Prisoner* (Nottingham: Spokesman, 1984) and Neville Alexander, *Robben Island Prison Dossier: 1964–1974* (Rondebosch: U of the Cape P, 1996).

local prison (where, among other things, Alan learnt how to smoke a cigarette like an inmate – you cradle it, it's precious). We talked, and we talked, often late into the night, about the play's gestural and vocal dynamics, its rhythmic patterns, its fierce physical and emotional demands, carefully unravelling its form from its content, trying to find its dramatic heart. And all the time I was aware of an increasing seriousness of purpose and responsibility towards the material, on all our parts.

The Island invites this kind of intimacy of engagement, for there are very few plays which collapse the boundary between actor and character more thoroughly or more poignantly. In the original production, of course, the character "John" was created by John Kani, "Winston" by Winston Ntshona, and although neither had actually been incarcerated on Robben Island, much of the fabric of the play is spun out of the story of their lives. For Gawaine and Alan, meanwhile, the degree of involvement with the fragmentation of their respective characters became so intense as to disturb the fixity of their sense of identity as performers. "It's OK when I don't know where Gawaine ends and John begins," Gawaine told me once, "but man, it's unnerving when I'm Gawaine playing John Kani playing John playing Creon. Which one of them is me?"

It should have been my job to intervene at such moments, to help these actors (both young and inexperienced) to understand and accommodate these slippages and elisions into their performance. But something strange was also happening to me, neither young nor inexperienced. Just as Gawaine had felt he was playing not only "John" but John Kani, I was finding it increasingly difficult as the weeks went by to maintain directorial distance from the play when we were rehearsing. It seemed to me as if I was wholly in tune in Fugard's original production and was re-enacting it; or, more complexly, as if his production was the palimpsest on which I was confidently superimposing my own. I was quite unaware of how dislocated, how decontextualized I had become. This was a West Indian production of a South African play directed by a European man, and consequently informed by all kinds of potentially discordant intercultural resonances. I just wasn't hearing these dissonances. In one memorable rehearsal a week before opening night, however, I was forced to listen.

We had been working on Scene Two, that powerful and pivotal scene during which the play's major peripeteia occurs: John is called out of the cell to be told that his sentence has been reduced and so he has only three months left to serve. Just before this, the two men have almost come to blows over Winston's sudden refusal to play the part of Antigone. Winston cannot bear to be laughed at, yet the sight of him at the start of the scene in Antigone's "titties and hair" has reduced

John to gales of uncontrollable hilarity, giving Winston a foretaste of what the audience reaction will be at the prison concert. John then tries to persuade Winston – in his most impassioned and eloquent speeches of the play – of Antigone's true significance and purpose:

> "You think those bastards out there won't know it's you? Yes, they'll laugh. But who cares about that as long as they laugh in the beginning and listen at the end. That's all we want them to do ... listen at the end!"[6]

But to no avail. Winston is now apparently implacably opposed to the idea: "Take your Antigone and shove it up your arse!" (59).

The scene had been causing Alan difficulties for a number of reasons. He found it hard to follow the mood and tempo swings, he was insecure about being alone on the stage (for the only time in the play), and above all, he did not like having to pretend to be a woman. It was the moment in the play when his character merged most closely with Winston's. Paradoxically, it was also the moment when he became least convincing as an actor, his body stiffening, his voice flat and without timbre. I had stopped him, once again, on his speech which begins: "Go to hell, man. Only last night you tell me that this Antigone is a bloody ... what you call it ... legend! A Greek one at that. Bloody thing never even happened. Not even history! ... Fuck legends" and ends: "I live my life here! I know why I'm here, and it's history, not legends. I had my chat with a magistrate in Cradock and now I'm here. Your Antigone is a child's play, man" (62).

I was pointing out the reasons for Winston's inability at this moment to transcend the barriers of race and gender, his desperation, his dreadful apprehension of the weight of history, when Alan interrupted me. Very quietly, he muttered: "And what the fuck do you think you understand about the history of my people, either there or here?" For a moment I thought he was talking in role. Gawaine seemed embarrassed, came over, put his arm round Alan. Alan was upset, started to apologize to me. But once again I had to stop him. I asked them both to be straight with me, for the production's sake, for my sake, for all our sakes. What was on their minds?

I should say that there's some, if limited, comfort for me in reading reports of the tensions and misunderstandings that grew between Fugard and Kani and Ntshona during the course of the original production. Nonetheless, the next hour was painful. I hadn't realized just how presumptuous, how culturally and historically ignorant, above all how *white* I'd seemed to them both. They felt I had become a kind of directorial Hodoshe (when I thought I was becoming Fugard!), forcing

---

6 "The Island," in Fugard, Kani & Ntshona, *Statements*, 62. Further page references are in the text.

them into their stage cell night after night, pushing them, correcting them, never satisfied. And they had a major concern which they believed I, as a metropolitan European, couldn't possibly understand: the mentality of the typical Barbadian audience. This, they assured me, was profoundly Christian and conservative (would deeply resent, for example, the profanity of the language and Winston's constant smoking), but, far worse, would fail to take the play seriously, and would undoubtedly laugh at Alan for what they'd see as his foolishness in dressing up as a woman. What I hadn't appreciated, they thought, was exactly how close Winston's anxieties in terms of audience reaction were to their own. They both feared ridicule, for themselves and for this play that meant so much to them.

I found it hard to accept what they were saying, and as in the original production (at least according to John Kani), we "fought and got very mad, and yelled."[7] At one point, as Alan once again voiced his concerns about impersonating a woman, I lost my patience, and with a hollow laugh told him I found such an attitude frankly incredible coming from a young man who'd been happy to perform as a male stripper. Alan merely "chupsed" (kissed his teeth) and turned away stony-faced. I finally asked why nothing had been said before. It was Gawaine who told me, a little ruefully: "we thought even if you listened, you wouldn't really be able to understand." I asked why. Gawaine shrugged. "You're a white man in a black country. How could you?"

In the event, our production, coinciding with election week in South Africa, played to full houses every night. Audience reaction was by and large extremely positive, though we had one or two walk-outs each night as well. At least one of these, I know, was because of the smoking on stage, not the politics or the swearing. People laughed where they were supposed to, and the feared ridicule never happened; indeed, many on each night were moved to tears as the lights faded on Alan/Winston's desperate face, such a poignant contrast to the radiant smiling face of a victorious Mandela that was lighting up the display in our foyer as it was lighting up the world. The crowning delight for all of us came a few weeks later, when we received a telegram from Fugard greeting us from "an old South Africa that is on the point of its rebirth," and giving our production his blessing.

In many ways, then, the production was a success, for all concerned, in all the ways that such success is usually measured. Cave Hill Theatre Workshop was firmly on the map, and we had earned considerable local kudos for the passion and truthfulness of the performances. Nonetheless, looking back now, it seems to me that in directing *The Island* I lost something.

---

7 Peter Rosenwald, "Separate Fables." *Guardian* (8 January 1974): 10.

For all the camaraderie and euphoria of the wrap-party – the signed programmes, the shared rum-punches – what had gone for good was my interculturalist innocence, my belief that a director's interventionist role is as neutral as the presence of a midwife during labour.[8] I'd learned in an acutely personal way the force of Rustom Bharucha's assertion that a meeting of cultures can easily become a collision, that it is "naive, if not irresponsible, to assume that a meaningful confrontation of any culture can transcend the immediacies of its history."[9] Even if you'd listened, Gawaine had said, we thought you wouldn't be able to understand. "Heavy words" indeed, to borrow John's expression at the end of Scene Two. Four years after this production of *The Island*, I'm still a white man in a black country. And like Athol Fugard, I'm still listening, even if I'll never really understand.

—— ॐ ∞ ——

[8] See Ariane Mnouchkine in Maria M. Delgado & Paul Heritage, *In Contact with the Gods? Directors Talk Theatre* (Manchester: Manchester UP, 1996): 187.

[9] Rustom Bharucha, *Theatre and the World: Performance and the Politics of Culture* (London: Routledge, 1993): 1.

Valley Song
and Beyond ⟨℞

Athol Fugard's Theatre of Intervention and Reconciliation in *Valley Song*

❧ Kristina Stanley

V*ALLEY SONG* IS ATHOL FUGARD'S FIRST PLAY to be produced since the 1994 democratic elections in South Africa. It suggests the possibility of a theatre of intervention functioning as a symbol of reconciliation, bridging the colonial and post-colonial division between the races.

Fugard positions himself as an agent of intervention and change in the role of the white Author and in this relationship with the two coloured (mixed-race) characters in the play, Buks and Veronica. The Author–Buks doubling (both parts played by the same white actor – Fugard himself in the premiere productions) problematizes the role of the white colonialist as patriarch. In this paper, I will first define the terms 'reconciliation' and 'intervention,' then address Fugard's awareness of the complex issues surrounding his characters, their relationship to place and identity. I shall then focus on the interventionist qualities of *Valley Song* and its production elements.

The process of dismantling apartheid and creating new sociopolitical structures has produced changes in the densely complex configuration of South African society. In this 'post-apartheid,' 'post-colonial' era, theatre practitioners have also had to make adjustments. Under apartheid, plays relevant to political struggle and resistance were labelled in various ways. Traditionally, three specific frameworks of reference, Afrikaans, Black, and English, were expanded to fit a variety of approaches; these fragmented into numerous groups, with deep rifts between.[1]

---

[1] For discussion of various colonial and post-colonial 'labels' and discourse, see: Temple Hauptfleisch & Ian Steadman, *South African Theatre: Four Plays and an Introduction* (Pretoria: HAUM Educational, 1984); Colleen Angove, "Alternative Theatre: Reflecting a Multi-Racial South African Society? *Theatre Research International* 17 (1992): 39–45; Andrew Horn, "South African Theatre: Ideology and Rebellion," *Research in African Literatures* 17 (1986): 211–33; Dennis Walder, "Resituating Fugard: South African Drama as Witness," *New Theatre Quarterly* 32 (November 1992): 343–61.

Categories include Steadman's and Hauptfleisch's "alternative theatre," Angove's "alternative, alternative theatre," the various theatres of "manipulation," "resistance," "acceptance and lament," and "criticism and confrontation," as well as "agitprop," "protest," "didactic" and "political" theatre." What "anti-apartheid" plays all had in common, regardless of approach or aesthetic, was an attempt to bring local and international attention to the colonial oppression of South Africa under Nationalist rule; "all South African theatre-makers of note during the apartheid era confronted apartheid's seemingly unavoidable commission."[2] A few years after the official end of apartheid, new attempts are being made to catalogue and re-interpret theatre within the South African context.[3] Writing on the current state of local theatre and its relationship to culture and society, Zakes Mda suggests that the political dynamic has become one of "reconciliation" rather than resistance.[4]

Mda is correct in his assertion; the political and social climate of South Africa, in particular since the 1994 election, may well be described in terms of "reconciliation." Nelson Mandela called for the nation to "forget the past" as the multicultural entertainment event that followed his speech heralded the push for a new and improved country:

> It was a "national reconciliation" in motion: *Many Cultures, One Nation*, a classic patriotic spectacle, smudged the sharp edges of these truths into a parade of superficial cultural styles that gave South Africans – trapped for so long in the fixed apartheid identities to which they were so arbitrarily allocated – a glossy song-and-dance dream of what they could be.[5]

A propos the effects of reconciliation on popular entertainment and media, Suzanne Daley argues that *Suburban Bliss*, a new South African TV sitcom featuring a biracial cast and parodying racism, exemplifies the current trend; during its first week on the air, the show won the top slot in the country's TV ratings system, a feat "unthinkable only a few years ago."[6] Marketing and retail firms have also responded; many magazines and television advertisements use multiracial images to promote the "rainbow nation." On the legislative front (and perhaps the most

---

[2] Carol Steinberg & Malcolm Purkey, "South African Theatre in Crisis," *Theatre* 35 (1995): 26.

[3] Temple Hauptfleisch offers an alternative way of addressing these concerns with a "cultural polysystem," involving eight broad categories of performance in South Africa. See "Post-Colonial Criticism, Performance Theory and the Evolving Forms of South African Theatre," *South African Theatre Journal* 6 (September 1992): 64–83. Rosemary Jolly also provides an insightful discussion of the effects of post-colonial criticism on the contemporary formation of cultural criticism in South Africa in her article, "Rehearsals of Liberation: Contemporary Post-Colonial Discourse and the New South Africa," *PMLA* (November 1994): 17–29.

[4] Zakes Mda, "Theatre and Reconciliation in South Africa," *Theatre* 35 (1995): 38–45.

[5] Mark Gevisser, "Truth and Consequence in Post-Apartheid Theatre," *Theatre* 35 (1995): 10.

[6] Suzanne Daley, "Sitcom's Ticklish Idea: Will South Africa Laugh?," *New York Times* (December 5, 1995): A5.

startling and controversial example of the prevailing political climate), the Parliament passed laws in May of 1995 to set up the Truth and Reconciliation Commission to investigate past human-rights violations, and to recommend compensation for victims, as well as to grant amnesty to perpetrators.

While Mda's definition of reconciliation demands a strict set of requirements involving themes of repentance, forgiveness, justice, and restitution, Colleen Angove emphasizes an "alternative" and less rigid, "hybrid" trend:

> This trend [to hybridize] gives an alternative perspective within Alternative theatre in which the reality of a polarized society is defined to present human beings from all racial and cultural groups, communicating, sharing and understanding one another's problems.[7]

What Mda does not address is the inherent nature of reconciliation: a 'return' or 'reunion' of two parties after an estrangement; since, for South Africa, that estrangement is tainted by almost five decades of Nationalist Party rule. Was there ever a history of true equality for all parties of different racial and cultural backgrounds in South Africa? Intervention certainly implies reconciliation, yet perhaps it goes a step further. Rather than simply bringing about "submission or acceptance," intervention attempts to affect or modify an action, thereby creating a different result. 'Intervention' is perhaps an alternative or more formidable term for describing the evolving sub-genre of post-colonial theatre; in these terms, intervention undeniably applies to Fugard's *Valley Song*.

The three-character play for two actors is a deceptively simple coming-of-age story about a vibrant young coloured woman named Veronica who dreams of becoming a singer and leaving the small Karoo town in which she has lived with her grandfather, Abraam Jonkers, commonly called "Buks."[8] Buks, hesitant to let her leave, is also confronted by the possibility of losing the small set of *akkers* [acres] to an outsider who wants to buy them. Veronica seems, in part, to represent youth and a future that must deal with the past while looking forward, wheras Buks and the Author represent the past and the fear of change. Veronica and Buks eventually leap these hurdles, confirming for themselves a new (and renewed) sense of identity. Fugard, along with his characters, looks forward to a new South Africa that must, in order to survive, successfully deal with the residual issues of the colonial experience.

---

[7] Colleen Angove, "Alternative Theatre," 44.

[8] *Valley Song* was first produced at the Market Theatre in Johannesburg, August 15, 1995 with Esmeralda Bihl originating the role of Veronica, and Fugard playing Buks/Author. It transferred to the Royal Court Theatre, January 31, 1996. The American premiere took place at the McCarter Theater in New Jersey, October 27, 1995 with Lisa–Gay Hamilton playing the role of Veronica opposite Fugard. Fugard has directed all of the premiere productions.

The colonial condition of *Valley Song* is introduced by the character of the Author, whose presence in Nieu-Bethesda exemplifies the residual economic control of the white middle and upper class after apartheid. The threat of an individual who has the power to take over the land begins to fragment and destroy Buks's sense of identity. A crisis of identity and dislocation faces Veronica and Buks; a dialectic between place and displacement for them has been created by a process of intervention, located within the text by the white Author. This white playwright (an autobiographical construct) is listed as "Author" and referred to by the other characters as "Master" and "the White man."[9] The Author acts as creator, colonizer, and agent of intervention; he considers buying the Landman house and the land on which Buks works, thereby threatening to displace Buks from the *akkers* to which he has no title although he has farmed them for more than thirty years. When Veronica asks how long "Master has been watching?" his reply, "A long time," suggests omniscience.[10] His motives, at times, appear almost whimsical, as though he were simply entertaining himself by withholding information and imparting it at his own convenience. The Author reasons that his search for identity is grounded initially in the need for change in his life. He claims he is "sick and tired of the madness and desperate scramble of life in the make-believe world of Theatre" (30–31). Ownership appears to motivate him; that sense of ownership which would give him the "peace" that comes with "sitting there on my *stoep* watching the sun set and admiring my land" (31). The land offers an illusory return to what he claims are "the essentials."

For Buks, the land represents his ancestral heritage and his uncertain future. The threat of losing his *akkers* is introduced early in the play when he expresses to Veronica his resolve concerning any future options: "Anyway, worry or not there's nothing we can do about it [...] If he [the Author] buys the land he can tell me take my spade and my wheelbarrow and go and that's the end of the story" (9). Buks, however, does worry, and concerns himself with the fate of the land. In the next scene he expresses concern in a prayer to his deceased wife: "And now there is this Whiteman looking at the house and the land. He is going to buy, Betty, I know it. And then what do I do?" (18). Continually bringing up the subject with Veronica, Buks insists at the same time that there "is nothing to do" regarding the impending sale (25). In his fatalism, he accepts the belief-system and identity of the oppressed and defeated: "because at the end of it ... there's nothing left ... it's all gone" (18).

---

9 Fugard makes no apology for the striking similarities between himself and the Author; both men are white, in their sixties, born in the Karoo, own land in Nieu-Bethesda and Port Elizabeth, and entertain careers as playwrights of international repute.

10 Athol Fugard, *Valley Song* (London: Faber & Faber, 1996): 20. Further page references are in the text.

Buks does not resist his positioning within the colonial ideal, believing that the only option is to accept defeat. His one hope is to appease the whiteman. To gain favour, Buks humbles himself before the Author with a wheelbarrow full of vegetables, offering not only his services to the potential landowner, but also those of his granddaughter. She later refuses to repeat the subjected life-style her grandparents led: "Here we are carrying on and talking just like the *klomp arme ou kleurlinge* [bunch of poor old coloureds] we've always been, frightened of the Whiteman, ready to crawl and beg him and be happy and grateful if we can scrub his floors" (28).

Veronica, in sharp contrast to Buks, indicates an awareness of the colonial condition that surrounds her. The *akkers* become a source of contention between Veronica and her grandfather:

> If I was my Oupa I would rather go hungry than plant another seed in the ground ...
> He's like a slave now to that little piece of land. That's all he lives for, and it's not even
> his. He talks about nothing else, worries about nothing else, prays for nothing else.
> (32)

She opposes Buks's obsession with the land, implying that it is an extension of colonization and earlier oppression. As Fugard places her at the transitional stage between child and adult, he suggests the transition as a metaphor for the larger transition of South Africa from apartheid to post-colonial. The seventeen-year-old argues in favour of "adventure and romance," but also wants to take advantage of the newly created economic and career opportunities that have been provided to her. Veronica's wish to identify with her mother, who left the Valley and its impressiveness in an attempt to create a better life, further exemplifies her urge to find other options for herself.

But Veronica's options are challenged by the Author, the intervening colonial presence and authority in Nieu-Bethesda. Homi Bhabha asserts that colonial conditions can also produce 'native' resistance to colonial authority:

> If the effect of colonial power is seen to be the production of hybridization rather
> than the noisy command of colonialist authority or the silent repression of native tra-
> ditions, then an important change of perspective occurs. The ambivalence at the
> source of traditional discourse on authority enables a form of subversion, founded on
> the undecidability that turns the discursive conditions of dominance into the grounds
> of intervention.[11]

Veronica's position at the end of the play, as it comes across in performance, signifies this form of subversion, and her relationship with the Author at times reflects that of her relationship with Buks. Yet the Author is not a surrogate father, and,

---

[11] Homi K. Bhabha, *The Location of Culture* (New York: Routledge, 1994): 112.

from their first meeting at the window of Mrs Jooste's house, he tries to substitute his own 'reality' for her growing identity and self-awareness. He disagrees with her, insisting that Alfred is being "sensible" when settling for a second-hand bicycle, rather than attempting and ultimately achieving something more. He also repeatedly tries to "reason" with Veronica concerning her own dreams and goals. While Veronica approaches life with the philosophy of not wasting it "on a second-hand dream" (23), the Author seems to claim that most dreams are too grand and unattainable.

At their next meeting, the Author gives Veronica the details of Mrs Jooste's death. After expressing his own fear of ghosts and the inevitability that one day he will "spook" the village, he attempts to deny her own dream: "it looks like your dreaming times in Martin Street are over, doesn't it?" (33). He also implies that the end result of "dreaming big" is bitterness and disappointment, particularly in a small Karoo town like Nieu-Bethesda:

> What I do know is that dreams don't do well in this Valley. Pumpkins, yes, but not dreams – and you've already seen enough of life to know that as well. Listen to me, Veronica – take your apple box and go home, and dream about something that has a chance of happening – a wonderful year for your Oupa on his *akkers* with hundreds of pumpkins – or dream that you meet a handsome man with a good job. (34–35)

In Bhabha's terms, this represents the "noisy command of colonialist authority." But as the Author torments her about the 'reality' of her condition, Veronica creates her own rules of recognition. The more he emphasizes the supposed limits to her options, the more she realizes she can take control of them. Delivering his final argument as a threat, the Author asks Veronica to picture herself in ten years time, like all the other women in the village,

> walking barefoot into the veld every day with a baby on your back to collect firewood [...] Because you know what you'll be dreaming about then, don't you? That I've given you a job scrubbing and polishing the floors of my nicely renovated old Landman house. (35)

Forcing Veronica to picture herself living a life in the colonial condition of her grandmother drives her to act. She questions the Author's authority, determined to assert control over the qualifying factors and to resist the colonial identity that is so strongly being forced upon her:

> Never! Now you listen to me. I swear on the Bible, on my Ouma's grave, that you will never see me walk barefoot with firewood on my head and a baby on my back – you will never see me on my knees scrubbing a Whiteman's floor. (35)

Thus, by way of intervention, the colonial power is resisted.

Although she does leave, Veronica insists that she will not forget the past, her grandfather, or the village; she has resolved the conflict, but without modifying her actions. She reassures Buks that the tragic series of events that her mother experiences will not be repeated. Buks may find assurance in knowing that his love and guidance have also enabled Veronica to prepare for the future. Here, again, Fugard offers the new South African experience as the larger and more global concern. Veronica also reconciles herself with the Author, who admits that she is more than capable of "passing the test": "I always had a feeling that you would do it, you know [...] The very first time I saw you dreaming on your apple box I had a feeling that one day you would be saying good-bye to the Valley" (52). Intervention motivates and enables change from the colonial condition. Yet reconciliation, for Veronica (and South Africa), does not include submission.

The Author directs the penultimate image of intervention at Buks. He encourages growth and development, the germination of the pumpkin seeds which have come to represent rebirth and other "miracles" of life. Is Fugard suggesting that the white colonizer is solely responsible for the rebirth of South Africa? He complicates the answer by casting the same actor as Buks and the Author. Although there has been some controversy over this specific production element, Fugard himself has implied that the two characters "are flip sides of the same coin."[12] Intervention in South Africa must occur at all levels within cultural and racial backgrounds. Fugard suggests that the white colonizer and the colonized coloured must both accept responsibility for change to occur. Theatre as a form of intervention implies reconciliation, yet the latter implies more than restoration. *Valley Song* illustrates theatre's potential for individual and societal change.

— ᢒ ᘔ —

---

[12] Personal interview, December 10, 1995, Any number of reviews and interviews responds to the subject of one actor playing the dual roles. Several of particular note include: Matthew Krouse, "Fugard's Fountain of Youth," *Weekly Mail and Guardian* (August 11, 1995): 33; Paul Taylor, "Valley Song," *The Independent* (February 8, 1996); Anon., "Song of dissent never finds its note of passion," *Evening Standard* (February 6, 1996).

Valley Song
Fugard Plays It Again

○ Toby Silverman Zinman

I HAVE SEEN ATHOL FUGARD PERFORM ONLY TWICE: in an anniver-
sary touring production of his earliest professional play, *The Blood Knot*, and
in the American premiere of his latest play, *Valley Song*. I am struck by how
remarkably similar these plays are – a similarity underscored in my mind's eye by
Fugard's presence in them – despite the intervening thirty-five years, and despite
the radical alterations in South African politics.

The theme, as I understand it, of both plays is 'home' – the place of belonging.
In *The Blood Knot*'s last lines, Zachariah asks, "What is it Morrie? The two of us ...
you know ... in here?" Morris replies, "Home ... we're tied together, Zach. It's what
they call the blood knot ...."[1] "Home" is defined as the "here," both the place and
the "bond between brothers" that keeps white-looking Morris and black-looking
Zach "tied together" – a locale which turns out to be psychological as well as ancestral and geographical. The last lines of *Valley Song* define 'home' as the valley
land that smells and feels better than any woman, as the Author tells Buks, the
Karoo earth for which both old men feel deep and abiding love, a tie that binds two
men, the white, wealthy and worldly Author and the 'coloured,' poor and provin-
cial Buks. Once again, 'home' is psychological as well as geographical, although
here historical rather than ancestral.

In the preface to *The Road to Mecca*, Fugard describes his drive through the Karoo to visit friends and what would be the source for *Valley Song* – his thought of
how pleasant it would be to have a country house there, "and escape from the city
if ever I felt like getting away from the world" while responding to the place with
some deep familiarity, since he had born there although obviously had no conscious recollection of it.[2] It is this magnetic force-field of home, not merely the
prospect of a city-dweller's getaway and dirt-cheap real estate, that is surely what
drew Fugard, as it drew *Valley Song*'s character, the Author, to return.

---

[1] Athol Fugard, *The Blood Knot* (New York: Samuel French, 1984): 81.
[2] Athol Fugard, *The Road to Mecca* (New York: Theatre Communications Group, 1984): vii.

When *The Road to Mecca's* Elsa, an outsider to the Karoo, refers to the region as "God without mankind," using Balzac to describe what she feels to be the awesome inhospitality of the place, Marius corrects her: "You judge it too harshly, Miss Barlow. It has got its gentle moments and moods as well ... As you can see [referring to the vegetable he has brought to Miss Helen], it feeds us. Can any man or woman ask for more than that from the little bit of earth he lives on?"[3] However unsympathetic a character Marius may be, he is surely speaking figuratively as well as literally here; the Karoo clearly feeds the soul as well as the stomach, and it is that sustenance that both Ou Buks and the Author know about in the miraculous pumpkin seeds. It is, after all, the wheelbarrow full of vegetables which Buks brings to the Author that convinces him to buy the obviously named Landman house in the Karoo.

I am more interested in theatre than in politics, and it seems to me that Fugard's recent drama – since his metaphorical return to the Karoo as his theatrical locale – has turned preachy and saccharine, providing little to look at and less to listen to. As an outsider, I have been struck by the fact that the most recent discussions of new works about South Africa resonate with similarities to *Valley Song* – for example, Charles van Onselen's book, *The Seed is Mine: The Life of Kas Maine, a South African Sharecropper, 1894–1985*. The title alone gives the clue: the land is both literal and figurative, both place and symbol, just as it is in *Valley Song*, and the symbol for the symbolic land is the seed: genuine Karoo pumpkin for preference, suggesting symbolically (and rather archly) in turn both the generation of children and the birth of the new political order in South Africa. The sharecropper whose life is chronicled by van Onselen is called by many names, but finally, as van Onselen puts it, "just Old Kas," like Fugard's sharecropper Abraam Jonkers, Veronica's Oupa, who "in the village" is called "ou Buks." I take as another example of similarity to *Valley Song* the rewriting of Ladysmith Black Mambazo's Sixties hit, *Nomathemba*, now a musical by Ntozake Shange, Eric Simonson and Joseph Shabalala. As Jon Pareles writes, "Given South Africa's history, no song about home is a simple love song."[4] It is part of my disappointment with Fugard's play that *Valley Song*'s songs about home are remarkably – I would say offensively – simple. The prosaic lyrics and the banal, repetitious melodies, combined with an actress's voice (which in the case of Lisa–Gay Hamilton, who premiered the role in the United States, is quite nice but far from thrilling or throbbing with undiscovered talent), leaves the audience certain that Veronica's dreams of stardom are foolish.

---

3 Fugard, *The Road to Mecca*, 42–43.
4 Jon Pareles, "A Parable of Lovers' Quest In Today's South Africa," *New York Times* (April 22, 1996): C11.

The political level is thus compromised, for if she represents the new South Africa, which the old South Africa has to let go to be free to discover itself and make its own mistakes, her conspicuous lack of talent and poetry posits failure. The best she can do is "Tomatoes and onions, / Cabbages and beans, / Quinces and peaches, / That's what summer means,"[5] which we are supposed to find charmingly innocent rather than deficient in imagination and linguistic juice. If Author represents a world of "pale, frightened white faces looking out at a world that doesn't belong to them anymore" (33), what does it say that Fugard has created so clichéed and pedestrian a voice – literally and figuratively – for the future? It is worth noting that Veronica feels no tie to the Karoo and longs to go to Johannesburg; the earth, she says, "gives us food but it takes our lives [...] That's why my mother ran away" (32). Does this suggest that South Africa is about to undergo the fundamental modern social revolution as the culture shifts from agrarian to urban? This tie to the land seems to be male, a function of gender rather than generation or race. It is worth noting here that in *Hello and Goodbye*, when the brother and sister are looking for their father's hidden legacy, the first thing they find is seeds ("Watermelons, pumpkins, onions – beans!"; 41), which Hester views as worthless but which Johnny wants to keep and plant. And, as Hester says, "Home sweet home where who did it means Hester done it" (26). Thus, when Johnny says, "I'll make a bargain. You take the money, all of it. I'll take the home," she replies with ease, "Fair exchange" (31). In *Playland*, which like *Valley Song* is a Karoo play, Gideon learns to count by walking with his father counting their cabbages – "counting our blessings" (11) as his Oubaas called it – a counting grotesquely transmuted into Gideon's battlefield counting of the Swapo corpses. Even the eleven-year-old boy at the end of Mark Behr's novel *The Smell of Apples*, having lost much of his innocence although not yet his privilege, looks out at the South Africa he loves, and thinks, "I don't know whether there's a more beautiful place in the whole world. Even with the railway-line. It's a perfect day, just like yesterday."[6] But not, significantly, like tomorrow.

In both *Blood Knot* and *Valley Song*, the relationship between the men and the home is of primary importance; female characters who appear to be central (as Veronica does in *Valley Song*) or merely threaten to appear (as penpal Ethel does in *Blood Knot*) are merely instrumental, dramatic devices to facilitate the interaction between the men and to provide an excuse for exposition. Veronica's lack of emotional involvement in her past and the naivety of her need for information – never

---

[5] Athol Fugard, *Valley Song* (London: Faber & Faber, 1996): 36. Further page references are in the text.

[6] Mark Behr, *The Smell of Apples* (New York: St. Martin's, 1995): 200.

having asked what her mother looked like, for example – makes her seem a plot-contrivance rather than a human being. That she is going to run away as her mother did, betraying everything her grandfather stands for and believes in, is announced in Buks's first appearance: he is singing a half-remembered song his Italian prisoner-of-war buddy taught him: we know, although he doesn't, that it's *Rigoletto's* "*La donna e mobile*," a song about the fickleness and unreliability of women. Singing, of course, is central to the *idea* if not the staging of *Valley Song*. That Veronica's goal is to be a popular singer with all the glamour and adulation typical of teenage fantasies is an interesting choice on Fugard's part. Significantly, it is not 'art' but showbiz. When the Author tries to convince her to dream a more realistic dream than becoming a rock star, the only options he offers are to "pray for hundreds of pumpkins" or " dream that you meet a handsome young man with a good job" (35). Why not advise her to dream about becoming a doctor or a teacher? The world of this play is bogusly divided between the 'real' world of land and vegetables and what the Author calls the "make-believe world of Theatre" (31). This noble savagery strikes me as standard-issue Romantic rubbish, a win–win situation for Fugard, who has written a *play*, after all, about the authenticity of the farm, condemning the "madness and desperate scramble of my life in the [...] theatre" (30–31). This disingenuous stance is additionally complicated by the play's being so baldly theatrical, insisting that the passion and the bare boards are enough. The actor – Fugard, in my experience – playing both the Author and Buks walks from one character to another, scene to scene, without any pretence of realism, of stage-set, of costume change, etc. In the production I saw, Fugard made no visible attempt to characterize each man by walk or gesture – he merely added a hat. More puzzling was the fact that neither the quality of voice nor the accent changed, so that it was often difficult to tell at the start of a scene which character he was playing at that moment. This simultaneous denial of theatrical illusion and insistence on it seems patently hypocritical, much like his condemnation in the dramatic vehicle of the fraudulence of theatre and "the nonsense from actors and producers and critics" (31). If the Author has come to some realization about what is important in life (which is to say, the land and its plenty), does *Valley Song* announce itself as Fugard's swan song?

In *The Blood Knot*, theatricality is both the point and the vehicle, the way the play self-reflexively reveals and shapes itself; and it is this loss that grieves me. The terrifying climactic scene when Morris puts on the costume, the accent, the walk, and the attitudes of the white man is really, of course, a play-within-a-play. Its point and its power reside in the theatricality of the act, the sudden assumption of another personality, another set of entitlements, another role – political as well as physical. The tension and the shock of that scene lie precisely in that moment when a dark-skinned actor and a light-skinned actor, playing dark-skinned character and light-skinned character, add the theatricalizing layer of play-acting to the play, making manifest not only the privilege and disenfranchisement of apartheid, but also the privilege and disenfranchisement of making theatre, the becoming of the Other, with all its attendant dangers and intoxications. Fugard gives us glimpses of this play-acting by characters in several plays, always adding a layer of dramatic density to the stage image by having us watch actors playing characters playing other characters. In *The Island*, the prisoners rehearse and then perform "The Trial and Punishment of Antigone"; in *Hello and Goodbye*, Johnny takes on his dead father's identity when he picks up his crutches; in *Sizwe Bansi Is Dead*, the whole plot as well as the entire theme of the play revolves around assuming another identity as an act of both subversion and rebirth as the character called "MAN" in the script officially ceases to be Sizwe Bansi and becomes Robert Zwelinzima. The theatricality of this play is intensified by the other actor playing both Buntu, Banzi's rescuer, and Mr Styles, the photographer, who theatrically conjures up all the characters at the factory where he used to work as well as his photographed customers.

The power of otherness as a concept, a vision of life, is necessarily more central to a play about apartheid than any other idea (in one of those *aperçus* vouchsafed only to outsiders, I realized that 'apartheid' meant 'apartness,' the state of being Other). In *The Blood Knot*, this idea becomes the way the play talks about itself, the otherness inherent in the whole enterprise of theatre, which is surely the most flagrant metaphor for the negotiation of otherness – the playwright's creation of a world made real and manifest, populated with real people embodying suddenly and temporarily *other* people, and the audience's (still *other* real people) act of watching those people having become *others*, identifying with them as both the character and the actor. Thus does theatre encourage in us that leap out of self which, in *Blood Knot*, is intensified by all the play-acting contained within it, not the least of which is Morris's years of 'passing' for the Other. Appearances can be deceiving – which is, after all, fundamental to 'passing,' and to drama.

Dennis Walder's eloquent discussion of the idea of the racially 'fractured' audience quotes Sartre on Richard Wright: "whatever the goodwill of the white readers may be, for a negro author they represent the Other."[7] Thus, Fugard's playing both roles in *Valley Song* seems an attempt to eradicate otherness in ways

---

[7] Dennis Walder, "Resituating Fugard: South African Drama as Witness," *New Theatre Quarterly* 4 (1992): 351.

so blatant that my heart breaks for his wish. In an interview at McCarter Theater, where *Valley Song* had its American premiere, Fugard spoke to this issue:

> Why not give the one character to a black actor? There are lots of black actors. Why hog it? You've already got a role for yourself. I'm still in the process of discovering why I did that. I know that I did the right thing. I know that this is what the play is about and there is a very specific stage direction that will say, when this play is published, that the role of the old man and the role of the author must be played by the same actor.[8]

And that stage-direction subsequently appeared in the published script. Doubling is at the ideological heart of this play, but not at its theatrical heart, and by this insistence on unearned physical, visual erasing of otherness, he robs the play of its tension. Of course, he has more than two roles in this production; not only is the Author's role compounded by the obvious suggestion of autobiography, but he was additionally both playwright and director. As Robert Greig put it, in reviewing the Market Theatre production in Johannesburg, "This is a one-man band."[9]

Imagine how ludicrous and unconvincing it would be if Fugard were to play Veronica's role. Otherness of gender and generation is apparently less tractable for Fugard than the otherness of race and privilege, revealing the exact site and focus of his political longings. In her provocative and astute discussion of *Playland*, Jeanne Colleran suggests that Fugard's "greater interest [is] in liberal values – here the transcendent values of forgiveness and mutuality – and in psychological drama over political theatre,"[10] an insight which seems to me to have great applicability here. Surely, in the politics of gay drama or feminist drama, the role-sharing would be reapportioned. In this apparent refusal to collaborate by "hogging it," by playing both roles, this rejection of intervention in the theatrical process and its consequences in *Valley Song* stands in direct contrast to the collaboration with Zakes Mokae in the process of the creation of *Blood Knot*.[11]

In a 1992 discussion with the South African novelist Lynn Freed, Fugard spoke about his collaborators: the actor Yvonne Bryceland; his set designer Susan Hilferty; and the actor John Kani.[12] It is interesting that he defined the difference between his collaborations with men and with women as the difference between "chemistry" and "alchemy" – in other words, between predictability and unpre-

---

[8] Mark Murphy, "A Conversation with Athol Fugard" (Audience Guide, McCarter Theater, Princeton NJ, 1995): 4.

[9] Robert Greig, "Fugard by Fugard suffocates the play and shields the audience," *Sunday Independent* (August 20, 1995): 21.

[10] Jeanne Colleran, "Athol Fugard and the Problematics of the Liberal Critique," *Modern Drama* 38.3 (Fall 1995): 402.

[11] Walder, "Resituating Fugard," 349.

[12] "Fugard's Treaty for the Warring Sexes," *New York Times* (26 January 1992): H23.

dictability – announcing that "in the new South Africa, women are going to have an infinitely more creative role than has been the case in the past."[13] Then, in 1994, he fashioned *My Life*, in a return to the improvisational, workshop style of collaborative theatre, by putting five young women on stage to perform extracts from their diaries, "filled with adolescent hope and naiveté," creating "an allegory for reconciliation."[14] *My Life* generated some negative criticism, as some people saw it as Fugard's "admission that he couldn't find his own words for a South Africa's new reality.[15] As though to compensate, *Valley Song* seems to swing to the opposite end of the creative spectrum and, borrowing that female voice of "adolescent hope and naiveté" from the preceding work, substitutes a totalitarian approach to theatre.

It seems to me that the loss of the collaborative impulse is linked to the loss of an acknowledgement of otherness, while the wholesale abdication of the playwright's creative control (as in *My Life*) is a surrender to otherness. In my attempt to puzzle out when I had ceased to be a Fugard fan, I realized that I admired *Blood Knot, Master Harold, Boesman and Lena, Statements After an Arrest*, but had found *Road to Mecca, My Children! My Africa!, Playland,* and *Valley Song* corny and cloying, where the heroic dignity of the Beckettian coping of the earlier plays had been replaced by wishful thinking and unearned dawns of new days. Beckett tells us, "hope deferred maketh the heart sick"; it also maketh art. Hope seems to have arrived in Fugard's drama, and with this intervention of hope comes the disappearance of ambiguity and ambivalence; grim dignity yields to syrupy optimism.

But beyond the political implication of otherness is an ontological otherness, crucial to which is the assumption of a fissure, the ineradicable, inevitable intervention of the Not-I. And it is in that fissure that drama is made; it is here that theatre triumphs. In the "Introduction" to *Blood Knot*, Fugard discusses the scene cut from the American production, in which Morris puts on Zachariah's coat. The missing lines go like this: "You get right inside a man when you can wrap up in the smell of him [...] your flesh, you see, has an effect on me." Fugard commented on this in the introduction to the playbook: "*You* are the other man, the other existence over which I have no control ultimately, yet somehow I feel that I've got something to do with it" (4). Thus Fugard's notion of the playwright's relation to audience and his notion of the audience's relation to character are, essentially, one: the recognition of otherness and a simultaneous refusal to capitulate entirely to

---

[13] "Fugard's Treaty," H23.

[14] Mark Gevisser, "South African Theater Faces a New World," *New York Times* (14 August 1994): H5.

[15] Gevisser, "South African Theater Faces a New World,", H5.

metaphysical isolationism, the brave unwillingness to relinquish connection while not presuming sameness. Fugard has intervened between his art and his audience, no longer trusting the medium of otherness; and both his art and his audience have suffered.

Questions from a
White Man Who Listens
The Voices of *Valley Song*

∞ Dennis Walder

M Y TITLE ECHOES THAT OF A FAMOUS POEM by Bertolt Brecht,[1] and my aim in using it is to suggest my position in the context of the present theme. Discourse always implies a position, and it is especially important to acknowledge this when we have to do with South Africa – a place perhaps less fragmented than before the nation began its current project of redefining itself as post-colonial, but still deeply alienated. Insofar as that process of redefinition involves all of us with an interest in the processes of decolonization, it involves us redefining ourselves too, or at least questioning who we are, and by what right any of us can claim to speak. To the extent that I think I have that right, it rests upon my having listened, although as a white man. By saying "although as a white man," I am trying to suggest a position involving both a certain distance from, and some complicity with, the material to which I have listened.

To what has this man listened? Much South African theatre – including, most recently, the play which set me thinking along these lines and prompted some of the questions I want to ask: Athol Fugard's *Valley Song* (1995). Whether or not you have seen this play, whatever you may think of it – and there have been some very strong noises both of approval and of disapproval[2] – I hope you will agree that it raises important questions about the present and the past, about the past *in* the present. It is a two-hander, with three characters: a seventeen-year-old 'coloured' girl, Veronica; her seventy-six-year-old grandfather, Abraam or "Buks" Jonkers;

---

[1] "Questions from a worker who reads" ("Fragen eines lesenden Arbeiters," 1935, *Svendborg Poems*), in Brecht, *Poems 1913–1956*, ed. John Willett & Ralph Manheim, with the co-operation of Erich Fried (London: Eyre Methuen, 1976): 252–53.

[2] Garalt MacLiam, "A *Valley* of wonderful dreams," *The Star* (August 17, 1995): 2 [Tonight]; Raeford Daniel, "Finest in Years," *Citizen* Johannesburg (August 17, 1985); Robert Greig, "Fugard by Fugard suffocates the play and shields the audience," *Sunday Independent* (Johannesburg; August 20, 1995): 21; Michael Billington, "The frustration of dashed dreams," *Guardian* (February 6, 1996): 2.

and the Author – a white man, who is obliged to listen to the other two, as the audience is obliged to listen to him. The same actor plays both Buks and the Author. The time is the present, the setting a small Karoo village. On one level, the play is about desire: the desire of the young woman to leave her rural backwater for the big city; and the desire of her grandfather to prevent her departure, to keep things the way they are. The white man's desire is for the land, which Buks has worked all his life as a tenant farmer. The play raises the question of who really owns the land. In South Africa, as in other settler-colonial territories in the process of decolonization, the basic demand of the historically dispossessed for the return of the land has to be met, although that is not proving easy. Nor is it in the play.

Valley Song also raises questions about the role and function of theatre in South Africa in the decolonizing present and the colonized past. The interventionist, or meta-theatrical, role of the character called Author, which has so far been played by the author Fugard, is of most interest here. In its opening production, the play begins with Fugard himself standing on the stage, speaking directly to the audience about 'his' village in the Karoo. He asks us to imagine the character Buks, whose role he takes on as he murmurs the fragmentary memory of a song Buks heard with the Cape Corps during the war. This introduces the theme of song as an expression of memory and desire. Fugard's role in the production, as writer, director, actor and two characters of different racial origins, repeats some of the more questionable aspects of his theatrical interventions over many years – the dominating, exclusionary, and patriarchal side of these interventions; but it also suggests a new move in the acting-out of a personal history tied up with the national history in profound and complex ways.

Fugard's theatre has always explored self-reflexive devices, through role-play, plays within plays, and interventionary frameworks such as John Kani's introductory monologue to *Sizwe Bansi is Dead* (1972). These devices derive from the undervalued or suppressed oral traditions of storytelling which still obtain in South Africa. Fugard, who insists he is above all a storyteller,[3] has tapped into these traditions. Nevertheless, his work also displays long familiarity with Western dramatic texts, conventions, and practice. From the post-colonial perspective, the question to ask is: how far does his investment in local cultural codes involve resistance to, or at least creative transformation of, the received theatrical models which the colonial experience has delivered unto him; and, on the other hand, how far does this commitment to the local also involve an imposition upon, even a

---

3 Athol Fugard, *Playland and Other Words* (Johannesburg: Witwatersrand UP, 1992): 73.

silencing, of those alternative indigenous voices and traditions he has drawn on, most famously in the collaborative practice which issued in *Sizwe Bansi is Dead?*

In other words – and this is the question I am really asking – how far is the space Fugard creates for the voices of others an illusion, and to that degree an attempt (unconscious, of course) to maintain white hegemony? We should beware of any simple connection between what happens in any one area of cultural production and in society at large. In the South African context of segregation and apartheid, the connection is simply inevitable, but not inevitably simple. During most of this century, establishment theatre in South Africa has involved mainly overseas works performed in urban theatres before separate or whites-only audiences – an implicit devaluation of the indigenous and the hybrid which continues into the present, despite the fact that the laws and subsidies which enforced segregation have gone; and we even find on occasion the opposite reflex, of overvaluing the local. Fugard's theatrical practice represents one of the most significant exceptions to this sorry story, standing as the first really formative example of successful creative interaction between Western and African traditions in South Africa. The only other partial exception is represented by the work of Herbert Dhlomo, who wrote and performed in the Thirties and Forties.

It is possible to go further back than Dhlomo, as a few scholars are beginning to do. But until more research is done, we are left with unrelated, if resonant fragments, such as that which opens Jill Fletcher's history of early South African theatre. Her story begins with the Portuguese explorer Vasco da Gama's encounter in 1497 with two hundred indigenous cattle herders in what is now Mossel Bay on the eastern seaboard. A group of herders began to play on flutes, making (according to Da Gama) "a pretty harmony for negroes who are not expected to be musicians," and they began to dance "in the style of negroes"; upon which the captain-major ordered the trumpets to be sounded "and we, in the boats, danced and the trumpet-major did so likewise when he rejoined us."[4] Colonial mimicry in reverse, it would seem. Or there is Stephen Gray's now familiar account of Andrew Geddes Bain and Frederick Rex's *Kaatje Kekkelbek* (Kate Chatterbox), a theatrical review of 1838, in which the Khoi woman of the title (played, incidentally, by a white man) satirizes Grahamstown life in a rich mix of Cape dialects, some of which later became Afrikaans – a language whose spokesmen fed it into the one body of solidly researched theatre history we have, reflecting the cultural assertiveness of their segment of South African society during the inter-war years.[5]

---

[4] Jill Fletcher, *Story of Theatre in South Africa 1780–1930* (Cape Town: Vleeburg, 1994): 11.

[5] Stephen Gray, *Southern African Literature: An Introduction* (Cape Town: David Philip, 1979): 52–57; F.C.L. Bosman, *Drama en Toneel in Suid-Afrika* (Cape Town: J. Dusseau, 1928), vol. 1.

But these moments of early performance and their fragmentary incorporation, intriguing and resonant as they are, hardly make up a history; and I am more interested here in paradigms than in the past. The appearance over the last two decades of a wide variety of hybrid, yet specialized forms, from trade-union and workers' performance to the rural community theatre which saves lives by teaching people about child nutrition and AIDS – this range of forms suggests the importance of freeing up the preconceptions about theatre which most of us who comment upon it hold – even if the criteria for interpreting and judging theatre then become more various, and less stable, than we might like.

For Herbert Dhlomo, Western and African drama stemmed from the same urge to re-create, through action, imitation, rhythm and gesture, the sacred and secular stories of the community, although their traditions had developed differently over time. What was needed in South Africa, he argued, was a South African aesthetic which brought together these traditions.[6] Mission-educated, Dhlomo himself wrote some twenty-four plays along broadly Western lines, none very successful or lasting – apart perhaps from *The Girl Who Killed To Save* (1936), about the nineteenth-century Xhosa prophetess, Nonquase. This was the first published play in English by a black South African, and it is a forerunner of Fatima Dike's ritualistic, Anglo-Xhosa play of the mid-Seventies, *The Sacrifice of Kreli* (1976), in setting and subject, if not in style. But, as I said, the first truly formative example so far of successful creative interaction between Western and African traditions in South Africa has been provided by Athol Fugard: in the collaborative 'township plays' (as I call them) of Sophiatown in 1958–59, above all in the New Brighton work of 1965–73. The influence of this New Brighton work has been acknowledged by many later local playwrights, from Maishe Maponya to Mbongeni Ngema. The township plays represented a new type of theatre in the country, intense, improvisatory, and 'poor'; a type of theatre which, for all its limitations, legitimized a transgressive, interracial space – at least provisionally.[7]

It may be that the very provisionality of representation in the theatre, a site of varying and specific performance, allows an escape from the implications of seeming to privilege one set of discourses over another in any such interaction. The theatrical mode is unlike other literary modes in its reliance on space as well as time, on the body as well as, or instead of, the text – which may indeed help explain the relative lack of attention theatre has received in the construction of liter-

---

6   See Ursula Barnett, *A Vision of Order: A Study of Black South African Literature in English 1914–1918* (London: Sinclair Browne, 1983): 228–29.

7   See Dennis Walder, *Athol Fugard: The Township Plays* (Oxford & Cape Town: Oxford UP, 1993): Introduction, xxiii–xxxi.

ary history in South Africa, despite the impressive flowering of theatre over the last two or three decades. That flowering, alongside the development of a neo-Marxist conception of cultural production among a number of white men who listened during the Eighties, led to studies (by David Coplan, Robert Kavanagh, Martin Orkin and Ian Steadman) of performance traditions more broadly understood. These studies demonstrated that theatre is tied to the time of its creation, thereby limiting the potential of any given performance. They also made it seem that, if some were allowed to speak, this was always at the expense of others – as in 1959 with the jazz opera *King Kong*, the inspirational product of a multiracial mix of urban South African performance traditions which, because of the destruction of its generating communities under apartheid, generated a series of exploitative, pseudo-African productions such as *Ipi Tombi* (1974), made and enjoyed for years afterwards by well-off and well-meaning whites at home and abroad.[8]

However, the terms of debate initiated by this influential recent approach are much more applicable to popular forms like township theatre or music drama than to the more formative and lasting, if minority, theatre work which has emerged out of the Fugardian intervention. It is important to recall that, just as the history of any written or printed text is also the history of its production, reception and status, so, too, is the history of any staged performance. But it seems to be forgotten, even by the neo-Marxists who go along with this formulation, that the relevant conditions are difficult if not sometimes impossible to discern; moreover, that, even if we could make them out, the determining relationship is *in the last instance* – whenever that may be. Certain works of art create a distance between themselves and their socially generating conditions which lends them a degree of autonomy. The really difficult question is: *how far* is any specific work autonomous? Yet the need to connect the history of a genre such as theatre to the histories within which it circulates seems to me self-evident.

How else, for example, are we to understand the changing responses to Fugard, Kani and Ntshona's *The Island*? Set on the notorious prison of Robben Island, this play began as an unscripted performance with a coded title in an obscure private club in Cape Town in 1973, so as to avoid the banning or imprisonment of its co-creators; it then reappeared in London five months later with *Sizwe Bansi* in a season of so-called Statements Plays accompanied by playbills with details of the apartheid laws, thus provoking the South African Embassy to complain that the plays "contained propaganda aimed at discrediting [the Embassy,] the Govern-

---

[8] David B. Coplan, *In Township Tonight! South Africa's Black City Music and Theatre* (London & New York: Longman, 1985): 173–75, 217–19; Martin Orkin, *Drama and the South African State* (Manchester & New York: Manchester UP, 1991): 73–79, 171–72.

ment, and White South Africans in general," followed by wider dispersal abroad, which in turn made possible the first 'open' production back home at the Market Theatre in 1977 – although not before the release from imprisonment without trial the previous year of Kani and Ntshona for unscripted remarks during a performance in the Transkei of *Sizwe Bansi* reflecting unfavourably upon Chief George Mantanzima, the so-called "Minister of Justice" in the territory. The revival of *The Island* in Cape Town's Baxter Theatre in 1985 by Kani and Ntshona included a public call for the "immediate release" of "Mr Nelson Mandela and all political prisoners and detainees"; while its award-winning reappearance in 1995 with the original cast led to appreciation in the local liberal press of a "protest" now safely "turned [...] into history."[9] This last response implies an idea of history as something too easily severed from the present – a perception enabling those whose identity remains invested in dated power-structures to forget what those structures meant in terms of tyranny, torture and imprisonment without trial. Protest may seem out-dated in today's South Africa. But the changing realities of present and past, as even this brief excursion into the reception of *The Island* shows, invite a fresh look at how we conceptualize history, including theatre history.

For me, this is part of the reconceptualization of literary and cultural studies generally in relation to the various kinds of ahistorical interpretation which have emerged within the post-war Western paradigm, from the New Criticism to post-structuralism (the latter including some versions of post-colonial criticism). If we reconceive the literary 'text' as the literary 'work': that is, as "a related series of concretely determinable semiotic events that embody and represent processes of social and historical experience," a critical method follows that embraces both the history of the work's 'textualizations' *and* the history of its reception. As Jerome McGann (from whom I borrow these terms) points out, these histories imply heuristic distinctions: "between the work at its point of origin, the work through its subsequent transmissions, and the work situated in the immediate field of its present 'investigation'." Of course, these topics and foci cannot be pursued in isolation; they are part of a critical dialectic which encourages *various* points of view, each illuminating the other rather than – and this is where I depart from McGann – an illusory whole, which literary works engage with, reflect, and/or reproduce.[10]

9 Dale Lautenbach, "An Island of Dreams," *Weekend Argus* (Cape Town; 2 November 1985); Justin Pearce, "Visions of a rainbow culture," *Mail & Guardian* (21–27 July 1995): 28.
10 Jerome McGann, *The Beauty of Inflections: Literary Investigations in Historical Method and Theory* (Oxford: Clarendon, 1988): 10.

The appropriateness of such a reconceptualizing, historicist, but multiple perspective within the South African present seems plain to me. One area of current
discourse I could draw on in support of my view is that which is revising the past
in the present as an antidote to so-called settler history, or to the old yet abiding
inequities of the white liberal, "Bantu, Boer and Briton" approach[11] I can recall
from my university days in Cape Town, and which I notice with alarm has been
resuscitated in the 1996 BBC television series *Rhodes*. Both Liberals and Marxists
have been suitably criticized for their reductionist assumptions about the past, and
for importing theoretical perspectives from the present into the past without due
consideration for the provisionality of the evidence, for "the complexity as well as
the directness, that exists between past and present, between Africans and Europe-
ans, between all subsections of the population – and that exists between similar
groups at different times and different places."[12] According to revisionist South
African historian Jay Naidoo, there is a sense in which "all history is contemporary
history"; "The past lives on in the present, through genes and culture, through
ideas and traditions; and the present, because the past has to be filtered through a
temporal present, lives on in the past." Naidoo goes on to offer alternative versions
of well-known and often documented figures and events in South African history,
each posed as a question, asking, for example (I quote a chapter heading), "Was
Gandhi's South African Struggle inspired by Race, Class, or Nation?" Naidoo avoids
the "careless and over-enthusiastic present-minded history" anathematized by
Harrison Wright.[13] But his offer is insufficient. Why? Because it is still what
Nietzsche labeled "monumental" history:[14] listening to those above, rather than to
those nearer the ground, where most of us live.

To explain what I mean, this is where I would like to bring in Brecht's poem.
"*Fragen eines lesenden Arbeiters*" or "Questions from a worker who reads," which
has itself a revealing micro-history.[15] It was written while the author was in exile
from the Nazis in Denmark, and first published in a Moscow periodical in August
1936. Before it could appear in the mammoth Malik-Verlag edition of his poems
and plays, published nominally from London but in fact from Prague, the invasion

[11] See W.M. MacMillan, *Bantu, Boer and Briton: The Making of the South African Native Problem*
(Oxford: Clarendon, 1963).

[12] Harrison M. Wright, *The Burden of the Present: Liberal–Radical Controversy over Southern African History* (Cape Town: David Philip, 1977): 107.

[13] Jay Naidoo, *Tracking Down Historical Myths: Eight South African Cases* (Johannesburg: Ad.
Donker, 1989): 9–10.

[14] Friedrich Nietzsche, *On the Advantage and Disadvantage of History for Life*, tr. Peter Preuss
(Indianapolis: Hackett, 1980): 14–19.

[15] Brecht, "Questions from a worker who reads," in *Poems 1913–1956*, ed. Willett & Manheim,
252–53 and Notes, 505–506.

of Czechoslovakia in March 1939 took place. Brecht already had in hand the proofs of the poem, along with the whole section entitled "Poems from Exile," which, however, then had to be reset in Copenhagen, where it became part of the renamed *Svendborg Poems* published there in May 1939. The outbreak of war in September, and the occupation of Denmark the following spring, interrupted deliveries, so that new copies of the poems were still turning up in London bookshops as late as 1946 – over ten years after "Questions" was first written, to be read by audiences who had gone through the cataclysmic events which had changed the face of Europe and the world. If anything, the poem was made more, rather than less, relevant by the passage of time. "Who built Thebes of the seven gates?" it begins. "In the books you will find the names of kings. / Did the kings hand up the lumps of rock?" Its subject is the nature of empire, and history; questioning the kind of history celebrated in national festivals and the chronicles of the great, which dominated the imagination at the time, and which still prevails, not only, but very noticeably, in South Africa today. "Even in fabled Atlantis / The night the ocean engulfed it / The drowning still bawled for their slaves." Considering these lines in the present makes one wonder how far that country really has released itself from the grip of the colonizing imagination.

"The young Alexander conquered India. / Was he alone? / Caesar beat the Gauls. / Did he not even have a cook with him?" Brecht's poem speaks on behalf of the nameless of history, the civilians, the women and children, the victims and rejects – those whose voices question the claims of the great and the good, as well as the infamous and wicked. Today, when hero-worship and nation-building are fashionable again, it offers a salutary reminder to listen to those voices.

"What could the majority of Soweto, born long after Nelson Mandela entered jail, make of him other than as a symbol or an icon?"[16] Or, I might add, what could an earlier generation, of white English-speaking 'liberal–lefties' like myself, make of him, tuned as we were to a European song of Marxist opposition, whose own heroes have toppled from their feet of clay? This is not to question the extraordinary achievement of Mandela, much less that of the broad movement to which he belongs, in bringing the country to democracy and a new constitution enshrining rights for all, regardless of race, class, creed or gender. Rather, it is to remind ourselves of the testimony of those anonymous many who have suffered and died in the process, and of those whose voices are even now liable to be drowned out by the shouts of triumph.

---

[16] Eric Hobsbawm, *The Age of Extremes: The Short Twentieth Century 1914–1991* (London: Michael Joseph, 1994): 329.

One such voice is suggested by the role of Veronica, the young woman at the centre of *Valley Song*. Fugard is not a playwright who deals with the past in any obvious sense, although he does write about his personal past, as, most obviously, in *"Master Harold" ... and the Boys* (1982), in which he ruminates about a defining moment in his early teens. But his abiding interest has been in the discarded, the lowly, those on the fringes of organized society – an interest intensified rather than produced by the racialized structures of South African society. His characters' limits are tested as much by their inner compulsions as by the inherited dictates of social and political discourse: hence the contradictory drive towards myth evident in, say, *Dimetos* (1975) on the one hand; and towards the realities of the streets on the other, as in *My Children! My Africa!* (1989). In his best work he is pushed beyond these alternatives, fruitfully invoking both, as in the collaboration which became *The Island* – which, it is very much the point, does not mention any of the heroes of the resistance, much less Mandela himself – who, by the way, played Creon in a Robben Island production of *Antigone*, the play at the centre of *The Island*.[17] The surprising achievement of *Valley Song* is that its simple, parabolic story registers a troubling awareness of contemporary realities, while reconnecting its audience with certain long traditions in the South Africa literary space, such as the *plaasroman* [farm novel], and the Karoo pastoral of Pauline Smith.

The setting is a Karoo village, the characters two "arme ou kleurlinge" (poor old coloureds) – a derogatory phrase rejected by Veronica even as she uses it because, she says, things have changed for them.[18] But how far have they? The story we listen to from the intervening Author reveals that Buks dreads losing his patch of lovingly tended earth to the incoming white man, while unwilling to ask for his new rights from the country's first democratic government.

BUKS   Your think those groot Kokkedoore are going to worry about me and my few akkers? Anyway, I don't think they even know where the village is. You told me yourself once that you couldn't find us on the map.

VERONICA   That was the school map, Oupa! Don't be silly now. The Government doesn't sit down with a school map and try to find all the places where it must do things. It already knows where everybody is. We had the elections here, didn't we? ... just like all the other places in the country. (26)

But old Buks, who has already lost both wife and daughter to the desire for change, is terrified of it, and clings to Veronica, whose need for fulfilment leads her to challenge his authority, even at the cost of his love. When Buks turns a deaf ear to her pleas for escape, she exclaims: "Now *you* listen to *me*, Oupa!"

---

17 Nelson Mandela, *Long Walk to Freedom: The Autobiography* (Boston MA & London: Little, Brown, 1994): 441.

18 Athol Fugard, *Valley Song* (London: Faber & Faber, 1996): 28; further references in the text.

This is a turning-point in the play, as well as in Fugardian theatrical intervention, which has moved from breaking what he used to call South Africa's
conspiracy of silence, speaking on behalf on the silenced others, towards offering a
space for others to speak – as in the immediately preceding work, *My Life* (premiered three months after the elections of April 1994), which gave five young
women of varying race and class backgrounds the opportunity to present their
personal biographies on stage. But things are more complicated than they appear,
as the microhistories of production, textualization and reception have already begun to reveal. Looking for that key phrase, "Now *you* listen to *me*, Oupa!" in the
published text, I found instead the much milder, even plaintive expression, "You're
not *listening* to me, Oupa" (41); when I asked the playwright to explain, he told me
that Lisa–Gay Hamilton – cast for the role in the production which American Equity forbade the 'coloured' South African actress Esmeralda Bihl to perform – had
found the original phrase too unassertive, and so she revised it; a revision Fugard
then allowed back into the play as it continues to be performed elsewhere in the
world, by Bihl.[19] So the printed text has already been overtaken by its production.

This change does not mean that the young woman's voice speaks for herself,
however – in the sense that, for example, Gcina Mhlophe's Zandile speaks for her
creator's personal experiences in *Have You Seen Zandile?*, a 1986 play which still
struggles for space in any current version of South African theatrical history, including Martin Orkin's otherwise exemplary *Drama and the South African State*, or
even Michael Chapman's new account of *Southern African Literatures*. In Orkin's
book, the striking emergence of women in South African theatres is marginalized
into what amounts to a postscript, where he argues that playwrights like Mhlophe
enlist our sympathy only to neutralize "whatever subversive thrusts appear to inform the work" by their "intimate and personal"[20] perspectives. Listening to Mhlophe, and others such as Fatima Dike, Sue Pam–Grant and Reza de Wet, as they
have been mediated by feminist South African critics (eg, Dorothy Driver, Miki
Flockemann and Marcia Blumberg), helps counter this form of cultural-materialist
orthodoxy by suggesting ways of thinking beyond familiar, gender-stereotyped
notions of subjectivity and inferiority. These notions deny women their voice and
agency, not so much by silencing (the old method) but by not listening. As Gayatri
Spivak suggests, the question "Who should speak?" may at times be less crucial
than "Who will listen?"[21]

---

[19] See Fugard interview below, 227.
[20] Orkin, *Drama and the South African State*, 231.
[21] Gayatri Chakravorty Spivak, *The Post-Colonial Critic: Interviews, Strategies, Dialogues*, ed.
Sara Harasym (London & New York: Routledge, 1990): 59–60.

Veronica is not denied agency; at least insofar as the Author-figure and her grandfather *are* obliged to listen to her, when she expresses her naive dreams of becoming a famous singer. The Author admits at the end of the play that the future belongs to her, while wishing that the Valley could "stay the unspoilt, innocent little world it was when I first discovered it. I am not as brave about change as I would like to be," he confesses, before she finally departs (53). The young woman's power lies in the future; his remains glued to the past. Insofar as that past continues in the present, he retains control. But then it is up to us, the audience, to resist him. By, for instance, taking the Brechtian perspective prompted by the gap between Author and his alter ego Buks; by recognizing that this is a kind of theatre which intervenes within the present state of transition, offering audiences the freedom to enter into a debate between present and past. The debate is about occupying space: the space to live, not just to survive, and the space to be heard, not just to speak.

Real freedom frees the oppressor as well as the oppressed; interestingly, Fugard claims this play has in some sense freed him, too:

> One of the things that I've been liberated from – maybe dangerously so – is a sense of having to speak for a silenced majority; of having to try and break a conspiracy of silence that was abroad in South Africa. Maybe there's been a dangerous liberation from that responsibility, and now the voice is only my own. I speak for myself, except that something I became conscious of in the writing of *Valley Song* – one of the wonderfully liberating aspects of the experience that I've gone through as a new South African – is that I'm now free to be a total Afrikaner, and that maybe I could even conceive of a scenario where I am a voice for the Afrikaner.

"*Dis wonderlik*," he told an interviewer at the Klein Karoo festival in April, 1996, where *Valley Song* was a sensation; "*Afrikaans neem nou sy plek in 'n groter werklikheid* [It's wonderful. Afrikaans is now taking its place in a greater reality]."

Is it time to listen to that Afrikaans voice, finding itself a new place in the present, by disengaging from its white supremacist past? Maybe. The point is, Fugard's theatre seems almost alone at present in engaging so readily with the shifting relations of power in South Africa, and in attempting to find a new perspective on the past. His Author-figure's nostalgia invites critical examination of the turn to the past in current South African theatre, a theatre summed up by one review of the 1994–95 National Vita Awards as "Looking back in nostalgia."[22] To mention the most notorious example, why does the co-creator of *Woza Albert!* and *Sarafina!*, Mbongeni Ngema, find nothing better to do with a scandalously large subsidy of over fourteen million rand than to create a *Sarafina 2* (December 1995), while

---

[22] Matthew Krouse, "Looking back in nostalgia," *Mail & Guardian* (October 6, 1995): 29.

local theatre starves of funds? Meanwhile, the protest writers of the townships, like Matsemela Manaka and Maishe Maponya, have fallen silent. Fatima Dike's research into her people's past has produced compelling drama since *The Sacrifice of Kreli*, such as the workshop production *Mantatisi, Queen of the Batlokwa*, which I saw young amateurs perform to an audience of ten in a small room in Cape Town in 1994; but her work as Writer in Residence at the Open University involved rewriting a play, *Glass House*, from her Space Theatre days in Cape Town in 1979.

Or is all this merely how things *must* seem, when theatre is understood as little more than a cultural form requiring national awards, institutions, festivals, administrators and buildings, all resting on a monumentalist notion of the past? Perhaps we should follow Brecht in questioning the distinction between what goes on in the theatre and what happens in the street. The public arena in South Africa is a space for representations of many kinds, not necessarily fictional or conventionally theatrical – a space where I can listen to theatre for development, where I can also hear Zanendaba, Mhlophe's group of self-taught storytellers, who help others to tell their stories, the stories of their lives but also of their people: the myths and fables which create and sustain a meaning for them in circumstances of continuing suffering and deprivation. For the barely educated, the illiterate, the women and children excluded from the centres of power, those anonymous multitudes whose waking hours are dominated by the struggle for existence, Zanendaba, and the few who are following their example, provide perhaps their only chance to tell their story, to speak and be listened to in the 'new' South Africa.

This chance to be listened to, minimal as it may seem, is after all the result of new freedoms: to move about the country at will, to talk about taboo yet everyday, intimate subjects, to treat theatrical performance as part of a continuum of cultural activity. One report on the opening of the Truth and Reconciliation hearings in East London City Hall in April 1996 described it thus: "From the moment Archbishop Desmond Tutu clambered up on to the stage it was apparent that the occasion was more one of dramatic performance than judicial enquiry."[23] Intended as a belittling comparison, the remark backfires. It reminds us that the theatrical (to offer an intervention) does not have to be on what is usually thought of as a stage; especially not in South Africa, where that stage has for so long been exclusive and excluding.[24]

[23] David Beresford, "Truth hearings beginning in South Africa," *Guardian* (16 April 1996).

[24] I would like to thank Liz Trew and Miki Flockemann for assistance in obtaining *Valley Song* reviews for this essay, which is a revised and abbreviated version of a paper first delivered at the "South African Literary History" Symposium, University of Essen, July 1996.

Lessons From a Fair Country

03 Jeanne Colleran

W ITHIN WEEKS OF EACH OTHER during the winter of 1995, two views of South Africa were on display on New York stages. The first, *Valley Song*, written by and starring Athol Fugard, completed two sold-out runs, marking another predictable success for the South African drama- tist, whose works enjoy an unparalleled history of receptivity in the United States.[1] The second, *A Fair Country*, nearly half of which is set in the coastal town of Dur- ban, in the Natal province of South Africa, had a less successful but nonetheless noteworthy run at Lincoln Center. *A Fair Country* was written by Jon Robin Baitz, an increasingly visible American playwright who had lived in South Africa as a teenager during the Seventies.

The two plays confront similar issues: preeminently, they are about genera- tional struggle, but each is concerned also with cultural struggle and the struggle over culture. Together, these familial and cultural/political considerations blend themselves into cautionary tales about American and South African futures. This overlap in theme and a shared aesthetic sense support the view that Baitz is more an heir to Athol Fugard than to any American playwright and gives to Fugard the son absent among new South African dramatists, In fact, Jon Robin Baitz's *A Fair Country* has already been compared to Fugard's *A Lesson from Aloes*, and clearly the theme of personal and political betrayal absorbs both writers. Other similarities between Fugard and Baitz are observable: both are fashioners of modern morality plays more than they are of political polemic: both are extraordinarily interested in the question of honourable conduct in the midst of complex and compromising historical situations: if Athol Fugard writes of reluctant colonizers, Jon Robin Baitz writes of reluctant imperialists.

Despite the historical sense that informs each playwright's world, Fugard and Baitz prefer to write domestic dramas in which the public and political invade and destabilize or destroy the private and personal. For this preference, Fugard and

---

[1] I discuss Fugard's popularity on American stages in "Athol Fugard and the Problematics of the Liberal Critique," *Modern Drama* 38.3 (1995): 389–407.

Baitz make themselves liable to criticism on either side of the equation; depending on the political interests of the audience member, either playwright's work can be criticized for its inability to elaborate convincingly the correspondence between private and public spheres. In both *A Fair Country* and *Valley Song*, political struggles overlay and exacerbate each other, but the correlation between them is often left unspecified, underdeveloped, perhaps purposely unexplored. Other problems nag each work: the ending of *A Fair Country*, for example, is abrupt and unsatisfactory, a virtual cliché of familial rapprochement. The language in *Valley Song* seems impoverished compared to that of Fugard's major plays; but, even more fundamentally, the play's premise – of a child wishing to flee the nest – offers far fewer dramatic possibilities than the switched passbook of *Sizwe Bansi is Dead* or the rebellious Afrikaner artist of *A Road to Mecca*.

In addition to specific analysis of each play, what I would like to do here is to look at them in tandem: first, to investigate how the depiction of the place and history of South Africa grounds a larger discussion of the idea of liberalism; and secondly, how this discussion in turn forces a re-evaluation of the critical boundaries of plays termed 'post-colonial.'

That both Baitz's play and Fugard's could command sizeable audiences on prominent New York stages is one index of the American interest in South African politics and the American admiration for South African theatre. Yet both interest and admiration are based on a vexed amalgamation of unfeigned esteem and unacknowledged self-interest. South African poet Breyten Breytenbach has described Africa as a "dark hinterland of the psyche,"[2] and his metaphor speaks to how African (here South African) cultural products can be used as a screen on which to project, with all the denial that accompanies these projections, masked but deeply self-referential concerns. In these plays in particular, South Africa is a screen on which to project either hope or despair at the viability of liberal politics; and, as the plays reveal, the demise of liberalism is an issue of crucial interest to both the South African and the American playwright.

Valley Song is built around two crises and one theatrical innovation. These features of the play, I will argue, are accountable for its ultimate re-inscription, despite its concern for the emergence of a new South Africa, of the liberal/colonialist paradigm. Both of the crises involve dispossession. Abraam "Buks" Jonkers, a 'coloured' man in his seventies living in the Karoo, ekes out a meagre existence for himself and his granddaughter, Veronica, by farming a few acres on the abandoned property of the white owners, the (unsubtly named) Landmans. Buks's first

---

[2] Breyten Breytenbach, "Why are Writers Always the Last to Know?," *New York Times Review of Books* (28 March 1993): 15.

fear, which is partially realized, is that the land will be purchased by another white man, and he will be thrown off it. His second fear, more fully realized, is that his granddaughter will leave him and the Valley to seek her fortune in the dangerous city of Johannesburg; this fear has been fuelled by the loss of his only child, Caroline, Veronica's mother, who had been lured away to the city in her youth, only to die there in childbirth. By the end of the play, Veronica does leave her grandfather (or Oupa) to try and make it as a singer and songwriter in Johannesburg. Veronica's ambition, while touchingly realistic in its naivety and youthful exuberance, is also painful to observe, since her songs and singing are excruciatingly devoid of talent. One example of the lyrics she composes will suffice:

> You plant seeds
> And I sing songs,
> We're Oupa and Veronica.
> Yes, Oupa and Veronica.
> You work hard
> And I dream dreams,
> That's Oupa and Veronica.
> Yes, Oupa and Veronica.[3]

Buks is not the only one who warns Veronica against leaving the Valley; she is also discouraged by the play's third character, the Author, the white man who eventually purchases the Landman property and who advises Veronica to cut her dreams to fit her opportunities. The most perplexing feature of *Valley Song* is Athol Fugard's insistence that the same actor play both Buks, the coloured farmer, and the Author, the new white landman. In performance, the character-change is signalled when the actor dons a woollen cap, which Buks wears and the Author does not. The single-author/double-character innovation is the feature most responsible for unsettling the calm surface of what would otherwise be a parabolically simple and genuinely moving drama.

The problems of such doubling are well illustrated by one of the Author's key monologues, where he explains Buks's sense of abandonment by God when, after a life of fidelity to church, family, and land, he loses his precious wife, daughter, granddaughter and soil. It is a doubly distressing speech, in part because the Author/character is either unaccountably omniscient or distressingly voyeuristic,[4] and in part because Buks, though passionate and eloquent, is not allowed to

---

[3] Athol Fugard, *Valley Song* (London: Faber & Faber, 1996): 48. Further page references are in the text

[4] One of the more unsettling moments of the play is when Veronica catches the Author watching her watch, through a window, a white woman's television."How long has Master been watching?" Veronica asks. "A long time," says the Author (20).

narrate his own spiritual crisis. However, the ventriloquism is not especially jar-
ring, since the Author has actually been directing the course of interpretation from
the play's opening moments. Because Fugard has written a narrative frame for the
drama's events, the play begins and ends with the Author's assessments. In performance, these judgements are further complicated by the playwright's assumption of the role of the Author. When Fugard walked onto the bare stage during the
performance I saw, the moment was riveting: Fugard's considerable personal
charisma, his stature as an internationally celebrated playwright, his reputation as
a skilled actor, and the decades-long admiration for his vigilant and courageous
denunciation of the apartheid regime, made it nearly impossible to separate the
Author from the playwright. Indeed, it is fair to say that Fugard's presence on stage
was the single most significant reason for the play's success in New York. The
elision between playwright and character was exacerbated further by the
conversational tone Fugard employed at the play's beginning; in the performance I
saw, Fugard began by thanking the audience for braving a raging snow storm to
make it to the theatre; intimacy and approval were established almost immediately,
and when Fugard drew a handful of pumpkin seeds from his pocket, explaining
they were white boer pumpkin seeds that he carried with him, the gesture seemed
more like an actor's talisman than the predetermined opening lines of the play. It
was, in fact, impossible to separate the improvisational from the scripted or to
pinpoint the exact moment when the playwright disappeared into the character of
the Author. Perhaps, he never did.

Consequently, when the Author describes Buks's anguish in terms analogous to
Job's predicament and puts the loss of Buks's daughter, granddaughter, and wife
on a par with the loss of his land, these judgements are largely accepted. The Job
analogy reinforces the play's preference for existential over political crisis, since it
places the generational struggle within the cosmological plight of the unjustly re-
warded just man. Yet, however much the Author/playwright would deem Buks's
suffering existential, the tale of inevitable human loss is tied to a tale that is historically specific and material: the ownership and stewardship of the earth. In this
entanglement, the moving simplicity of Buks's grief and the doctrinaire views of
the Author crowd out political critique. Clearly the losses are not equivalencies.
Buks's status as a squatter with neither political nor economic capital sufficient to
alter his state is a direct result of apartheid. Nor can Caroline's or Veronica's desire
to flee the Valley be drained of history or economics: the lack of opportunity for
either young woman, and Veronica's specifically stated desire to do more than
scrub a whiteman's floors, are similarly connected to the recent racist past. Only
the event of the death of Buks's wife is politically without implication; though

Fugard intimates elsewhere in the play that all deaths have historical and political consequences, since "white spooks" haunt the village and the coloured labourers have themselves become part of the soil (33). Despite the frustrating hints that Fugard does recognize the material circumstances that have caused Buks's losses, the Author nonetheless prefers narratives of generational difference or of restless, creative temperaments. The maddening refusal to name historical causality or to allow Buks to offer his own explanations produces a dynamic that brings to mind Edward Said's analysis of the insular world of Joseph Conrad's *Heart of Darkness*. Describing how the politics and aesthetics of Conrad's novel are both imperialist, Said makes a comment applicable to the dramatic structure of *Valley Song*:

> If we cannot truly understand someone else's experience, and if we must therefore depend on the assertive authority of the sort that Kurtz wields as a white man in the jungle or that Marlow, another white man *wields as narrator*, there is no use looking for other, non-imperialist alternatives; the system has simply eliminated them and made them unthinkable.[5]

The frame of *Valley Song* enacts the kind of circularity that Said goes on to describe as "not only aesthetically but also mentally unassailable."

What motivated Fugard's decision to use one actor doubly as both Buks and the Author? Inevitable, it seems a forced identification, an obligatory alignment of the two as brothers of the soil, with equal entitlement. The Author does concede that the "earth is the Lord's" and that Buks has an ancestral claim to his acres. Yet, despite his reservations and his desire that "God had countersigned the Title Deed" (31), the Author goes on to purchase the abandoned plot, and he does so when Buks, in an effort to force some recognition of an entitlement secured through years of labour, offers him a wheelbarrow of vegetables. In the Author's own words, "That wheelbarrow load of vegetables did it" (30). How could he "pass up the chance to own a piece of native Karoo earth that would allow me to brag and boast about my own pumpkins [...] my own beetroot [...] my own potatoes" (30)? Reservations about claim and entitlement quickly evaporate, and in the end, the Author has resurrected an apartheid-era relationship, allowing Buks to stay on the land that he will continue to work and will never own. The play's symbolic close has the Author claiming, without apparent irony, to have reinvigorated Buks after the departure of his granddaughter by giving him seeds to plant, seeds which will produce "flat, white, Boer pumpkins" (54).

In the course of this 'post-colonial' play about the emergence of a New South Africa where courts of appeal and the voting box will supplant the "arme ou

---

[5] Edward W. Said, *Culture and Imperialism* (New York: Random House/Vintage, 1994): 24 (emphasis mine). Further page references are in the text.

kleurling," the crawling and the begging, colonialist relations and paradigms remain intact. Said's assertion that at "some very basic level, imperialism means
thinking about, settling on, controlling land that you do not possess, that is distant,
that is lived on and owned by others" (7) is an apt summary of the Author's actions. Moreover, the attitudes of both ruler and ruled, particularly the Author's
paternalism towards Veronica and Buks's own resistance to modernization, are
consonant with the attitudes which first sustained imperialism and later nurtured
liberalism. In the former, the acceptance of subordination, according to the historian D.K. Fieldhouse, made "empire durable."[6] In terms of liberalism, the preference for individual rapprochement over systematic change, is clearly the path the
Author follows. To be fair, the text reminds us that Veronica does claim protection
by law and seeks equal representation and equal opportunity, and the Author acknowledges that he is both fearful and jealous of the changes Veronica will know.
But in the Valley, the Author would prefer to stand outside of history and have the
village remain the "unspoilt, innocent little world it was when I first discovered it"
(53). Such critics as the North American ones who regard the play as testimonial
drama or as another of Fugard's "reports from the front"[7] are guilty of standing
outside of both history and geography, failing to recognize that a 'post-colonial'
drama that does more to re-inscribe the categories of the last and less to advocate
the aspirations of the new nation offers at best only ambivalent testimony.

Said also suggests that while "direct colonialism has largely ended, imperialism, as we shall see, lingers where it has always been, in a kind of general cultural
sphere as well as in specific political, ideological, economic, and social practices"
(9). It is this sphere that is the subject of Jon Robin Baitz's play, *A Fair Country*.
Written by one who spent much of his childhood in South Africa, and who was
partially educated there but has since returned to his native country, Baitz's play
gives us the opportunity to watch non-South African characters attempting to understand South African society and their relation to it. South Africa, in *A Fair
Country* is the "dark hinterland" or screen described above. It is a play which
grapples with what Rob Nixon has described as the "vexed sense of half-shared
histories" that marks American and South African relationships, and which had
led to "an illusory sense of mutual intelligibility."[8] Hence, one of the key values of
this play is its exposure of how South Africa has been constructed by non-South
Africans and to what purpose. Baitz's drama capitalizes on the American characters' horror at apartheid, which they regard as an anomalous, aberrant form of

---

[6] Quoted in Said, *Culture and Imperialism*, 11.

[7] Fugard, *Valley Song*, back-cover text.

[8] Rob Nixon, *Homelands, Harlem, and Hollywood* (New York: Routledge, 1995): 3.

racism unique to South Africa. Ultimately, *A Fair Country*, like its more accomplished predecessor, *Angels in America* by Tony Kushner, is a play of "self-reckoning" which must "trace the trajectory of its habitual destructions."[9]

Nearly half of *A Fair Country* is set in South Africa, specifically in Durban. Like the Karoo valley, the locale has actual geographical and historical status within the play, but it quickly becomes a figurative pole. In fact, one of the more fascinating aspects of Baitz's visual construction of the play is its movement from highly particularized settings – the back yard of the Durban household and the cold, modernist apartment in Amsterdam – to nearly bare stages meant to represent an airport in Central Africa or the jungle of Mexico. The staging of *A Fair Country* insists both on the impossibility of standing outside of history and culture and on the exilic condition of rootless Americans. But the spawning-ground for the problems of the Burgess family is located – at least initially – in South Africa.

A Fair Country is the story of a family, Harry and Patrice Burgess and their two sons, Alec, a student at Columbia studying journalism and Gil, a high-school student. In 1978, just two years after the Soweto uprising, three of the family are living in Durban, where Harry is a cultural affairs attaché. His efforts to increase cross-cultural understanding enact a meta-commentary on the play's own assessment of the role of art as political commentary or political action. Harry brings American artists out to tour in Africa, and his choices are clearly aligned to American nationalist values. Here Baitz allows himself to lampoon political correctness, Sixties hipness, and earnest populism. Harry sponsors plays by ex-convicts performing in something with the less-than-subtle name *The Idiot's Delight*, and he brings Burl Ives-like folk artists to sing and clog their way into African hearts, and black American dancers who provide him with the self-satisfaction of seeing "the South African police vomiting with rage" at the effect one of his dance groups has on young black South Africans.[10] Harry and Patrice also sponsor the predictable post-performance cultural rapprochement in the form of late-night parties.

Unfortunately for Harry's efforts, it appears that his wife has violated a key principle of diplomatic conduct: she has vented her pent-up frustrations on the family's black South African maid, who is subsequently carted off to jail. Patrice, a drinker, smoker, and sayer of the repressed, unvarnished truth, is worrisome to Harry, who ascribes her hysteria to the difficulty of living in apartheid South Africa, a conclusion/rationalization that Patrice espouses as well. In order to remove

---

[9] Una Chaudhuri, *Staging Place: The Geography of Modern Drama* (Ann Arbor: U of Michigan P, 1996): 249.

[10] One wonders, after all, why the Author does not advise Veronica honestly about her level of talent or at least, if he sees promise in it, give her some leads to pursue.

his distraught wife from South Africa, Harry provides what he believes to be an inconsequential list of his elder son's black-activist friends to his diplomatic superior, who in turn submits the list to the CIA. Harry's incredible naivety – the natural consequence of clinging (even while living in South Africa) to a belief in apoliticality – gets his family out of South Africa, but, within two years, his elder son has been assassinated, the persons on the list have been detained or have died, the marriage breaks up, and Gil the younger, now openly gay, son repudiates both his parents.

Clearly, Baitz, like Fugard, wishes to explore differing generational responses as well as the impact of the political context upon personal lives. But there are important differences in the way that Baitz examines how these private tensions intersect with larger political issues, and his plays offer a kind of analysis that Fugard's dramas often do not, even as they fail to achieve the kind of admirable economy and empathetic appeal that Fugard's do. Reconciliation is Fugard's perennial theme. But if, in *The Blood Knot*, the actual blood-brothers Morrie and Zach must reconcile themselves to remaining connected against a world that will never incorporate them, they have been replaced by the time of *Playland* with metaphorical brothers – the white man, Gideon, and the black man, Martinus – who exchange personal forgiveness and model what Fugard clearly believes is necessary in the larger, public sphere. *Valley Song* is an extension of the value Fugard places on charity, personal reconciliation, and benevolence over political solutions.

While Baitz's *A Fair Country* shares with Fugard's drama a concern for how private tensions are played out against larger political dynamics, the play does not suggest that individual agency can solve systemic problems. While Baitz's play depends upon an exchange of confessions that also structures works like *Playland*, *A Fair Country* suggests that, if personal reconciliation is largely a fragile hope, then cultural understanding hangs on an even more tenuous thread. For example, immediately after Patrice has her black maid arrested for her angry, pot-smashing outburst, she and her younger son, Gil, attempt to puzzle out what has just happened. Patrice hypothesizes that the problem is "role confusion": as an egalitarian American, she is uncomfortable in the class- and race-conscious role of the South African matron. Patrice simply refuses to play "at being some goddam lump-ankled white Anglican housewife managing" her servant's every move.[11] Patrice delivers this defence – a smug assertion of American ethical superiority – even as she wipes her maid's blood from her sleeve. But Patrice is temperamentally mercurial and ethically conflicted, hence a source of growing bewilderment for her

---

[11] Jon Robin Baitz, *A Fair Country* (Johannesburg: Witwatersrand UP, 1992): 19. Further page references are in the text

son. When Gil wonders whether the maid's violence is a form of "that impenetrable African anger," Patrice chastises him for making some sort of "racial test case" out of a personal clash (18). The about-face she enacts, from suggesting that socially inscribed roles inhibited her relationship with the maid to her claim that their differences were merely "personal," is reversed yet again: "Was it cultural?" Patrice asks rhetorically. "I'll give you that" (19).

One American critic has read this scene as exemplary of the corrupting effects of having to live in South Africa. The explanation, like one of Patrice's own, hits a convenient but inaccurate mark. Rather, Patrice's inability to explain her anger is an indication of the enervated state of sociopolitical analysis in America, but it is also indicative of the failure of liberal politics in America. The remarkable insight of *A Fair Country* is that the failure of the political analysis is symptomized as personal failure; thus the failure of liberal politics remains mysterious, beyond the characters' powers of recognition.

To put this dynamic in more specific terms: Harry and Patrice are so inept at political analysis, of seeing how their own small actions are interpellated within – and partly predicated by – a larger system of social and political gestures meant to conserve the status quo even as it makes small shows of enfranchisement, that when an incident such as "the maid going berserk" makes this abstract problem something that must be addressed, the Burgesses turn most easily to personal blame. Patrice, however, despite her capriciousness and her contradictions, has a more complex social vision than her husband, the petty diplomat, does. For, just as Patrice cannot define for herself an effective way of dealing fairly with employees habituated to authoritarian treatment, her husband cannot articulate the value of his work, the worthiness of the very enterprise which obsesses him. At best, inviting American folk-dancers to clog their way from Cape Town to Queen's Town is a benign activity; at worst, as is the case in *A Fair Country*, it is not diplomacy or cultural exchange but a ruse for covert activities. Again, like his wife, Harry suspects what he also endorses, but he too lacks the critical political discourse which would allow him both to interrogate and to replace his liberal assumptions. And, as good liberals, Patrice and Harry take personal responsibility for what cannot be addressed publicly. In short, the Burgesses are experiencing a crisis for which they have no language or conceptual map. Their crisis is a crisis of alterity of the kind described by Sanford Budick as a "failure of culture, in relationship to otherness, that was the frame of [social] undertaking."[12] The Burgesses' view of cultural ex-

---

[12] Sanford Budick, "Crisis of Alterity: Cultural Untranslatability and the Experience of Secondary Otherness," in *The Translatability of Cultures*, ed. Sanford Budick & Wolfgang Iser (Stanford CA: Stanford UP, 1996): 5.

change is a version of neo-colonialism, one which is a view from the centre that insists that the "world is heterogeneous but ultimately one; that cultural difference is transportable, and if it is not it is not likely to be interesting."[13] The notion of un-bridgeable differences in culture – the fact of incommensurability – cannot be entertained. So much have the Burgesses invested in the triple myth of cultural exchange as cultural understanding, the beneficence of liberal politics, and the efficacy of American earnestness, that they are not merely Innocents Abroad but Idiots Abroad.

Just as the Burgesses fail and self-destruct, the liberal, self-legitimating dream of America as global peacemaker also fails in *A Fair Country*. As Fugard does in *Playland*, Baitz sets his play against a historical example of failed liberalism: the demise of the Carter administration during the Iran hostage crisis. Ultimately, *A Fair Country* maintains that efforts at cross-cultural understanding lead as often to ambiguity, to unintelligibility, and to a recognition of incommensurability, as they do to insight. Getting to a fair country, to a fair assessment of a country, is impos-sible when one version of a national identity (the 'idea of South Africa'), frequently a strategic demonization as in the case of Iran and Iraq, or simply a wilful distor-tion, as in the case of South Africa, is pitted against another, equally mythic version of national identity (the 'idea of America').

Baitz's play contributes both to ongoing dialogue about the future of America's secular faith in liberalism and to discussions about the relationship of art and poli-tics. By making the confused Harry the Voice of America, the play asks questions such as: who gets to represent a national? – a Fugard? a Ngema? a rural folk-mu-sician, an urban poet, a black rapper, Disney? Who authorizes this representation of nationhood and what relation does the representation bear to economic values or political agenda, both tacit and overt? How much culture is translatable? And what is the cost involved in the transition? What is the relation between art and polity? *A Fair Country* is no abstract tract on these theoretical concerns; it does not explore any of them exhaustively; it merely raises most of them, which in Ameri-can theatre is perhaps remarkable enough. Most searingly of all, Baitz's play suggest the extent to which an entirely private agenda – Patrice's hysteria – drives public conduct, and has far-reaching consequences. If Baitz's play is to be read as parabolically as *Valley Song*, the suggestion made is that American narcissism is costly and dangerous.

In many ways, Baitz's play is far less polished than Fugard's. Some linkages are left unexplored, like the notion of blood-sacrifice raised in the play's opening

---

[13] Elleke Boehmer, *Colonial and Postcolonial Literature: Migrant Metaphors* (Oxford: Oxford UP, 1995): 236.

scene and the blood-sacrifice of the elder Burgess son. And Patrice's evolution at the drama's end into a conciliator and concerned mother is difficult to fathom, given her earlier role as the anarchic figure who both reveals and destroys. The truce forged between the two remaining Burgesses is a delicate one; and, like the odd symbolism that ends *Valley Song*, the bond between mother and son is formed in opposition to a common, unseen native Other who might steal Gil's archaeological find – the cultural artefact he wishes to conserve.

Despite these weaknesses, Baitz's play suggests a more coherent correspondence between the historical periods it invokes – the liberal dream and Jeffersonian faith of the Carter years; the smiling self-interest of the Iran–Contra Reagan years – and the effect of these historical moments on individual lives. Like the hostages released only after Reagan's inauguration, the Burgesses have been held captive by their own uncritical idealism and the menacing underside of American diplomacy. Baitz goes further, too, to suggest not only the intersection of the individual and the national community, but of the nation and the world. Baitz's play attempts to enlarge simpler paradigms of post-colonial drama, suggesting a greater reciprocity of influence than is figured in the usual imperialist narrative. He wishes to forge a new, geopolitical theatre. Baitz also exposes cultural exchange as cultural appropriation or cultural imposition. Ultimately, Baitz's play offers no effective alternative to political liberalism, and *A Fair Country* clearly mourns this loss. Unlike the triumphant ending of *Angels in America*, where the new world-order will be insistently diverse, *A Fair Country* ends in exile and to a large degree in pessimism. Perhaps this exilic point of view has brought Baitz to Nadine Gordimer's assessment of the American future where "History is against you." Perhaps it explains Fugard's nostalgia and hope and Baitz's discouragement and near-resignation. Liberalism is at a dead end in the United States, for, as Gordimer rightly states:

> White Americans cannot give to blacks a lost identity; black Americans are reluctant to accept that that identity cannot be found in an avatar of apartheid. They are all Americans, and whether the whites like it or not, and whether the blacks like it or not, a common destiny has to be worked out. Alas, Martin Luther King is dead and you have no Mandela.[14]

Yes. Alas.[15]

————— ℰ ℛ —————

[14] Nadine Gordimer, "Blacks Apart," *New York Times Magazine* (8 June 1997): 48.

[15] I would like to thank Marcia Blumberg, Dennis Walder, and Toby Zinman for several valuable discussions of South African theatre which helped to enrich the present essay.

Illustrations

PLATE 1:   Mark Fleishman and Jenny Reznek, *Medea*
(Jay Pather and Bo Petersen, January 1996)

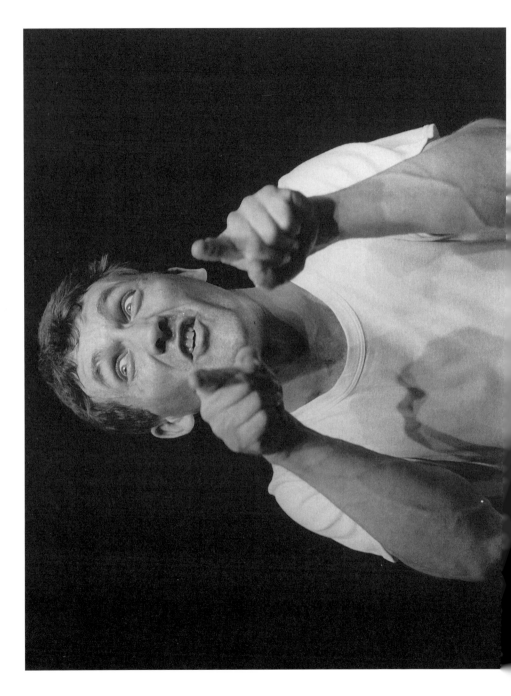

PLATE 2:   Andrew Buckland, *The Ugly Noo Noo*
(Andrew Buckland, July 1988)

PLATE 3:   Athol Fugard, *Boesman and Lena*
(Bill Currie and Nomhle Nkonyeni, July 1993)

PLATE 4:   Athol Fugard, *Valley Song*
                     (Esmeralda Bihl and Athol Fugard, July 1995)

PLATE 5: Junction Avenue Theatre Company, *Sophiatown*
(Ramolao Makhene, Siphiwe Khumalo, Arthur
Molepo and Patrick Shai, February 1986)

PLATE 6:   Junction Avenue Theatre Company, *Tooth and Nail*
(Megan Kruskal and Daphne Hlomuka, July 1989)

PLATE 7: Gcina Mhlophe, *Have You Seen Zandile?*
(Thoko Ntshinga and Gcina Mhlophe, August 1987)

PLATE 8: *Madam & Eve*
(cartoon reflecting on the *Sarafina 2* fiasco,
Mail & Guardian, June 14, 1996, page 30)

PLATE 9:   William Kentridge and the Handspring
Puppet Company, *Faustus in Africa*
(Adrian Kohler and Basil Jones, April 1995)

PLATE 10: Fatima Dike, *So What's New?*
(Doris Sihula, Nomsa Xaba, Motshabi Tyele,
and Petunia Maboa, 1990)

PLATE 11: Gcina Mhlophe and Janet Suzman,
The Good Woman of Sharkville
(Pamela Nomvete, June 1996)

Performing Race, Gender and Sexuality ❧

The Body of Change and the Changing Body in the Plays of Junction Avenue Theatre Company

ᘂ Anne Fuchs

I
T IS FASHIONABLE TODAY for theorists both inside and outside the theatre to consider postmodernism as no longer a dismal sequel to modernism but, rather, as a movement which may precede or even predict the birth of new forms of cultural expression. Not surprisingly, perhaps, this was realized in South Africa even before such Western literary pundits as Jean–François Lyotard, or Eugenio Barba, or Patrice Pavis contemplated a more positive future for the arts. In South Africa, the prime factor governing postmodernist forms has been social fragmentation. I suggest that in the case of a theatre company such as Junction Avenue, the representation of social fragmentation eventually led to a fragmentation of the personae in the dramatic text, and of the actor's body as iconic image on stage. Paradoxically, apartheid itself was disintegrating, its essentialist structures doomed to disappearance, before new forms of social order could be born.

The necessity to overcome fragmentation should have led the arts, particularly the theatre, towards syncretism or some form of coming-togetherness as a reflection or prediction of post-apartheid utopia. This is a reversal of the situation world-wide, with the end of so-called utopias, from the late Eighties, to nationalist fragmentation from Latvia to Burundi. My purpose here is to discuss notions of fragmentation and syncretism in the work of Junction Avenue Theatre Company, in terms both of the body politic and of the 'speaking body' in performance.

When they workshopped *The Fantastical History of a Useless Man* in 1976, the white male-dominated group of actors had their own identity problems; they were, as Barney Simon was later to put it, *Born in the RSA* (1985), and as such were confined to the margins of a specific post-colonial society. The exploration and criticism of this white fragment, albeit an empowered fragment, of South African society, may be seen in hindsight to be a prelude – if not to commitment, at least to

disengagement from the reigning body politic. But to realize one is useless, to sati-
rize one's roots, one's present activities and the Progressive Party which represents
one's parents in the all-white parliament, could only be described as minimal
change.

In Patrice Pavis's 1996 study of theatre, Bakhtin's notion of the chronotope in
narrative is adapted to theatrical form.[1] Pavis suggests that the relation chronos/
topos may be extended in the performing arts to form a triangle composed of time,
space and body/action. For the spectator, the time and space of the theatre are
both imaginary and concrete; and it is the body of the actor, composed of time and
space, which will at the same time also mediate between time and space. Applied
to the workshopped productions of Junction Avenue from *The Fantastical History*
onwards, one can see that there was always a fixed point to the triangle – that of
space, whether imaginary (the fable) or concrete (the space of performance). This
fixed point was that of apartheid – a spatial term in itself, a space affected by and
related to time (as in Coetzee's novels). But time itself moves on, and as the time-
point moves, so will the action embodied concretely on stage.

We can thus take as our first triangle the space of apartheid and the time-point
of 1976 in *The Fantastical History*, which enquires into the origins of the young
white male of this period. What seems to characterize and connect the sequences
of this first Junction Avenue play is verbally expressed in "The Song" which forms
a kind of Brechtian prologue to the play. The theme is "rupture":

> The sympathetic liberal is working to repair
> The ruptures in the structures that are spreading everywhere…

followed by

> For the colonial structure
> Is just about to rupture.[2]

During the first act of the play, this "rupture" in the time and space of the Soweto
riots is mediated concretely by bodies *"bursting through"*; the spectator is witnessing the births leading to the historical central point of the play, 1950. First, the
actors playing Van Riebeeck and Van der Stel burst physically through two huge
ten-rand notes: it is the birth of the first Dutch colonialists. Then Cecil John
Rhodes, the man who "brought Christian civilisation to the savages and fish and
chips to Africa," is born from the body of the British Empire – a headless body
symbolizing Queen Victoria (34). The Act ends with the Mother opening the 1950

---

[1] Patrice Pavis, *L'analyse de spectacles* (Paris: Nathan, 1996).

[2] "The Fantastical History," in *At the Junction: Four Plays by the Junction Avenue Theatre Company*, ed. & intro. Martin Orkin (Johannesburg: Witwatersrand UP, 1995): 25. Further page references are in the text.

International Gladiolus and Azalea Show; she cuts the ribbon, her waters break, and the Useless Man *"pops his head through the table"* (47).

Act Two begins with the body of the young white man concealing a sub-machine gun. 1950 is also the birth of apartheid, but from this moment on, the predominant mode of rupture becomes rejection. From the Group Areas Act to Sharpeville, the black majority will be increasingly rejected; Republic Day becomes a memory of being given a flag and confirming the master–servant relationship between white and black. But this first part of the second act is narrated, not tangibly embodied on stage; the young white man's concrete reality is far from black experience and is embodied in cocktail parties, Beatlemania, and the going–away party which supposedly endows him with civilization. On his return from Europe, he rejects his parents' plans, goes to University to find himself, rejects Christian Education (or biblical studies) and Fashion (or fashionable revolution), and is allotted sociological research on "bourgeois toilet habits." These habits are mimed on stage and shown by the Compère to be the ultimate in individualism and the desire for privacy. Then, through his involvement in student politics, the young white is subject to recuperation by the system: suitable occupations proposed for him include opposition journalism, progressive school-teaching, and radical law. His subsequent refusal of revolutionary violence as an alternative (*"He reaches to take [a] gun, but is unable to do so"*) leaves him with no option but to become a "useless man": "the most I can do is be the least obstruction" (60). This final attitude is represented during his last speech by the bodies of the other actors who *"collapse onto the floor in cramped grotesque positions"* (59).

Martin Orkin notes the shifts in gender representation between the different Junction Avenue works.[3] It is obvious that, in *The Fantastical History*, the women embody passive and conservative stereotyping; even the mother figure has no creative role to play, since both the Useless Man and Cecil John Rhodes emerge of their own volition from the manipulated bodies of the Mother and Queen Victoria. That Rhodes should be played by a girl in drag whose head represents, before parturition, the head of the Queen seems, at most, to unsex both the Queen and Rhodes.

For this (1950) space/time/body triangle of departure for the Junction Avenue Theatre Company, the 1976 time-point of production will not allow on stage a corporeal representation of empowerment for either the 'other' races or the 'other' sex, so the subject-actant is very firmly the young white English-speaking male, and the female figure will not even constitute, as in traditional plays, the object of

---

[3] Introduction to *At the Junction: Four Plays by the Junction Avenue Theatre Company.*

his quest. It is only in a Brechtian epic narrative mode that blacks may be shown as victims of colonial policy or within the master–slave relationship. A very tentative rhetorical question regarding the situation of women, while connecting it with racial difference, is introduced in the "bourgeois toilet" sequence: "Do you believe in the artificial barriers between man and woman? Do you not believe in the equality of all members of the human race?" The potential of this question was slightly undermined by a woman running out screaming after presumably having seen a man in the ladies' toilet. But, as the Compère remarked in a rather ambiguous statement, "The bourgeois is unable to respond to the concrete problems of women and the need for their liberation" (56–57).

To sum up *The Fantastical History* in terms of 1976: the social fragmentation of South Africa was only represented on stage as a positive energy or force by the white male fragment. The 'rupture' ironically images both the birth-pangs of this element and the possibility of rejection by the natural successors to bourgeois liberalism (the study of toilet habits can, of course, be seen as a study of rejection; one is, in every sense of the term, re-ejecting what one has absorbed).

If we now move to 1978 and *Randlords and Rotgut*, we may notice that the time-swing will have forced a corresponding displacement of the body/action presented in a concrete form. This production was commissioned by the History Workshop of the University of the Witwatersrand and based on their research into different ways of looking at South African history. This might not have proved to be a very different viewpoint from that of *The Fantastical History*, but what completely changed the translation of history into theatrical terms was the addition, to the original group of devisors, three black actors who had all performed with Workshop '71 – Siphiwe Khumalo, Ramalao Makhene and Arthur Malepo.[4] In the story of randlords juggling with their profits both as mine-owners and as purveyors of alcohol, trying to manipulate the black workers through the church, another fragment of society is concretely present on stage: the black workers forced into the mines by taxes and land appropriation. Body-language, both as shown and as represented verbally, takes on a new importance; for the first phase of the play, the keynote is the black Nduna shouting "Tighten up your balls";[5] and this first sequence ends with the image of a miner physically trapped in the mine-shaft. The space/time/body action of this play constitutes a trap – we consider the real bodies on stage: they are those of actors still trapped in 1978's apartheid. The bodies of the three black miners are subject to the extremes of violence through beatings,

4 See Robert Kavanagh, *Theatre and Cultural Struggle in South Africa* (London: Zed, 1985).
5 "Randlord and Rotgut," in *At the Junction*, ed. & intro. Orkin, 80. Further page references are in the text.

and to even more refined assault during disinfection by DDT. The stage directions must have been difficult to follow: *"He* [a miner] *is laid out flat and the following mime of violence is enacted: a pole is forced up his anus and the orderlies twist his body over itself by means of the pole. He is passed through the air and finally thrown into the dip head first, and then dragged out and laid aside"* (83). Their bodies have been degraded by sex and alcohol (the rotgut of the title) and reduced either to animal status – *"they* [the white exploiters] *feel the flesh of the worker as if they were at a cattle auction"* – or to a mere algebraic unit. Death through alcohol poisoning or rockfall is ever-present. The repression which became all-powerful in the apartheid state – represented, for example, by the torture and death of Steve Biko – is reflected in the situation of the trapped miners of the late-nineteenth century: "We are locked in your compounds! We are guarded by your dogs! We are beaten by your thugs!" (127–28).

The black actors from Workshop '71 also brought with them their African cultural heritage, already adapted to Western stage-forms in such plays as *Survival* (1981). In *Randlords*, they use worksongs which express their situation in a language not understood by the white bosses or the white audience. The *a capella* singing was to become an important feature of Junction Avenue performances; in this instance, it signified a search for a way out of the trap: "The day will come when we stand together and storm out of the tunnels into the street. We will find the word that unites us, we'll discover our communal song" (113–14). Junction Avenue also started to take part in the new black theatre tradition, a tradition of Grotowskian poor theatre, relying heavily on body transformations and mimicry, which had started with the Serpent Players and Workshop '71 and which reached its climax with *Woza Albert!* in the early Eighties. This episodic, physical, and at the same time often very witty form seems to be based on traditional African story-telling modes.[6] In *Randlords* there are important sequences based on the well-known, traditional 'trickster' character: the miners trick and deceive the white shift-boss through physical imitations of drunkenness and laziness.

The 'trap' situation is also applicable to the white historical characters, who are trapped within the capitalist system, divided or fragmented among themselves (as they try to reconcile the interests of the mines and the distilleries), between the Afrikaners and the British, and finally between the British upper class and the 'self-made man' Samuel Marks: "Mr Marks, if you want to make a good impression, I think you must be very conscious of posture" (92). This fragmentation of the rul-

---

[6] See Anne Fuchs, "Re-Creation: One Aspect of Oral Tradition and the Theatre in South Africa," *Commonwealth* 9.2 (1987): 32–39, and Mark Fleishman, "Workshop Theatre as Oppositional Form," *South African Theatre Journal* 4.1 (1990): 88–118.

ing class (already met in *The Fantastical History*) is not only carried further by that between black and white but also by the divisions created between blacks, in particular between the 'boss boy' who aspires to become a mine policeman, and the other workers.

The empowerment of the male black South Africans by their bodily presence on stage, their performance skills, and the beginning of organized resistance in the dramatic text all seems to have had a strange effect on gender relations in a play apparently only concerned with male confrontation. The one female character, Rosie the prostitute, brought into the compound to service the miners, is interesting because she is *"overly white,"* as the text states (82), and is neither English- nor Afrikaans-speaking, but German. Was this unconsciously the desire by the company not to put an English-speaker or Afrikaner in the position of woman as a stereotyped bodily *object* on stage? Perhaps it was a role which actress Astrid von Kotze, herself a German aristocrat, had no qualms in assuming and upon which she made a strong imprint, transforming Rosie into a subject-actant oppressing the black male workers.

Although it is not possible to analyze each of Junction Avenue's productions here in any detail, before arriving at the final fragmentation and more complicated gender relations established in *Tooth and Nail* (1989), it can be said that Junction Avenue in the early Eighties began to explore contemporary themes separating white (*Will of a Rebel*) and black actors (*Dikitsheneng* and *Security*). It was at this time that Ari Sitas and Astrid von Kotze became more and more involved in black trade-union theatre, and eventually left Johannesburg for Durban.[7] With the return of Malcolm Purkey, the company went back to documenting South African history, first with *Marabi* – moving on to the Thirties and Forties in Doornfontein – and then to their best-known play, *Sophiatown*, first performed in 1986. The forced removals of the Fifties took place after the birth of official apartheid, which meant that for spectators over the age of forty it was well within living memory. 1986 in South Africa began with hope, with the UDF, but was followed by despair and defeat with the successive states of emergency. School boycotts, violence and police raids paralleled a vibrant intellectual life. It was all reflected in *Sophiatown*. The fragmentation of black society portrayed in the play suggested a social, generational and gender fragmentation, despite its emphasis on ethnic unity. The opposite may be said for the only white character – who is distinguished by the blacks as white, but Jewish. Once again, this is due in part to the composition of the company, but it also represents the growing, deep splits in the white commu-

---

[7] Astrid von Kotze, *Organize and Act* (Durban: Culture and Working Life Project, 1988).

nity at large. Junction Avenue was by this time male-dominated rather than white male-dominated, and this accounts for the stereotyping and passivity of the black women characters. We remember seeing *You Strike the Woman, You Strike the Rock* in the company of the black actors and devisors of *Sophiatown*, who reacted to the militant all-woman cast with loud hissings and exclamations of "Sis" during the performance. But male or female, as for *Marabi*, the whole cast constitutes an enormous step towards the "body of change," in that the play is a refined celebration of black township culture. It is probably an example of theatrical syncretism at its best, with its mixture of South African languages, traditional and contemporary music and dance forms, storytelling, intimate family scenes, and the hard politics of the outside world.

Sophiatown was a popular success; *Tooth and Nail* was a critical success. The time of the latter's creation was 1988–89: for South Africa this was the time of the final explosion while also the still hypothetical end to the fragmentation of apartheid. The structure of the plays has moved away from Brechtian episodic epic; the episodes composing *The Resistible Rise of Arturo Ui* are performed in progressive sequence, and even the scenes of *Randlords and Rotgut* progress from the installation of the first distilleries, through prohibition, to accepted illegal drinking; from the new miner's arrival in the compound to his education completed by the old hands; but *Tooth and Nail* has moved to postmodernism. The individual episodes of the play (now called "fragments") can be performed in any sequence; they are fragments of the lives and thoughts of many different characters, both black and white, male and female, at a point in time which the director Malcolm Purkey called the "interregnum" (Gramsci's phrase) or the "bitter times between the old and the new."[8] The play was subsequently reworked for the Grahamstown Festival of 1991: that is, after the release of Mandela and the beginning of talks to dismantle apartheid. At this crucial point in time, the space/time/body-action, referred to by Purkey himself as "the metaphor of the play," is that of flood. The biblical myth of the Flood and Noah's ark was used, and the question asked was how people were to survive during this period of cleansing and healing. Malcolm Purkey and Martin Orkin have both explained in detail how the fragmented structure is reflected in the fragmented images of different characters, played by both full-size puppets and actors (as in the case of the photographer Saul or the white madam Madelaine), or by two characters functionally bound together (such as the activist Sifiso and the Interpreter, or, once again, Madelaine and her houseboy Angelo).

---

[8] Malcolm Purkey, "*Tooth and Nail*: Rethinking Form for the South African Theatre," in *Theatre and Change in South Africa*, ed. Geoffrey V. Davis & Anne Fuchs (Amsterdam: Harwood Academic, 1996): 162.

However, the stereotyping of female roles continues in this new work. Orkin's opinion is that there is a "perceptible shift in the Company's representation of women," which he attributes to women's (presumably feminist) intervention in the making of the play.[9] But as far as the black women are concerned, there is merely a development of the Mamariti/Lulu or mother/daughter, traditional/ radical situation. White Letitia, admired for her independent subject-attitude, in-carnates desire – but isn't she just a logical development of the Rosie–Ruth charac-ters who also (to a lesser degree) fed off apartheid violence and were destroyed by it? Letitia is married to a white man and has a black lover. Again, no change: Junction Avenue have never portrayed a white man desiring a black woman. Admittedly, Princess at the end of *Sophiatown* allegedly departs into exile with a Dutchman; but this is not seen on stage. Madelaine is also a development of the white women of *The Fantastical History*, her role as defender of European civiliza-tion now permanently fixed within the language of the operatic aria, and defini-tively unsexed when played by an actor.

To conclude: the body of change as shown in these plays reaches a crisis of fragmentation; the personal concrete changing body is also split by the use of pup-pets. Language is split by difference and interpretation, but also by repetition and non-sequitur. This appears to be a typical postmodern technique, in which time loses its goal and space its meaning. I suggested at the beginning that postmod-ernism in South Africa was also a prelude to new forms. *Tooth and Nail* paradoxically retains its syncretic form, preserving the empowerment of the black male devisors who proclaim their message of survival, to "learn to read the signs." But we may ask whether, on another level, there is not also the empowerment of black women. I am not talking about the obvious role of Thandi as an activist – rather, of the power of resistance and solidity given to black women compared with either the frenzy or the rigidity of white women, here both equally con-demned. Their rock-like quality was, of course, that of the Vusisizwe Players in *You Strike the Woman, You Strike the Rock* back in 1986, but it has also been por-trayed in a very different context: that of Reza de Wet's play, *Diepe Grond* (1986), where the black nursemaid looks on and survives, while the white children fran-tically play out roles dictated by the past. "So what's new" in the lives of South African black women (as Fatima Dike has asked[10])? Why it is that, since 1991, Junction Avenue have chosen to go back and repeat *Sophiatown* and *Marabi*? These two classics of Junction Avenue are indeed still relevant today, in that their syn-

---

9 Orkin, *At the Junction*, 235.
10 Fatima Dike, "So What's New?" in *Four Plays*, compiled & intro. Zakes Mda (Florida Hills, S.A.: Vivlia, 1996).

cretic form remains a model of the genre; but has the company outgrown its own structures? Fragmentation of the devisors had already taken place in 1982; a second breakaway occurred when William Kentridge joined forces with the Handspring Puppet Company in the early Nineties. Can the company survive and advance so that the post-apartheid space and time will reveal newly empowered bodies, including those of black women, in theatrical forms whose syncretism may be influenced not only by the Western world but also by Greater Africa, the Orient, and South America?

Revaluing Women's Storytelling in South African Theatre

ৎ Marcia Blumberg

There was a time in African culture when the setting of the sun announced that it was time for story-telling [...] The television and the radio and the disco are taking over [...] That kills something of the child's imagination [...] Our stories are fresh because they've been suppressed for so long.[1]

When women "spin a story" they illustrate the political significance of personal narratives for performance theory [...] In their story-telling process, women come to see that their personal experiences have social origins.[2]

To tell a story is to activate a dream.[3]

T HREE WOMEN IN SOUTH AFRICAN THEATRE shared an engagement with their work during the London conference, treating us to diverse modes of storytelling in their performances. I would like here to make yet another voice audible, that of Gcina Mhlophe, who received an honorary doctorate from the Open University in 1994. At that time, Dennis Walder's presentation attested to her participation in many facets of South African theatre, emphasizing her use of storytelling in different forms and venues as a vehicle of intervention:

It is for her contribution as a writer and artist to that larger struggle [...] to be heard [...] that we honour Gcina Mhlophe [...] She performs in schools and fringe theatre venues around the world, and now lives by storytelling [...] for Gcina and her group of self-taught traditional story-tellers, Zanendaba ["Bring me a story"], it means telling the truths which have been lost, which have not yet been heard [...] They help others to tell *their* stories, the stories of their lives but also the stories of their people.[4]

---

[1] Gcina Mhlophe, quoted in Tyrone August, "Interview with Gcina Mhlophe," *Journal of Southern African Studies* 16.2 (June 1990): 330–31.

[2] Kristen M. Langellier & Eric E. Peterson, "Spinstorying: An Analysis of Women Storytelling," in *Performance, Culture, and Identity*, ed. Elizabeth C. Fine & Jean Haskell Speer (Westport CT: Frederick J. Praeger, 1992): 157–60.

[3] Breyten Breytenbach, "Why are Writers Always the Last to Know?," *New York Times Book Review* (28 March 1993): 16.

[4] Dennis Walder, "Presentation of Gcina Mhlope for an honorary degree of Doctor of the Open University" (April 1994); unpublished MS.

The involvement of Mhlophe and women from Zanendaba[5] in storytelling is a re-cuperative practice directed at oral history and South African culture. The individual and sometimes collective empowerment of the women makes this performative form a vital aspect for the en-gendering of voice in South Africa.

Mhlophe's activities have brought a greater awareness of the art of storytelling and have widened its appeal and value, especially for black South Africans, who, Ellen Kuzwayo reminds us, "have owned [their] stories while owning so little else."[6] Mhlophe is keenly aware of the valorization of written stories and particular narratives exemplifying the might of colonial structures that simultaneously devalue, and sometimes erase, the practices of the oral tradition. Prizing the repository of stories, values, history, mythology, and a world view of a particular culture, she knows it requires ongoing performance to facilitate its transmission:

> TV and going to the moon are great, but storytelling is number one. There is that person-to-person contact, which is crucial, and it has spirituality. I have yet to meet a storyteller who wants to compete. There's no competition: I tell you that story of my people, you tell the story of your people.[7]

In foregrounding the communication between storyteller and listener, Mhlophe not only points to the dynamic of sharing amongst equals, she also appreciates the opportunity stories provide both to learn and to improve understanding, since stories, amongst their many attributes, carry personal and community histories.

Analyzing the material conditions for production of these performances, Mhlophe pragmatically asserts their benefits: "people of different political persuasions could share in storytelling. And children of different financial standing could be reached very cheaply [...] It's very cost effective."[8] The practical effect of minimal costs translates into accessibility for audiences of all ages and political stripe; levelling the economic considerations brings inclusivity. Mhlophe utilizes traditional folk-tales but also creates new stories to maintain freshness and engage her listeners. She also realizes how much the context for storytelling has altered over the decades and emphasizes the need to be always aware of the particular audi-

---

[5] Gcina Mhlophe prioritizes the following for Zanendaba: training a core of professional storytellers; conducting in-house workshops, sending storytellers to organizations and schools upon request; building the resources of the Institute in order to conduct research into African folklore; hosting exchanges between storytellers from around the world and especially with Africa; holding regular storytelling performances and creating an annual festival (*South African Outlook*, 54).

[6] Ellen Kuzwayo, *Sit Down and Listen* (Claremont, S.A.: David Philip, 1990): ix.

[7] Gcina Mhlophe, quoted in Yvonne Fontyn, "The world is listening to Gcina's tales," *Weekly Mail & Guardian* 10.20 (20–26 May 1994): 36.

[8] Mhlophe, quoted in Tyrone August, "Interview with Gcina Mhlophe (1993)," *Politics and Performance: Theatre, Poetry and Song in Southern Africa*, ed. Liz Gunner (Johannesburg: Witwatersrand UP, 1994): 280.

ence: "I often tell stories in a theatre or classroom. My grandmother told me stories around the fire at home."[9] Nokwanda Sithole considers that

> the stories have changed territorially because of changing audiences and environments. Mhlophe has also done a lot of adapting in her different projects: You can tell the same story to university, high school, primary and little children, but have to do it differently for each group.[10]

These varying occasions for the performance of stories nevertheless provide rich opportunities for reconnecting with traditions and narratives of the past and for revaluing them within the context of a country in flux.

As an interventionary practice in another mode, "Mhlophe believes that storytelling can play a role in redressing distortions to African history and pride – particularly for young children who cannot read."[11] Storytelling offers one method to combat the poor educational practices, and the perhaps even poorer relationships between students and their teacher, which are the legacy of apartheid; it also provides a more creative, participatory, less authoritarian approach. Yet the question of intervention raises other problems when we consider the contrast between the engagement of storytellers as performers and that of academics whose research involves collecting stories. One journalist cautions: "In scholarly hands, [...] the record is dry, flat and often incorrect."[12] Sithole also warns that recently

> there has been a conscious drive by black people to record black history, but this has happened to a limited extent. There has also been a tendency towards an academic approach – not accessible to the majority of people for whom the exercise is meant.[13]

These issues of who speaks for and to whom, and of the quality of listening, as well as such related problems as the dynamics of sisterhood, require sensitive analysis.

How do stories work in order for them to be recaptured and transformed? Women's "spinstorying" has been regarded as "a rich and intricate verbal art [that] combines different story types and different ways of telling stories,"[14] and

---

[9] Mhlophe, quoted in Bobby Rodwell, "Gcina Mhlophe," *Speak* 37 (1991): 6.

[10] Nokwanda Sithole, "Once Upon a Time," *Tribute* (November 1989): 20.

[11] Sithole, "Once Upon a Time," 18.

[12] *South African Outlook* 121.4 (May 1991): 53.

[13] Sithole, "Once Upon a Time," 18. Desiree Lewis's reminder, "the right to interpret black experience in South Africa has been a white right. Blacks may have emotions and display their experience, but cannot be credited with self-knowledge or interpretation" ("The Politics of FEMINISM in South Africa," *Staffrider* 10.3 [1992]: 20), challenges critics and academics to reflect more carefully on their practices. My approach utilizes the playwrights' statements to bring their voices to the fore in a dialogue with their playtexts and the writing of other critics; yet I am ever mindful of my situation as a mediator as I listen to the various voices, interpret the different texts, and shape my own writings.

[14] Langellier & Peterson, "Spinstorying: An Analysis of Women Storytelling," 157. Sincere thanks to Dennis Walder for drawing my attention to this article and for sharing his then unpublished manuscripts and other material on the work of Gcina Mhlophe.

conceptualized as the often private performance of personal narratives. Mhlophe's storytelling workshops transform the private into a more public form, yet still provide a supportive environment. As women participate in the narratives of other women's lives, they perceive commonalties and assess differences; most important-ly, they feel part of a community rather than dealing with various oppressive conditions in isolation.

> Spin suggests the curvilinear structure of kernel stories that spiral from conversation to story to conversation to story. Personal narratives spin connections and interweave women's lives [...] Women focus on personal narratives because they cannot draw upon a shared history at a social level when their history is particularized, depreci-ated, regulated, and silenced.[15]

"Spinstorying" exemplifies the dynamics of communication between women and the performance of stories imbricated in their lives and histories. Across many cultures, patriarchal systems have silenced and regulated women in oppressive ways. Mhlophe's storytelling therefore energizes women's voices in South Africa, making them audible and valuable; it also helps to restore them to the community at large, where they have been mostly silenced yet have always belonged.

How does Mhlophe employ the practice of storytelling in her own theatrical stagings? Central to Mhlophe's play *Have You Seen Zandile?*[16] is the performance of words rendered concrete in the practices of storytelling, the ritual of praise poetry, the recuperation and narrativization of personal history. From the vantage-point of young adulthood, Zandile remembers and revalues her personal history, which forms a significant part of the extended silence, the unspoken, forgotten, or ne-glected stories, of her community. The recall and shaping of memory translates into its narrativization in the plays. Zandile's quest for the memories of childhood directly relates to her absence from and desire for a reunion with her grand-mother; Gogo, in turn, searches for Zandile over many years and retains her grandchild's artefacts and gifts, which constitute a personal memory-bank and a cultural treasure-trove.

Zandile's enactment of scenes from her youth comprises fourteen discrete fragments set in the context of apartheid South Africa over two decades from the mid-Sixties. While the larger political picture informs her situation, the play

---

[15] Langellier & Peterson, "Spinstorying," 173–74.

[16] *Have You Seen Zandile?* premiered at the Market Theatre, Johannesburg in February 1986 and returned in July 1987. It won a Fringe Festival Award at the Edinburgh Festival in 1987 and toured to Basel, Zurich, and London. Its American premiere in Chicago in 1988 was followed by a season in 1989 in Baltimore and Knoxville, Tennessee, with the Carpetbag Company. My thanks to Gcina Mhlophe for talking with me about her work in London in 1993 and on subse-quent occasions in Toronto. Most of all I thank her for challenging me to think long and hard about my positioning and role in this work.

stresses the personal as political. Zandile's world is turned upside-down when she is abducted by her Xhosa mother and removed from the city and her Zulu granny's loving care. Zandile is unacquainted with the Xhosa language and culture and unused to rural traditional ways, but her alienation is somewhat ameliorated by her desperate attempts to communicate with Gogo and her determination to learn all about her people and their history. In fact, the play renders concrete the contention that "the personal is not only political, as feminists have said, but sociological and historical as well."[17] All of these facets obtain in what has sometimes been dismissively regarded as a "woman's story." The deliberate mix of languages, Zulu, English, and Xhosa, emphasizes the rich cultural heritage that signifies Zandile's history and that of her creator, but also reminds spectators that these are three of eleven official languages in South Africa, all of which represent the stories of many diverse peoples.

The title, *Have You Seen Zandile?*, precedes a phrase, "a play originated by Gcina Mhlophe, based on her childhood," then names three women, Mhlophe, Maralin Vanrenen, and Thembi Mtshali. These markers, as well as the dedication "to the memory of my grandmother, Gogo, who deserves praise for the storyteller in me," point to the collaboration of the three women and to a different kind of collaborative inspirational work through memory, the spiritual presence, and the love for the techniques of storytelling instilled by Mhlophe's grandmother. The acknowledgement that the play is "based on" her childhood takes spectators into the liminal space of autobiography, suggesting that her life-story is a starting-point for the stories in the play, much as her storytelling employs, reworks, and renews folk-tales. It is instructive to assess the play in the light of Jane Watts's rationale for what she sees as a common writing practice among black South African writers:

> whatever genre they take up is likely to be used as a *vehicle for this autobiographical search* [...] Writing becomes a request for reassurance that they in fact *have* an identity, that they have rescued the fragments and shards of a personality from the systematic official attempt to eradicate it.[18]

Watts's perspective offers a very narrow view of black writers and devalues the autobiographical genre, denying the creativity of the writers and the range of material produced in South Africa. Mhlophe's play deliberately employs aspects of the genre that provide the writer with tools of self-discovery and at the same time extends the process to concerns wider than cultural and gender implications.

---

[17] Wini Breines, *Young, White and Miserable: Growing Up Female in the Fifties* (Boston MA: Beacon, 1992): x.

[18] Jane Watts, *Black Writers from South Africa: Towards a Discourse of Liberation* (London: Macmillan, 1989): 115 (my emphasis).

The play also realizes the argument that "self-definition in relation to significant others [...] is the most pervasive characteristic of the female autobiography [...] for women it is relational."[19] Zandile's relationships with Gogo, her mother, her invented and actual friends, and other women constitute the dramatic and emotional structuring of the play. Even scenes that feature one actor on stage include other female interlocutors, so that relationality "is the most pervasive characteristic." Zandile's abrupt, unwanted relocation and separation from Gogo provide opportunities for this internal dialogue, which is at once personal and representative of issues and cultural practices within the communities.

Miki Flockemann's admiration for the dynamic of *Have You Seen Zandile?* as a "sort of 'counter discourse' to what has been called protest theatre, because of the way it goes into area of personal life and experience" elicits Mhlophe's printed response: "If I could write about the masses I can also write about myself, I'm one of the masses!"[20] Challenges that her play lacked relevance since it seemed to eschew the liberation struggle provoked a rejoinder from Mhlophe:

> I've done plays that deal with the political conflicts and with the police and the shooting and the dying and detentions [...] [T]his is the first different play [...] I was getting quite angry, "Do you think we spend our lives marching in the streets?" [...] "We do washing sometimes, sometimes we fall in love, sometimes children get born."[21]

This response came at the same time as Albie Sachs's controversial paper "Preparing ourselves for freedom" reacted to a rather narrow focus on the politics of liberation as the *sine qua non* of artistic work.[22] Furthermore, Flockemann's contextualization of the play's setting stressed the relevance of its trajectory in the present:

> First workshopped then performed [...] in 1986, the play is set in the period between 1966 and 1976 – though the "horizon" of the play seems more in keeping with developments in the 1990's, transcending the post-Sharpeville, pre-Soweto period of the actual time of the play.[23]

---

[19] Bella Brodski & Celeste Schenck, ed. "The Other Voice," *Life/Lines: Theorizing Women's Autobiography* (Ithaca NY: Cornell UP, 1988): 8, 9.

[20] These citations are taken from an unedited version of "Gcina Mhlophe in conversation with Miki Flockemann and Thuli Mazibuko, Cape Town, 2 August 1994" (forthcoming in *Contemporary Theatre*, 1999. My thanks to the editor, Lizbeth Goodman, for providing this material.

[21] Quoted in Patrick Kagan–Moore, "The *Zandile* Project: A Collaboration Between UT, Carpetbag Theatre, and South African Playwright Gcina Mhlophe; An Interview," *Drama Review* 34.1 (Spring 1990): 119–20.

[22] Albie Sachs, "Preparing ourselves for freedom," in *Spring is Rebellious: Arguments About Cultural Freedom by Albie Sachs and Respondents*, ed. Ingrid de Kok & Karen Press (Cape Town: Buchu, 1990): 19–29.

[23] Miki Flockemann, "*Have You Seen Zandile?* English or english – An Approach to Teaching Literature in Postapartheid South Africa," *AUETSA [Association of University English Teachers of Southern Africa]* (Fort Hare & Potchefstroom, S.A., 1991): 510–11.

This speaks directly to the opposite dynamic in Athol Fugard's *The Road to Mecca* (1985) and *Playland* (1992), which, while written in the past decade (the latter even set in 1990), depict attitudes and mind-sets reminiscent of the Sixties.

The play begins with an empty stage but is soon occupied with Zandile's performance as an eight-year-old child in dialogue with a newly invented friend. There is an obvious depth of affection between herself and Gogo, and the importance of storytelling is brought out as Gogo performs the story of the woman on the moon. The latter staging realizes storytelling not only as a formative influence on the young Zandile but also as an integral component of their tradition. Spectators witness the interaction of the teller's performance and the listeners' participation, see the educative potential, and realize how the story acts as a *caveat* about moral choices: a mother's desire to care for her baby supervenes over a prohibition about Sunday work, for which she and her baby are cruelly punished with banishment to the moon and permanent separation from the rest of the family. This story provides an ironic parallel with Zandile's situation later in the play: her mother kidnaps her, removing her permanently from contact with her beloved Gogo. Yet the mythic mother does everything she can for her baby, who remains with her although they are both banished.

Another scene combines the comic and the serious in a significant demonstration of the effects of storytelling as Zandile performs for the putative pupils, flowers in Gogo's garden. She enacts multiple roles: the teacher, Miss Zandile; herself and her imagined friend, Bongi, as schoolgirls; and, in addition, the pupils' response. Reiterating Gogo's cautionary tale about the danger of the white car that arrives and takes naughty children "to a far away place and nobody's going to see you ever again,"[24] she emulates the authoritarian structures of her school. Comedy arises from self-reflexive strategizing for her class when they receive a visit from the school inspector. Exhibiting an understanding of role-playing and appeasement, Zandile informs the students about the inspector's linguistic handicap – he can only understand English. As she assigns "white names" to the flowers, she observes in amazement: "Do you know what name the inspector gave me today? Elsie. And I don't even look like an Elsie!" (20). Mhlophe explains how her father's stories taught her the significance of names: "Our names have meanings; and when you're told the meaning of your name, when you meet other people, that's the beginning of the conversation."[25] In other words, their African names provide a genealogy and place the interlocutors in specific contexts, which the assumed

---

[24] Gcina Mhlophe, Maralin Vanrenen & Thembi Mtshali, *Have You Seen Zandile?* (London: Heinemann/Methuen, 1988): 19. Further page references are in the text.

[25] Quoted in Patrick Kagan–Moore, "The *Zandile* Project," 122.

English names erase. The final tableau represents Zandile's frustration at the students' mistakes in the rendering of a Zulu song and her violent reaction as she breaks the flowers (students). In contrast to the harsh education system, which spawns violence, Gogo lovingly remonstrates with her: "Everything that grows has feelings" (23).

The arrival of the white car at the end of the school term violently disrupts the anticipated vacation, as the vehicle facilitates her abduction. Scenes from the Transkei evoke linguistic and cultural alienation; Zandile alleviates her unhappiness by telling stories to the children in the fields, but, most importantly, she tells her story to Gogo in the form of letters that are destroyed by her mother. Between Zandile's attempts to reach her, Gogo shows the photographs and asks spectators, "Have you seen Zandile?" (34). This question, which reverberates with the significance of its function as title, places audience members in a disturbing scenario of complicity, since they have witnessed the abduction and do know the answer but are bound by theatrical convention to remain silent in response to Gogo's desperate plea. Perhaps, at this moment, the dilemma of the spectator, who finds herself in a morally untenable situation, partly replicates but also exposes the difference in the situations of many South Africans, who knew to a greater or lesser degree about the intolerable conditions and injustice of apartheid, yet were complicitous in their silence and inaction.

Zandile's proudest moment also involves storytelling, as she invokes her grandmother and recites a praise poem in Xhosa for her teacher on his retirement. That this scene derives from personal experience is confirmed by Mhlophe's joy at the memory of her discovery of the ritual of praise poetry, "That's the poetry that I grew up on. That's the poetry that inspired me to become a writer."[26] Zandile's pride in her performance of the praise poem is evident, but is contrasted with the appearance of Gogo on the other side of the stage in an isolating spotlit area. Gogo's gifts mark her continued affection for Zandile, as does her anticipation of their meeting sometime; as she places these presents in a suitcase, this bag and its contents become an overdetermined signifier for their once-loving relationship and its loss, as well as a repository for her childhood dreams.

The final scene represents Zandile's return to Durban to search for Gogo, but her dreams of an anticipated reunion are shattered when she hears about her granmother's recent death. As Gogo had taken solace in storytelling about her granddaughter, so Zandile sustained herself on stories in the absence of her grandmother through the presence of her transmitted tradition. This final tableau is the

---

[26] Quoted in Peter Gzowski, "Gcina Mhlophe interviewed on CBC," *Morningside* (18 May 1995): 1, 2. Thanks to the CBC for supplying the transcript of the radio interview.

most poignant moment of the play: Zandile, isolated in a pool of light, opens Gogo's suitcase and takes out the wrapped gifts, which she places on one side while she unpacks in turn the three dresses from her childhood. *"She then holds all three dresses closely to her, hugging them and sobbing. The lights slowly fade to black"* (77). The gestures and images, the dramatic structure of bonding, forced separation, and a discovery that creates a certain finality but no emotional resolution – these are, indeed, aspects that are immediately understood despite cultural difference. So, too, is the pain of multiple losses: that of her cherished grandmother, her childhood, the missed years of non-communication, and the never-to-be-restored bond with her mentor and muse. Peggy Phelan's interrogation of the conjunction of objects, memory, and loss is especially pertinent to this situation:

> The speech act of memory and description [can] become a performative expression [...] The description itself does not reproduce the object, it rather helps us to restage and restate the effort to remember what is lost. The descriptions remind us how loss acquires meaning and generates recovery – not only of and for the object, but for the one who remembers.[27]

The dresses signify Zandile's lost innocence, the abruptly terminated joy of childhood, and the painful separation and now final loss of her Gogo. Spectators are assured that this "loss acquires meaning and generates recovery" by Mhlophe's construction of her story as that of Zandile, and her avowed intention to devote time and energy to storytelling.

The specificities of the South African situation create a complex problematic and demand closer attention. As Susan Bennett remarks in another context, "cultural baggage is not an optional extra; it must be carried everywhere."[28] Gogo's suitcase is a repository of artefacts for Zandile, but the dresses are the most significant items, since they are metonymic of her life and are also among the few possessions that she calls her own. Her positioning at the conjunction of issues of race, class, gender and economics marks her transformation from a child to a young black woman restricted by structures of apartheid, customary law, and patriarchy. These dresses thus signify her dreams and their enforced curtailment. Zandile's allusion to Gogo's gift of a new dress as she performs the role of Miss Zandile signifies her aspirations for a career as a teacher – one possible option for a well-educated young black woman in South Africa in 1966, in contrast to the millions of black women employed as domestic workers. In addition, Zandile's separation from the dresses, which represent one component of her urban life and

---

[27] Peggy Phelan, *Unmarked: The Politics of Peformance* (London: Routledge, 1993): 147.

[28] Susan Bennett, "Mother Tongue: Colonized Bodies and Performing Cultures," *Contemporary Theatre Review* 2:3 (1995): 108.

its potential, foregrounds some of the material effects of her abduction and the co-
ercion to adopt the practices and fulfil the expectations of a traditional rural life.
That Zandile is prohibited from wearing shoes to supposedly facilitate her work in
the fields is of a piece with Lulama's explanation that her daughter's dreams of
teaching are inappropriate: "Are you going to teach the goats?" (38). Quite apart
from their more universal implications, the dresses, as a marker of Zandile's disrupted childhood, serve as a vehicle for manifold factors which stage interventions
specific to South Africa.

In South Africa and on international stages, Mhlophe's performance of storytelling is invested with the force of the personal as political and the extended force
of the personal as a metonym of the community and its politics. As the oppressive
structures and their attendant silences break down, so the voices engendered in
storytelling can articulate and activate new dreams. Will spectators be listening
attentively and feel empowered?

Gay Theatres in South Africa
Peter Hayes, Pogiso Mogwera, and Jay Pather

❧   Michael Arthur

A MONG THE MANY ITEMS in South Africa's expanding catalogue of remarkable achievements can be included a constitutional clause unique among nations: the Republic of South Africa is the only country in the world with the rights of its gay and lesbian population enshrined in the very fabric of its constitution's basic statement of human rights:

> Every person shall have the right to equality before the law and to equal protection of the law. No person shall be unfairly discriminated against, directly or indirectly [...] on one or more of the following grounds in particular: race, gender, sex, ethnic or social origin, colour, sexual orientation, age disabilities, religion, conscience, belief, culture or language.

Of course, as with so many items in its impressive catalogue, this symbol of inclusion exists more as promise than reality in the provisional new South Africa. In the trenches of the everyday, life has not suddenly become free and easy for South Africa's gay and lesbian communities, which face continued prejudice and struggle because of their sexual orientation.

The particulars of the gay and lesbian experience in South Africa have begun to emerge on the printed page, in a growing body of non-fiction studies, novels, short stories and poems. Such anthologies as *Defiant Desire* and *The Invisible Ghetto*[1] offer numerous examples of the ways in which race, class and sex intersect in gay South African life. But there has been little if any discussion of the ways in which theatre has served as a medium for expressing these experiences, and the activist/interventionist implications.

This is a considerable omission, considering that some very interesting local works examining gay South African identities from within the community have appeared in recent years. Specifically, the director/performer Peter Hayes, the

---

[1] *Defiant Desire: Gay and Lesbian Lives in South Africa*, ed. Mark Gevisser & Edward Cameron (New York: Routledge, 1995); *The Invisible Ghetto: Lesbian and Gay Writing from South Africa*, ed. Matthew Krouse (Johannesburg: COSAW, 1993).

dancer/actor/writer/choreographer Jay Pather, and the director/writer Pogiso Mogwera have both individually and (at times) in combination begun creating theatre works which explore the parameters of South African performance, while exposing the complexities and specificities of gay South African experience. This paper, drawing primarily on a joint interview I conducted with Peter, Jay and Pogiso during the 1996 Grahamstown Festival, and further informed by texts of their plays and my viewing of several of their productions, will provide a very brief overview of both their goals and work and some peripheral indication of the challenges specific to their lives as gay/theatre-practitioner/activists.

(I think it worth mentioning first that, as *Defiant Desire* and *The Invisible Ghetto* indicate, there is some substantial lesbian writing and political activism. I am not aware of any consistent theatre work dealing with South African lesbian identity. Furthermore, even in *Defiant Desire*, gay articles outnumber lesbian articles by about five to one. Doubtless owing to the double oppression of women/lesbians, representations of South African lesbians remain less visible than gay male representations.)

Like many artists working from within marginalized communities in South Africa, Peter, Jay and Pogiso seek a balance between, and combination of, art and activism. On the one hand, they are educated, skilled artists, graduates all of university theatre departments (not that this is a requirement for skilled art); Pogiso and Peter attended university in Cape Town, while Jay studied dance and theatre in South Africa and the USA, where he received his MA from New York University. Jay's résumé, in particular, is notable for the wide array of parts, both gay and straight, that he has played, and for the many pieces he has danced and choreographed. It would not be an exaggeration to say that he is one of South Africa's finest performers in any category. On the other hand, all three are conscious of prejudices prevalent in both gay and straight communities, prejudices which in their work they seek to address and overcome; each told me about encounters with closeted gays who view their theatre activity as "rocking the boat," while the very real theatre of gay-bashing remains the most extreme, yet all too often chosen, option among those resistant to the inclusion of openly gay people in South African society. As a consequence, Peter, Jay and Pogiso's activist messages are directed at both gay and straight audiences. Peter says his "gay theatre work" has

> always [had] two very definite strands that run parallel. One is about affirming a gay audience, about saying "this is us, this is our lives." And making that special through theatre. And the other is about educating the straight audience. [...] straight audiences who have seen [my plays] end up saying. "I didn't expect to relate to so much."]²

---

² All quotations are from my interview with the artists (Grahamstown, 6 July 1996).

For Pogiso, whose base is in Mmabatho (Swaziland), the necessity of educating straight audiences is foremost: "You have whites in an understanding era at the moment. You know, more understanding. Blacks [...] understand but not really. [...] I mean, in most black townships it's thought of as trash to be gay." Consequently, Pogiso's work in Mmabatho is intended to emphasize black homosexuality as a reality while pointing out how closed-minded attitudes amongst both gays and straights are hurtful.

Nevertheless, Peter, Jay and Pogiso all have a conscious desire to create performances with artistic merit, 'good' theatre which is essentially political. Their activism is dependent upon speaking from within the gay experience, and so they all find the balance between artistic detachment and political intervention particularly difficult to achieve. As Jay says,

> we've got some kind of integrity as artists and so you think, you don't want to be apolitical by backing away from the gay issue, but by the same token you want [the play] to survive as a work of art as well. I think there's a big tension in all of that [...] I think maybe there's a point forward as far as gay theatre in that when more of the issue settles down within the communities then there will be drama about people, there will be theatre about people.

Another, related burden emerges from the tension between the roles they play in their work and the fact that one of their primary goals is to wed their personal gay identity to their art; all consider their most significant strategy and achievement to be that of making the gay presence visible. This manifests itself differently for Pogiso, whose professional role so far has been as director and author, than for Peter and Jay, who also perform. Pogiso's work emerges from his role as drama teacher with the Mmabana Cultural Centre in Mmabatho. While most of his performers are predominantly straight students, Pogiso insists upon presenting himself as openly gay within the organization and its community, while having the students work on his material – material which deals with gay subject-matter. He sees both of these strategies in terms of an activism protected by the promises of his new society:

> Isn't Reconstruction and Development [meant] to teach people about homosexuality, that it's fine, it's OK? That we're not saying you should be homosexual but you should accept those who are? [...] In Mmabatho I've changed a lot of attitudes [by being "out"]. This one guy said to me, "this is the first time I am talking to a gay person." [...] [I said] "this is the first time you've opened your mind and your acceptance of opinions to a gay person."

For Peter and Jay, the visibility factor is related more to their role as performers; that is, by making it clear to their audience that they, like the characters they play and the subject-matter they deal with, are gay, Peter and Jay believe that they remove the viewer's "comfort factor." Peter and Jay's first significant production together, *The Homosexuals: Out in Africa* (1992), was, as far as Peter knows, the first play to be "directed, written and performed by a group of gay men who were out in South Africa." Over the last decade or so, South African stages have hosted such American plays as *The Normal Heart*, *Angels in America*, *The Night Larry Kramer Kissed Me*, the camp musical *Boy Meets Boy*, and *Love, Valor, Compassion!* – all plays with predominately gay characters and gay-specific themes. While expressing admiration for many of these productions, Peter, Jay and Pogiso each criticized general tendencies in these works on the basis that: (1) the subject matter was not South African; (2) the performers in the plays were often presented publicly (in reviews and publicity, etc) as heterosexuals playing gay roles; and (3) the presentation of the plays, as slick, well-produced local versions of international fare, tended to minimize their potential for challenging South African attitudes about gay lifestyles. (When I asked Pogiso how he liked *Love, Valor, Compassion!*, he was generally enthusiastic – especially about all the naked guys – but criticized it for being too safe. "Where's the homework for the audience?" he asked.) About *The Homosexuals* specifically and his work in general, Peter says: "I didn't want the audience to be able to *separate*. Didn't want to give them the comfort zone of being able to sit there and say 'well, thank God he's going home to his wife and child'."

On the other hand, despite this potentially charged rhetoric, associating life-experience with acting qualifications – which, taken to its extreme, might seem to suggest that only gay performers should play gay roles, only straight players should play straight roles, and only ancient Greeks should perform *Medea* (and, perhaps, I, as a heterosexual scholar, shouldn't write this paper) – despite all this, both Jay and Peter express frustration with the limitations imposed by critics who confuse them with the roles they play. Peter especially complains that many who saw his monologue *Get Hard* (1992) didn't realize "how much of it is acting. People just generally thought 'Peter Hayes was on stage – he did have a script but he was just being himself'." Jay identifies this as an extension of homophobia, and likens it to the racism he has experienced as an actor:

> It's like a black person couldn't really play a character, they always play themselves [...] the establishment press [...] don't see marginalized groups as actually having that much artistic integrity. I've often felt that, even when I was in a mini-skirt and shaved legs and stuff, that they wouldn't see it as you working within a character.

Nevertheless, the use of their 'selves' in their work is calculated to add an experiential texture to the 'reality' of the stories that they tell and to increase the effectiveness of their work as activist interventions in audience attitudes.

As for those stories, Peter began his work in 'gay theatre' in 1992 as director, producer and co-creator of *The Homosexuals: Out in Africa*. His breakthrough came with his performance in *Get Hard* – perhaps ironically, when one considers Peter's emphatic claim that gay South African theatre should be South African in subject-matter; *Get Hard* is an adaptation of the American performance-artist Tim Miller's monologue *My Queer Body*. With Miller's permission, Peter reconceived the work, localizing references and personalizing the stories, while shifting Miller's focus on AIDS-related issues to gay-bashing, a concern more relevant to gay men in the South African context. (A significant difference between American and South African gay experience is the impact of HIV/AIDS: in South Africa AIDS is primarily – although, of course, not exclusively – a syndrome with dire consequences for the heterosexual black community.) *Get Hard* was a tremendous success for Peter; he played to sold-out seasons at Grahamstown (in 1992 and 1993) and toured the country, even performing at the State Theatre in Pretoria (interesting, when one considers a fantasy-sequence in the work which imagines the inauguration of South Africa's first black-lesbian President in the State Theatre at Pretoria). Primarily due to the tremendous popular response to *Get Hard*, Peter was invited by the Grahamstown Festival Committee to create a work as part of the 1995 main season. The piece, *Journey*, might be likened to Fugard's experiment *My Life* (1994), in that its premise was that the stories were drawn from young people (in this case, people in their twenties) from around the new South Africa. An extended workshop production (the chosen performers 'journeyed' around the country while they developed the piece, drawing their scenes from people and experiences they encountered), *Journey* included gay and lesbian issues as part of its depiction of the new South Africa. In 1996, Peter directed and produced *The Stories I Could Tell*, which was performed in Melbourne, Australia and Cape Town. (At the 1996 Grahamstown Festival, Peter presented two pieces: *Dogs*, a play dealing with submerged racism and violence, which he produced, acted in, and directed; and *1,000 Cranes*, a theatre-for-youth play set in Japan in the years after the dropping of the atomic bomb, which he produced and directed. Neither play, though both socially committed works, specially addresses gay issues.)

Jay, in addition to his main job at the Playhouse in Durban, has been one of Hayes's primary collaborators on *The Homosexuals*, *Journey*, and *The Stories I Could Tell* and has created several dances and solo performance pieces as well. The general form of Hayes and Pather's collaborations has been the extended monologue; most of the pieces are confessional in tone and style. Even *Journey* was primarily a series of solo pieces, with a few smaller scenes featuring two or more members of the group. Although they speak of challenging their audiences, their style is not very confrontational; their choice of material, primarily the open depiction of gay subject-matter, is their most subversive practice. With the notable exception of Hayes in *Get Hard*, which required him to step nude into the audience area, the works tend not to break the Western, traditional, separated actor/audience relationship. Jay and Peter's most recent collaboration, *The Stories I Could Tell*, moves beyond the simple monologue, in that one of the primary goals of the piece was to subvert cultural forms with content; each of the four pieces in the work utilized different storytelling traditions. For example, the work featured a praise poem to a gay lover, as well as a scene in which an Indian son's homosexuality becomes apparent in a traditional dance performed for his father.

In keeping with his function as drama tutor for the Mmabana Cultural Centre in Mmabatho, Pogiso's 'intervention' in attitudes towards homosexuality takes place in both the classroom/drama-lab and the theatre. Since almost all the students who perform his scripts are straight, tensions have arisen between him and both his bosses and nervous parents. In 1995 he wrote a play called *Dumela Bangani*, which addressed violence against gays in the townships. His 1996 work, *Hanging Oopside Down*, was primarily a dance piece which had a few scenes featuring male partnering, including sections he has been adapting from a book of gay poetry.

Again, the work was performed by his students. There is some irony in the fact that, compared to Jay and Peter, Pogiso is limited in what he can do by virtue of his subversion being paid for, as he says, by the "gravy train"; the cultural centre with which he is associated has a multi-million working budget. And with great budgets come great responsibilities: his primary task as far as his employers are concerned is to provide his students with a good arts education, while exposing the Arts centre's work to the community and at the various South African arts festivals, especially Grahamstown.

Like much work emerging from within the shifting cultural landscape of South Africa, the gay theatre endeavours of Peter Hayes, Jay Pather and Pogiso Mogwera might best be thought of as occupying a space between the promises of a new society and the everyday realities of the present. Their work is often rough along the edges; they haven't yet found the requisite balance between commitment and quality; economic realities figure strongly in their ability to pursue their variously committed arts agenda. The primary challenge for them now is to sharpen and focus both their work and their conception of their audiences. As South African artists who foreground a gay identity, they describe their mission as the presentation of good work that disrupts notions of sexual and cultural norms, work that affirms a gay audience and unsettles the assumptions of straight audiences. This mission is strongly informed by both the theory and the practice of American and European gay theatre artists. However, unlike the politicized work of these better-known and more experienced gay theatre artists/activists, Peter, Jay and Pogiso work in a society where the primary cultural agenda is the creation of a national consciousness inclusive of the population's diversity, in terms of racial, cultural, religious, and/or sexual identity. Only through continued explorations of the expressive possibilities afforded them by the new paradigms of their society will their work emerge as truly significant. But they are working to bridge the gap between their ideals and their life and work. This is one of the most exciting features of cultural production and intervention in the provisional new South Africa.

Theatre in/ and Education ℭ⅊

Rainbows and Spiderwebs
New Challenges for Theatre in a Transformed System of Education in South Africa[1]

∞ Michael Carklin

> THAMI   [...] I have tried very hard, believe me, but it's not as simple and easy as it used to be to sit behind that desk and listen to the teacher. That little world of the classroom where I used to be happy, where they used to pat me on the head and say: Little Thami, you'll go far [...] that little room of wonderful promises, where I used to feel so safe has become a place I don't trust any more. Now I sit at my desk like an animal that has smelt danger, heard something moving in the bushes, and knows it must be very, very careful.[2]

IRST PERFORMED IN 1989, Athol Fugard's *My Children! My Africa!* highlights the crisis facing education at the time, and reminds us that it was not just a crisis characterized by inequitable resourcing, underqualified teachers, lack of facilities and fundamentally skewed education philosophies (although all of these were crucial). It manifested itself at the level of the individual pupil, particularly black pupils, who found that the world of school became a threat, a place of militancy in which violence not only flourished but became a force of self-preservation. South Africa during the Seventies and Eighties, and as recently as the early Nineties, was a country in which it became necessary to have large organizations with names like the "National Education Crisis Committee" (NECC) and to coin terms like "the lost generation" to describe pupils of school-going age during that time.

One of the images that seems to characterize the period for me is that of the spider. Thinking back to my own childhood, I am reminded of a rhyme: "'Come into my parlour,' said the spider to the fly." A sinister air, a web of intrigue, shrouded the country, and there was a very real sense of being flies caught in this

---

[1] This essay updates a paper originally presented at the South African Theatre conference in London and subsequently published in *Research in Drama Education* 2.2 (1997): 203–13.

[2] Athol Fugard, *"My Children! My Africa!" and Selected Shorter Plays* (Johannesburg: Witwatersrand UP, 1990): 173.

larger, restraining and all-powerful net. While the education crisis is far from over, post-apartheid South Africa is now faced with a fundamentally changed context in which new philosophies, new policies and renewed enthusiasm once again raise the possibility of seeing the classroom, in Fugard's terms, as the "little room of wonderful promises."

Transformed contexts

There is little doubt that the world faced by South African school pupils in the latter half of the Nineties and into the twenty-first century is very different from that faced by pupils in the early Nineties. The images have changed – now we have become a nation chasing after rainbows and pots of gold (which we hope will not be taken by hijackers on our way home through the streets of Johannesburg). Rather than being cowering animals scenting danger in the bushes, we have had the sense of a nation coming together to celebrate the *amabokoboko*,[3] and, as we step out of the apartheid cocoon, hopefully transformed into something more beautiful than we were before, we face a new web. Not the web of the menacing spider, the sidekick of *"die groot krokodil,"*[4] but a huge web spun by an interesting new species of spider. A species that does not say "come into my parlour," but that says "there are millions of parlours out there, which one would you like to explore?" I'm referring, of course, to the World Wide Web and the vast opportunities for networking that this offers.

This suggests that pupils' life-experiences demand skills and insights which the education system inherited from our past era is simply unable to offer. Their world has become one characterized by new experiences of cultural mixing and multilingualism, of a renewed contact with the rest of the world. South Africa is a country in which censorship laws have virtually disappeared and a whole world of experience that was kept from people is suddenly available and – for some South Africans – abundant; it is a strange mix of what some might term 'First-' and 'Third-World': both a developing country, and, in some respects, quite a developed one. The image of a "rainbow nation," although needing to be treated critically and with a certain amount of caution, is nonetheless a symbol of the positive embracing of multiplicity within our society.

As we venture into a world of post-colonialism, we are also faced with something of a postmodern landscape of eclecticism, choice and multiple perspective.

---

[3] The *amabokoboko* is the name given to the Springbok team that won the Rugby World Cup in 1995. The event was characterized by an unprecedented show of unity among all South Africans.

[4] An Afrikaans phrase; literally, 'the large crocodile.' It became one of the names used to designate the former President, P.W. Botha.

The 'grand narratives' – as they formed an impression upon my mind, for example, through years of learning about the "Great Trek" in school history – have been challenged, and we are faced with a confusing choice of his- and her-stories. Unlike Vladimir and Estragon in *Waiting for Godot*, it is not a case of "Nothing to be done"[5] but a question of "What can we do and how should we do it?" (And of "Do you think there is money available from the Government with which to do it?").

It is not all positive change, of course. Part of the new landscape (or variety of landscapes) is scarred by violent crime. The jackals have not gone into hiding, but have used change to their advantage. And while the great "Gathering of the Beasts" in the form of the Truth and Reconciliation Commission called on people to reveal their spots or show their true stripes, the vultures and hyenas waited anxiously for their pickings.[6]

New philosophies ... new policies

In short, in exploring possible levels of intervention we need to take close cognizance of the changing world of South Africa, which demands an education system that requires a radical redefinition of self and society by pupils, parents, and teachers. The philosophical underpinnings of a reconstructed system of education stress child-centred, experiential forms of learning, whilst the Reconstruction and Development Programme, the initial blueprint for South Africa's transformation, described the arts as a crucial part of South Africa's human resource development.[7] More recently, the launch of the Curriculum 2005 process[8] has set the stage for the introduction of 'outcomes-based' education. Integrated schools, revised curricula, and the need for fresh and innovative resources provide a context in which theatre intervenes as both a medium for development and a medium for creative expression.

The Nineties in South Africa have been concerned with meeting the challenges of change head-on as frenetic work in all aspects of reconstruction has taken place to turn new philosophies into policy statements, to galvanize support, to turn vision into legislation. The opportunity to contribute to policy formulation has been

[5] Samuel Beckett, *Waiting for Godot* (London: Faber & Faber, 1965): 1.

[6] The Truth and Reconciliation Commission (TRC) was the body under the chairpersonship of Archbishop Desmond Tutu which conducted hearings into political acts of violence committed during the apartheid era. While submissions were made by people from all sides of the country's conflict, it was particularly the killings and violent oppression by the security forces of the apartheid state that were exposed.

[7] African National Congress, *The Reconstruction and Development Programme: A Policy Framework* (Johannesburg: Umanya, 1994): par. 1.4.8.

[8] Department of Education (South Africa), *Curriculum 2005: Lifelong Learning for the 21st Century* (Pretoria: Department of Education, 1977).

significant, with a real sense, for the first time, of consultation and progressive thought. In terms of drama and theatre, the set of resolutions adopted by the broadly representative National Arts Coalition (in 1993), the widely consulted Arts and Culture Task Group Report (ACTAG) (1995), and the subsequent White Paper on Arts, Culture and Heritage all include positive reference to the arts in education, the result of vocal lobbying on the part of the arts and education community. In addition, Curriculum 2005 includes Arts and Culture as one of eight core learning areas. The challenge now, of course, is to be able to turn such policy statements into practice – which is considerably more difficult.

Theatrical intervention

In considering some of the ways in which theatre can and often does intervene, I would emphasize the distinction between learning *about* drama and theatre, and learning *through* drama and theatre. The relationship is not dichotomous, and quite often one might be learning about theatre at the same time as learning through theatre. But they both represent potential aspects of intervention. I further suggest that such intervention happens both overtly and covertly (but always intentionally). I focus on three areas of intervention: first, theatre studies as part of the formal school curriculum; secondly, dramatic techniques as a methodology for the teacher; and thirdly, theatrical interventions in the school by outside groupings.

Theatre studies in the curriculum

Under the previous system, a very smart number of schools offered drama as a subject of study up to matriculation level. This is still the case. These schools are mainly in KwaZulu–Natal province and tend to be the previously 'white' or 'Indian' institutions. In addition, there are a few private schools in the other provinces which offer the subject.

It would seem that one key area of intervention is the development of drama and theatre as a subject of study, and the process has begun with some effect. Thanks to the lobbying of arts educators, policy documentation now embraces the idea of arts education, and a syllabus is in place which firmly roots theatre studies in a South African context. For the first time, the White Paper on Education states:

> Education in the arts, and the opportunity to *learn, participate and excel in dance, music, theatre, arts and crafts* must become increasingly available to all communities on an equitable basis, drawing on and sharing the rich traditions of our varied cultural heritage and contemporary practice.[9]

---

[9] R.S.A., *White Paper on Education and Training, Government Gazette* 357.16312, Notice no. 196 of 1995 (Pretoria: Department of Education, 1995): 2 (emphasis in the original).

This is couched within a broad educational philosophy that favours child-centred, experiential approaches to learning and teaching. This is in stark contrast to previous policy, where arts in education were constantly faced with marginalization and usually seen as subjects for 'talented' pupils only, or for 'weaker' pupils who could not cope with maths or science. Part of the reason that the arts have been accorded 'Cinderella' status has been a misunderstanding of the kind of educational experience they can provide.

The drama curriculum is not simply a wallpapering of the previously inadequate syllabus. It should be examined in the light of the ACTAG Report, which states:

> What we are calling for, is a re-evaluation of the values, assumptions, aims and objectives which have underpinned the curricula of the past and a reconceptualisation in terms of the needs and interests of learners and their communities.[10]

A key indicator of intervention taking place is the revised transitional syllabus drafted by the National Education and Training Forum (NETF) Subcommittee on Drama during the latter half of 1994.[11] The work of the committee was guided by three main principles, and these seem to indicate some of the various levels at which theatrical interventions can take place within the school.

First, the committee was guided by the idea that our ways of seeing or experiencing and expressing our local South African world are generally more immediate, whereas our experience of the rest of the world tends to be mediated to a greater degree. This implies that our study of and through drama and theatre should start with our immediate experience, then broaden to incorporate the rest of the world, rather than be rooted in a study of European theatre, as has been the case in the past, with South African and African studies regarded as an appendage.

A closer look at the syllabus shows that South African plays and historical theatre studies now make up a major portion of the curriculum. Theatre History, for example, begins with the idea of Ritual in an African Context, and then turns its attention to South African theatre studies, which includes the township musical, Black Consciousness theatre, and South African playwrights and performance forms such as gumboot dance, *volkspele* [traditional Afrikaans folk-dances], *toyi-toyi* [military/protest/celebratory step], *Kaapse klopse* [Cape Malay street dances], *isicathamiya* [Zulu choral singing], *mokhibo* [Sotho dance form], protest theatre, workers' theatre, workshopped theatre, educational theatre, and satirical review. It

---

[10] Arts and Culture Task Group (ACTAG). *Draft Report Prepared by the ACTAG for the Ministry of Arts, Culture, Science and Technology* (Pretoria: ACTAG, 1995): 257, para. 5.1.

[11] This transitional syllabus takes the place of the syllabus used under the previous education system and will eventually be replaced by the 'outcomes-based' Curriculum 2005.

then broadens out to include the rest of the world – Africa, Europe, Asia, and America. A list from one of the schools in Grahamstown which offers drama as a subject includes set plays such as *Woza Albert!*, *Sophiatown*, *Cincinnati*, *"Master Harold" ... and the Boys*, *Saturday Night at the Palace*, and *The Hungry Earth*.

At an interventionary level, the introduction of such a syllabus to schools is crucial, in that it represents a reclamation and re-exploration of South African cultural expression. Through coming to terms with theatre studies as offered by such a syllabus, the potential is there for pupils not only to become conversant with the idea of theatre and theatricality, but for pupils to come to terms with 'history' from the perspective of cultural histories. This has close ties to the idea of the oral tradition in South Africa, where the telling of history through performance practices is a fundamental part of community expression. Theatre thus intervenes in throwing new light on the past, providing the opportunity to reconceptualize self and society through dramatic expression.

The second guiding principle in the construction of the syllabus was the methodological approach of a praxis which aims at creating learning situations "in which students can experience and then be skilled with ways of thinking about those experiences critically."[12] Based on the thinking of Paulo Freire, this is the key to much Educational Drama and Theatre (EDT) practice, and in many ways represents theatre at its most democratic. Like Augusto Boal's Forum Theatre and Image Theatre, it suggests a theatre of participation and activity, in which one breaks down not only the boundaries between the actor and the spectator (in Boal's words the "spect-actor") but also those between the teacher and the learner. As EDT practitioners have passionately argued, the teacher is no longer the all-knowing authority, but becomes an (authoritative) member of the community of learners, facilitating the process of exploration and reflection. Thus, if the first principle makes a major intervention in the education system in terms of content, this second principle intervenes in terms of methodology, challenging the conventional chalk–talk teaching practices that have been so much a part of South African schools. This leads directly to the third principle, to which we have already alluded: that drama should be promoted as a way of 'knowing' – both knowledge about drama and knowledge through drama.

Unfortunately, the fact of the matter remains that it is a very limited number of schools that offer drama as a subject – none of the 'black' schools do, nor do most integrated state schools outside of KwaZulu–Natal.

---

[12] National Education and Training Forum, *Guide to Speech and Drama Syllabus: Standards 8, 9, 10 (Grades 10, 11, 12)* (Pretoria: NEFT, 1994): 1.

Drama methodologies

Taking this into account, it would seem that a more effective form of intervention in the education system would be the promotion of drama as teaching methodology across all subjects. Through theatricalizing (and I am thinking here of active participatory theatre), a major intervention would be made at the level of teaching and learning methodologies. At the Ilitha Arts Education Conference held at Rhodes University in April 1995, the major call from delegates, who were drawn from across the country, was for teacher training and development in the arts.[13] The value of interactive learning techniques is not lost on many teachers, and the challenge becomes the creation of effective in-service training programmes which see to the implementation of high-quality development.

In many ways, this is one of the most covert levels of intervention, through which theatre methodologies become integral to teaching methodologies; at the same time, theatre itself changes and is transformed. I say "covert," because it has a sense of the 'subversive' about it. While, philosophically, change in education has been quite radical, in practical terms schools are still the same hierarchical, authoritarian places they always were. What better way to intervene than to subvert the system by introducing notions of theatre into the training of teachers? Of course, this is not a new idea, but within the South African context, such methodologies provide an exceptionally useful medium for creating learning situations for multicultural and multilingual classes in which pupils themselves become key resources.

Intervention from outside

The above refers to theatre intervening from within the school system. The other way that theatre intervenes, of course, is from the outside. South Africa has a long history of Theatre in Education (TIE), often based most strongly in university drama departments. However, it has been felt that the 'one-off' interventions that have characterized TIE in the past need to be reconsidered. Much more effective intervention is needed in which a sustained impact can be made. The DramAidE Project is an example which uses multiphased interventions, and, very significantly, begins to link directly to the syllabus in terms of the life-skills development that forms a core part of the new Guidance curriculum.

DramAidE was initiated in KwaZulu–Natal province in 1992 under the leadership of Lynn Dalrymple. It has now spread across that province, with new

---

[13] The proceedings of the conference are available in the *Ilitha Arts Education Conference Journal* (Ilitha Arts Education Project, 1995).

projects set up in the Eastern Cape (based in Grahamstown) and Gauteng (based in Johannesburg). It is concerned with HIV/AIDS and life-skills education in secondary schools, using drama and theatre methodologies. The Eastern Cape project is an example of the kinds of intervention that are taking place.

This project has four phases of intervention: on the first visit to the school, the team conducts a needs-analysis workshop with each standard (grade) separately. They use Image Theatre techniques to catalyze and facilitate group debates. Images used focus on specific research questions that differ according to standard and developmental factors. For example, images may depict scenes of peer pressure, or various attitudes to sex. The important thing is that they remain open to interpretation and become good indicators of pupils' own perceptions, experiences, and understanding. At this phase, the team also runs a workshop with teachers to introduce them to the project and to the idea of interactive learning techniques. The second phase is a life-skills workshop, again with each separate standard. Here a series of catalyst scenes are presented multilingually by the team in the roles of members of a youth club. Issues from the needs-analysis workshop are problematized, and Forum Theatre is used to examine various potential solutions. Some of the scenes will form part of the storyline of phase 3, the play.

The play is performed for the whole school, and the team has committed itself to exciting work. Clearly, educational efficacy relies on polished and innovative theatricality. It is this phase in particular that interests me in terms of theatrical intervention. The play developed by the Eastern Cape team has caused some controversy within DramAidE more broadly. When performed at an "all-teams forum" in Durban, there was some criticism from members of other teams of the symbolic/metaphoric nature of the work; many argued that the message needed to be spelled out for pupils in what I understood to mean pure didactic theatre.

The Eastern Cape team, however, defended their theatrical decisions, which are aimed at meeting the changed context of life in South Africa head-on. They not only see the world of multiplicity and intertextuality out there, but consciously employ these concepts in designing and executing the work. The play is multilingual, and the team is very conscious of the importance of physical expression. Gesture, for example, becomes a crucial part of the communication process. A mixture of puppetry, drama, Image Theatre, Forum Theatre, dance, physical theatre, song, and praise poetry makes for an eclectic piece which both challenges the audience and provides multiple layers of meaning. It acknowledges that each pupil faces different experiences and will relate differently to the work.

An interesting influence on the development of the play has been the team's composition. There are six members: three university honours graduates; three "community theatre practitioners" without tertiary training. The team is unique within DramAidE in terms of its makeup. In developing the play, the work has included a strong staff-development component in which each team member has been responsible for running workshops with the rest of the group. These might include, for example, facilitation skills, gumboot dancing, *mapantsula* [fashionable young urban black] dance, Forum Theatre, physical theatre, and mime.

This does not mean that in developing the play one is left with a mishmash of "rainbow nation" aesthetics in which ballerinas in gumboots become the order of the day. Rather, it is a conscious transformation of the collective performance resources of the group into work that is visually exciting and challenging, and that sees the need for expression beyond the limitations of the spoken word. It also draws on notions of Theatre for Development in using cultural forms with which the pupils might be familiar, but then goes further in challenging them with possibly new theatrical experiences. The team leader for the pilot-project, Nan Hamilton, describes the process of creating the play as "finding a modern ritual response to the [AIDS] crisis."[14]

The fourth project-phase is an open day, hosted by the school, for which pupils have prepared their own plays, songs, or poems, thus really needing to come to terms with the issues. The project also included a past competition with the theme "HIV/AIDS in my Africa Dream ... mind, body and soul." At present this model is being developed to include interventions in clinics and with parents and teachers.

I wrote earlier of the cocoon from which we have emerged. Nan Hamilton has a similar view of DramAidE's work, which she calls "Worming In and Flying Out": the intervention requires a worming in, but the result is one of transformation:

> As a pilot project we were asked to worm out ways into a school system and "culture of learning" which often felt like a vacuum; to worm our way into each other's lives as we confronted our fears of death and terminal illness; to worm our way into opening up young people's hearts to talk about their hopes, risks, realities, to recognise oppressive, abusive behaviour as not normative; to worm into a coherent mix of culture and style that would engage and teach, and reinforce the value that things can be different. Through this action–reflection process we have experienced transformation and the necessary discomfort of the unknown. The internal team process is what we need to realise in schools so that young people too can self-actualise and learn to fly.[15]

---

[14] DramAidE Eastern Cape, *DramAidE Eastern Cape Pilot Project: Final Report* (Grahamstown: Rhodes University, 1996): 8. It should be noted that these comments about DramAidE refer specifically to the 1996 pilot project. During 1997/8, DramAidE Eastern Cape has continued to develop, with Likhaya Ngandi taking over as Team leader.

[15] *DramAidE Eastern Cape Pilot Project: Final Report*, 8.

Conclusion

I began this paper with the image of the cowering animal. Clearly, the education system we want is not one in which pupils learn out of fear. Nor, however, is it one in which we train a highly skilled troupe of Pavlovian pupils to salivate every time the school bell rings. The way in which theatre intervenes demands a critical engagement with the process of exploring and learning.

I have discussed three basic modes of intervention: as a subject of study at school; as a methodology for teachers; and as a vehicle used by an outside agent.[16] While these are not new modes, in the sense that other countries around the world have developed and introduced such approaches over previous decades, and in the sense that South African drama educators have been arguing for the importance of such approaches for many years, the current South African educational and sociopolitical contexts provide a firm base for such interventions to take place.

The launch of Curriculum 2005 (1997) with its focus on developing skills, critical thinking, attitudes and understanding reinforces the potential for drama and the arts. Coupled with a political context embracing diversity and demanding a "culture of learning" in all schools, it would seem that the time is ripe for introducing drama into schools in a much bigger way than is currently available. All three areas of intervention can contribute to the developing of pupil-centred, holistic, multicultural learning programmes, but the challenges are immense, especially in terms of teacher education and resource development.

The need for resource development is particularly apparent if one considers the shift of emphasis in the syllabus towards a South African focus. Lack of accessible documentation on South African theatre, and general inexperience among many current drama teachers regarding the history, theory and performance of drama and theatre in Southern Africa, mean that programmes need to be researched, developed and implemented which support teacher education at both pre-service and in-service levels. While it might seem strange to many that South African teachers are generally ill-equipped to teach South African theatre, this situation highlights the education legacy that is currently undergoing transformation, one in which eurocentric syllabuses negated the validity of our own experience in Southern Africa. This, however, also suggests that there are exciting possibilities for innovative resource development and re-exploring ideas of theatre and dramatic performance in terms of a context which draws strongly on both indigenous oral traditions and Western theatre. Debates on syncretism, physical expression and storytelling in the theatre become central to a curriculum seeking

---

[16] These are selective areas of intervention; there are, of course, other issues to be considered, such as the 'school play' or the place of dramatic literature in language and literature syllabuses.

to support multiplicity. This provides a challenge to theatre and education researchers committed to fostering drama at secondary-school level and developing fresh notions of identity and community for the learning experience.

The significance of South Africa's having only recently embraced democracy should not be underestimated; in many senses, we are only now coming to terms (in a practical way) with the many possibilities that child-centred, active learning offers. The challenge of transforming an entire teaching force that in the main has become used to unilingual, unicultural transmission-teaching highlights the immense task of intervening not only at the level of *content* (changing curricula), but also at the level of *methodology*. In this light, drama and theatre seem particularly appropriate for use across the curriculum, especially in a country with such varying levels of education and literacy and strong communal performance traditions.

Transformation is not a swift process, and it will undoubtedly take many years for significant, well-rooted changes in education to take place. It therefore seems that theatrical interventions by outside agents are of additional importance: not only do they provide innovative educational experiences for the pupil, but they also expose teachers to the opportunities for drama in the classroom. This is particularly so in programmes such as DramAidE, which do not rely on one-off interventions but which are multiphased, developmental or progressive approaches, including work with the teachers themselves.

I have sought to examine the ways in which theatre intervenes in South Africa's education system. Intervention, suggesting conscious mediation aimed at effecting significant change or development is potentially one of the most far-reaching contributions that theatre can make in the national school-system to the process of radical transformation, stimulating the imaginative, creative and critical growth of the country's young people. While policy statements support the introduction of drama at various levels, the reality is that this is unlikely to happen unless arts educators intervene with well-researched and strategically applied programmes. It is hoped that, in so doing, we can help our young people to spread their wings and open their minds to new insights and experiences.

> African Child
> Your wings will grow
> Then
> You must fly.[17]

—— ℰᴏ ᴄ꞉ ——

---

[17] Poem by David Rubadiri, in *Growing Up with African Poetry: An Anthology for Secondary Schools*, ed. Rubadiri (Houghton, S.A.: Heinemann, 1989): 79.

Theatre for Reconciliation
David Lan's *Desire* as an Interventionary Vehicle

℘   Hazel Barnes

Truth and reconciliation

> A woman circles the stage on an old bicycle and exits. The people of her village watch as she sets out to ride up the mountain and demand her village's share of government rations. Her sister, crippled in the war of liberation, hobbles forward and shouts after her, "Freedom, keep going! Keep going, Rosemary!"[1]

THIS, THE CONCLUSION TO DAVID LAN'S PLAY *DESIRE,* has significance on a number of levels. The image embodies the reconciliation of conflict within the character of Rosemary, her acceptance, both literal and figurative, of the spirit of Freedom and thus her responsibility for the continued well-being of her community. The bicycle circling, an image associated throughout the play with the female spirit of Freedom struggling to inhabit Rosemary (and through her ensure that truth is heard), signifies wholeness, a wholeness won through the rituals of ancestor worship which compel the three male characters implicated in the death of the village girl, whose *nom de guerre* is Freedom, to confess and thus accept responsibility. The public acknowledgement of the truth leads to the healing of Rosemary, the realization of her power, and the unity and reconciliation of her village. The conclusion has significance beyond the play: it resonates with the hearings of the Truth and Reconciliation Commission that have occurred in South Africa since 1996; it also illustrates the empowerment made possible through symbolic processes such as ritual or theatre.

April 27, 1994 signalled the beginnings of the transition to democracy in South Africa. For many South Africans it also symbolized the triumph of rationality and negotiation over the passion and brutality of warfare. For many white South

---

[1] David Lan, *"Desire" and Other Plays* (London: Faber & Faber, 1990): 176.

Africans it seemed as if a hopeless and bloody civil war had been averted; as if the positive spirit of compassion, compromise and inclusivity had at last prevailed over the antitheses set up by colonialism. This triumph was celebrated nationally by South Africans during the inauguration of President Mandela. It was celebrated with all the euphoria of victory, for South Africa *had* been at war, as the evidence heard by the Truth and Reconciliation Commission makes clear. In the few years since April 1994 this euphoria has abated, as the challenges lying ahead and the pain still lingering from the past have become more and more evident. The recognition of the impact of the past on the present is the basis on which policies for the future are being built. Initiatives such as the Reconstruction and Development Programme and the Truth and Reconciliation Commission bear this out. The commission was led by Archbishop Tutu, representing religion and its essential role in reconciliation, and by Dr Alex Boraine of the Institute for Democratic Alternative South Africa, representing the function of principled public responsibility.

The purpose of the Truth and Reconciliation Commission has been described as one of bearing witness.[2] This witnessing had two functions. One was that of discovering the truth so that an accurate history of recent events could be determined and written. This was essential in a country where press censorship and clandestine government operations made the truth inaccessible over many years. The second function of bearing witness was to reveal the humanity of fellow South Africans to each other. The Truth and Reconciliation Commission allowed South Africans, divided from each other in the past, to sit together in the same room hearing each other's experiences. The public reporting of each session by the media ensured that all South Africans had the opportunity to learn about each other's experience of apartheid. It ensured that those whites who had not been able to believe in the reality of government atrocities acknowledged them. This public hearing confirmed that the experience of oppression was real; that the denials of torture and suffering by those with power – the District Surgeon who didn't see the injuries, the Magistrate who didn't hear the complaint – were fabrications. The pain and suffering of apartheid has had many faces, and the struggle for liberation has resulted, in some cases, in the death and mutilation of the innocent. These oppressive situations demand public acknowledgement; the common humanity of all South Africans, both perpetrators and victims, needs to be affirmed in order to foster empathy with and understanding of the experiences of others. Both the struggle to find a more equitable way of living together and the commission of

---

2 I am indebted to Ilan Lax of the KwaZulu–Natal/Free State Truth and Reconciliation Commission for this information. He spoke at a seminar on Truth and Reconciliation in South Africa held by the Critical Studies Group, University of Natal, Pietermaritzburg, on 4 June 1996.

unspeakable acts of violence need to be recognized and owned. Confession and cleansing are seen as essential prerequisites for creating a more just future.

The Truth and Reconciliation Commission was responsible for a number of different types of hearings. Victim hearings were instituted to restore people's dignity through their own accounts of political trauma. The Commission selected examples which were illustrative, found all the records of the events, heard the account of the event, and made a recommendation that the tellers involved were found to be victims. Their suffering was publicly acknowledged. Event hearings examined particular events such as the Trust Feed Massacres and forced removals, and the Commission looked for patterns of command and abuse in order to discover how various parties such as vigilante groups and political parties functioned. Hearings also involved the political parties: the former government, the ANC and other political parties, as well as the NGOs, testified. Finally, the Commission probed other apartheid issues such as land claims, justice, prisons, and gender-inequality.

South Africa is not alone in recognizing the need for truth and reconciliation; there have been over forty such commissions operating in the last twenty years. But the South African Truth and Reconciliation Commission was unique in choosing a central course between the more common extremes. The one extreme, represented by the Nuremberg Trials, is that in which the victors prosecute the vanquished. The other extreme is exemplified by Zimbabwe, where the hearings of its commission have never been made public, on the presumption that Zimbabweans are "turning over the page and making a new start." The South African Truth and Reconciliation Commission, accentuating its symbolic role, chose to make hearings public, and also granted amnesty to most perpetrators who make a public confession of apartheid crimes. This choice gave rise to controversy, but affirmed the government's belief that forgiveness and reconciliation are primary.

They are also central themes in the play *Desire*, which climaxes in a scene of confession. Set in a village in the Zambezi valley immediately after the War of Liberation, the play explores the community's need to understand the truth surrounding the death of a young woman, Freedom, who had fought with the guerrillas, and their need to hear the perpetrator's public acknowledgement of culpability. This truth is made all the more poignant and relevant to our situation in South Africa by the complex loyalties evident in the predicament of civil war. The metaphor which embodies this need for veracity and makes it available to an audience is the phenomenon of spirit-possession, an important aspect of ancestral religion. Freedom is able to make her fervent need for the public acknowledgement of the truth strikingly obvious through her spirit's possession of a childhood friend, Rosemary.

In his ethnographic account of the Dande people, *Guns and Rain*, David Lan elucidates the important function performed by traditional religion and by its shamans in the struggle for liberation. The opposition between traditional African values and spirituality and European settler values became an important means of strengthening the guerrilla cause, enabling the guerrillas (who were most often strangers) to integrate with local populations, and further distanced those populations from chiefs tainted by colonial values and loyalties.[3] This emphasis on marginalized African belief-systems as a source of resistance, resilience and discernment is crystallized in *Desire*, and is what makes the play a viable vehicle for engagement or intervention by black theatre students in South Africa.

Context

The University of Natal, in common with most South African universities, has undergone a process of transition during the past decade. One of the main features of this transition has been the increasing attendance of black students at formerly "whites only" universities. This has meant that black students, historically separated from white culture and educationally disadvantaged, have been thrown into a milieu in which they have felt alienated, undervalued and sometimes inadequate. In interviews, both black and Indian students have identified feelings of inferiority and passivity as the main legacy of apartheid.[4]

During the past decade, black students have pushed for the transformation of curricula at universities. In the Drama Studies Department at the University of Natal, Pietermaritzburg, this has resulted in the development of courses on performance studies in place of the traditional history of Western theatre; the inclusion of indigenous texts, the development of community theatre, and the social application of drama in education and development. To the staff of the department, all white, it has felt like a major shift of focus, away from eurocentricity. White students do not uniformly welcome the politicizing of their studies. Black students, however, still find the department alien. Their main criticism lies in the use of the Hexagon Theatre, a prestigious and flexible theatre laboratory seating between 300 and 500, which in their perceptions privileges performances that demonstrate a predominantly Western, as opposed to African, world-view. These

---

[3] David Lan, *Guns and Rain: Guerrillas and Spirit Mediums in Zimbabwe* (London: James Currey, 1985).

[4] Interviews with Teboho Hlahane, Shanita Jugmohan, Mzi Mdingi, Beatrice Motene, Reuben Ngubane, Sehlula Ngubane, Katherine Smart, Ntutu Spelman, Alexandra Sutherland & Stellar Zulu (conducted by the author, June 1996).

shows comprise American musicals, contemporary plays by South African, British and American playwrights, and visiting productions by professionals of all races. Our smaller experimental theatre, seating eighty, is used predominantly but not exclusively for plays directed and workshopped by students. These vary from versions of South African classics, through workshopped plays on a variety of social and political issues, to playscripts of American or British origin. The common feeling among black students is that the plays, particularly those in the larger theatre, are unlikely to be of interest to them.

One may argue for the importance of such plays in terms of their value as cultural icons, their literary and historical significance, their addressing of important human issues or their theatrical innovations; but such arguments do not bring in multicultural audiences. Many white students express their boredom with plays dealing with political issues ("Apartheid is dead; why are you still thrusting it down our throats?") and are more intent on pushing theatrical practice to its limits in terms of form and subject-matter. Their main concern is to perform, direct or create theatre in the international forum, and they tend to resent what they perceive as a parochial focus. This difference of interests splits students within the department. The dichotomy between African perceptions of the function of art and those of the 'centre' – an emphasis on "the social function of writing over its function as a tool of individual expression"[5] – underlies this difference.

Choosing *Desire*

Desire appeared to be a play that might help bridge the gulf in the expectations and aspirations of our student body. For black students, the play presents an African world-view through the meticulous re-creation of cultural signifiers by the social-anthropologist/playwright. Lan presents African values and spirituality; moreover, he celebrates them as a powerful source of strength and wisdom.[6] The play deals with important contemporary issues in Africa: the struggle for liberation, the establishment of democracy and gender-equality, the synthesizing of traditional beliefs and current doctrine, the problem of duplicity and betrayal. For white students, here is a play written by an established European playwright dealing with vital local concerns alongside the broader issue of the efficacy of belief-systems, while using a modern mainstream theatre form, a striking dramatic metaphor, and providing challenging characterizations.

---

[5] Bill Ashcroft, Gareth Griffiths & Helen Tiffin. *The Empire Writes Back: Theory and Practice in Post-Colonial Literatures* (London: Routledge, 1989): 126.

[6] Lan, *"Desire" and Other Plays*, xii.

As a director and teacher in a South African university, I wanted to work on a play that provided for cross-cultural exploration by a multiracial cast. Furthermore, the script should affirm an African world-view and put black cast members in the position of those who knew and understood the cultural parameters within which we needed to work. At the same time, I had no wish to discount other cultures; rather, I considered the focus on belief-systems within the play (which is one of a trilogy dealing with this theme), as ideal for cross-cultural exchange. That the play was written by a white South African-born playwright who had lived as an anthropologist amongst the Dande people depicted in the play added a dimension of conscious analysis to the cultural practices we needed to explore. This self-reflexivity could then be extended to ourselves, the creators of this production, as a diverse cultural grouping, enabling us to reflect on our own cultural beliefs in relation to those of the characters in the play. It also allowed us to become aware of our own ritualistic practices and professional beliefs, as a group of theatre practitioners bound by a common enterprise.

The setting of the play in a remote village in the Zambezi valley offered a helpful dynamic. It was African enough to feel familiar to black students, affirming the relevance and importance of black experience, yet distant enough to be examined with detachment. This enabled the cast to explore sensitive issues relating to violence, gender and religion without feeling personally implicated in the discussions. The multiracial nature of the cast was important in ensuring that the African experiences and focus of the play could be seen to have a wider interest and relevance, especially in response to the experience of marginalization during apartheid. It seemed valid to expose white students to the alienation inherent in being immersed in a different culture – a common experience for black students moving into the university environment. A secondary healing function might also occur in the exploration of issues of responsibility and reconciliation in relation both to the subject-matter of the play and to the student's own experiences of apartheid. For students of acting and theatre, the play provided an opportunity to explore a Western acting style (selected realism) in the context of familiar characters, setting, issues and themes, thus extending their performance repertoire. This style was different from that used in most forms of black theatre in South Africa.

The rehearsal process

The first week of rehearsals involved exploring themes from the play and building group-cohesion. My main focus lay with the group's personal and cultural responses, primarily towards the issues of violence and religion.

The problem of violence was one that aroused strong responses, especially among the male cast members. All three of the black males involved had experienced township violence in one form or another, and improvisations around bush warfare sparked off vivid recall of their involvement, often forced, in raids and counter-raids against rival political groups. To a certain extent, the telling of these personal experiences was veiled in generalities; but a sense of understanding and support was clear, especially among those black women who had suffered the terror of such raids. This situation was complicated by the different experiences of violence of the white cast members as victims of both black criminals and freedom fighters, and of exposure to random violence in the form of muggings and car-hijackings. Young white males also experience the gratuitous violence of all-male high schools based on English public-school traditions, and until very recently the threat of military service. The implications of national service primarily concerned violation of personal autonomy and complicity in the imposition of apartheid through service in the townships. It might also involve the violation of national borders and the destabilization of neighbouring states. Exploration of this theme had the potential to polarize racial attitudes; it certainly emphasized difference.

Discussions and improvisations around the issue of religion provided a fruitful ground for intercultural exploration. Several clear-cut positions became apparent. Certain students were openly atheist; some of these were interested in discussions on religion from a philosophical and psychological standpoint; others were guardedly disdainful of the perceived 'primitivism' of ancestral religion and spirit-possession. Another group of students expressed their personal tensions in trying to accommodate both Christianity and traditional practices. It became clear that it was important to these students to be known as Christian, but at the same time they did not wish to deny their Africanness or insult respected older family members for whom traditional worship was an important expression of culture. Responses from the student with a Hindu background helped to reinforce both the broad applicability of a spiritual impulse and the cultural specificity of religious symbolism and expression.

This oblique approach to the text was taken for a number of reasons: to explore beliefs and attitudes shaped by differing cultures; to explore our experiences as South Africans in relation to issues of colonization and the struggle for liberation; and to build interest in the chosen text. This latter motivation addressed students who expressed uneasiness with the notion of performing characters from a different culture, particularly when presenting such culturally specific modes of behaviour as spirit-possession. Also, second-language students have often articulated their difficulty in reading scripts in English (although all of them appreciated the accessible English used by the playwright), and improvising around the major issues seemed a useful way to encourage discussion, build interest, and work with the personal experiences and expertise of the cast.

Theme-based rehearsals moved to a detailed examination of the culture represented in the play, thereby placing the black cast members in the position of advisors on cultural practices, but also challenging them to discover the differences between their own experiences and those of the characters. Documentaries on traditional African rituals,[7] particularly spirit-possession; and representations of African belief-systems in traditional art forms[8] provided rich sources, as did interviews with Zimbabwean and Zambian nationals.[9] In addition, Lan's ethnographic writings were invaluable in building a composite understanding of the thinking and beliefs of the characters.[10] In researching the period of warfare in Zimbabwe which immediately predates the action in the play,[11] it became apparent that the possession of a relative or friend by the spirit of a dead guerrilla was a fairly common experience at this time and an effective method for dealing with the untraceable disappearances of loved ones during bush warfare.[12] The whole cast enjoyed this process of research and felt that it was vital in order to have a better understanding of the play and its portrayal of the specific Dande community.[13]

The rest of the rehearsals proceeded with textual analysis, the building of character, the creation of emotional understanding, and the exploration of form to create effective performance. The focus placed on the text – involving explorations of theme and symbol (Grotowski), analysis of structure, rhythm and climax as well

---

[7] Margaret Thompson Drewal, *Yoruba Ritual: Rites and Ceremonies* (African Systems of Thought Series; Bloomington: Indiana UP, 1992); David Muir, *Road to the Stamping Ground* (NOS–TV Holland & Polygon Pictures, RM ARTS, 1984); Christopher Roy, "Yaaba Soore: The Path of the Ancestors," and "Dance of the Spirits," in *Art and Death in Africa* (School of Art and Art History, U of Iowa P, 1986); and Klaus Schmidt, *Inculturation in Malawi* (Munich: MISSIO München, 1994).

[8] E.J. de Jager, *Images of Man* (Alice, S.A.: Fort Hare UP, 1992); Mary H. Nooter, *Secrecy: African Art that Conceals and Reveals* (New York: Museum of African Art, 1993); and Susan Vogel & Francine N'Diaye, *African Masterpieces* (New York: Center for African Art, 1985).

[9] Douglas Dziva & Austin Allan, Religious Studies Department, University of Natal, Pietermaritzburg (interviews conducted by the author, August 1995) and Charles and Bob Kizito, with David Pike (interviews with author and cast, August 1995).

[10] David Lan, *Guns and Rain*, and "Spirit Mediums and the Authority to Resist in the Struggle for Zimbabwe," in *Collected Seminar Papers on the Societies of Southern Africa in the 19th and 20th Centuries* (University of London, Institute of Commonwealth Studies) 13 (1984): 152–61.

[11] Julie Frederikse, *None But Ourselves: Masses vs Media in the Making of Zimbabwe* (London: Heinemann Educational, 1982) and Gay Seidman, David Martin & Phyllis Johnson, ed. *Zimbabwe: A New History* (Harare: Zimbabwe Publishing House, 1982).

[12] Irene Staunton, ed. *Mothers of the Revolution* (Harare: Baobab, 1990).

[13] Interviews with Teboho Hlahane, Shanita Jugmohan, Mzi Mdingi, Beatrice Motene, Reuben Ngubane, Sehlula Ngubane, Katherine Smart, Ntutu Spelman, Alexandra Sutherland & Stellar Zulu (interviews conducted by the author, June 1996).

as character,[14] creation of a "through line of action" for each character (Stani-
slavsky), and emphasis on the sociopolitical statement predominant in each scene
(Brecht) – was a new approach for the black cast members and served both to integrate their academic theatre studies and to give them a sense of having gained in
understanding and competence through the production.[15]

The main challenges for the cast in performing the play were in understanding
the traditional belief-system represented therein; working through personal experiences of violence in the struggle for liberation; depicting the spirit-possession
ritual; depicting the particularities of Dande culture; and giving proper weight to
the confession scene. White students experienced cultural alienation; one withdrew from the production, the other preferred a peripheral role. One black male
student withdrew when renewed memories of war caused trauma, while another
regarded the evocation of memories as useful material upon which to draw.

The ritual of ancestral religion during which the spirit-possession and the confession occurs takes up the whole of the second half of the play. The ritual itself is
the means by which the importance of reaching the truth is clarified. The inherent
power of the female characters as the protagonists in the ritual, combined with the
knowledge of the black actresses in the main roles, helped to create a convincing
and commanding presentation. Using personal knowledge gained through observation of spirit-possession, the actresses were able to bring authenticity and
authority to their roles. They also worked with the choreographer to create the
presentation of the ritual and to induct the other actresses into its mysteries. Their
contribution was supported by the drumming of those in the cast not directly involved in the ritual. The multiracial nature of the creative process was enhanced
here by our expert white drummer, who was able to create the necessary rhythms
under the direction of the black actresses. Knowledge and observation of Hindu
firewalking ceremonies (one of which takes place annually in Pietermaritzburg),
and a Hindu cast member's familiarity with and acceptance of trance-states facilitated the acceptance and practice of the ritual.

The accurate depiction of Dande culture (confirmed by Zimbabwean and
Zambian nationals in the audience) proved surprisingly attainable, and all cast
members enjoyed the concrete assistance (provided by Charles, Bob, and Kizito in
August 1995) with specific behaviours such as greetings, gestures, speech habits
and customary physical postures.

---

[14] Robert Benedetti, *The Actor at Work* (Englewood Cliffs NJ: Prentice–Hall, 1976).
[15] Interviews with Teboho Hlahane, Shanita Jugmohan et al.

Audience reaction

Many black students felt that this was a play that they could relate to – one depicting Africans and the African perspective – and they felt motivated to attend. Some were particularly impressed by the convincing portrayal of spirit-possession. Audience members from other racial groupings found this scene extremely powerful, noticing particularly the authority of the women characters. The 'transcendental' nature of the ritual was convincing, working metaphorically to persuade audiences of the effectiveness of strongly held beliefs. This focus on the re-creation of ritual was thus affirming rather than marginalizing.

Some black audience members also enjoyed being able to explain and inform others about the traditions observed in the performed. A number of local high-school pupils attended the production. One local teacher (Anton Immelman from Epworth High School) remarked that his pupils had been very interested in the issues of the play and that he had noticed that the black pupils had informed the white pupils about the meanings of the African tradition. They were, for a change, in the position of those who know.

The enthusiasm of black audiences and cast members for the production was surprising in that they had been exposed to productions of black protest theatre such as *Asinamali!* and *Woza Albert!* and black drama students had themselves directed and performed in plays by South African playwrights such as Zakes Mda and Athol Fugard, as well as workshopping plays themselves. The powerful presentation of a traditional African world-view by a multiracial cast motivated audience acclaim. The black cast members appear to have appreciated the multiracial aspect of the production and felt that it had bridged the usual divide between plays that black students take part in and those that interest whites. One student's response to a questionnaire given to the cast is instructive:

> Most plays directed in the department one can categorize into a certain class – but this opened doors for all – and it is my wish that the department direct more plays of this nature since they are:
> 1. relevant to our present culture and knowledge
> 2. they are more didactic for other cultures to know about other hidden or deep cultural backgrounds
> 3. they open doors for every student to participate.

Two of the white students enjoyed working in a multiracial cast and appreciated the insights gained into an African world-view. Four colleagues commented on the evident growth in self-confidence among the student cast and the affirming nature of the production experience. They applauded the play's recognition of gender-equality in the power realized by the women characters through their control of religious ritual. They enjoyed the way in which the playwright dealt with important cultural and political issues, without using the rhetoric of protest, but through the metaphor of story, character and images. They praised the commitment and hard work of the cast and their evident bonding into a productive team. They saw evidence of a growth in acting-technique in the presentation of richly complex characters whose psychology and thinking were fully understood.

Conclusion

The production of *Desire* proved to be an important, affirming experience for most of the cast members and for many of the black students in the audiences. This affirmation lay mainly in public recognition of the value of African culture. However, because *Desire* is a contemporary play dealing with contemporary issues, the production was not seen as Africanist, or as an exercise in decolonization. Issues of democracy, gender, religious beliefs and even truth and reconciliation were seen by the cast as vital concerns for discussion. The views of black cast members interviewed were essentially syncretic; while they were prepared to respect tradition, their ambition is to be part of the contemporary world. They see a democratic future for South Africa although they are very aware of the legacy of privilege in traditional chieftaincy. They regard the present South African society as one divided along urban–contemporary and rural–traditional lines that time and education will alter in favour of the former. All the black women in the cast claim they have no intention of making traditional marriages, as the *lobola*[16] system implies possession. These women consider economic independence as their only guarantee of an autonomous future.

During rehearsals, race relations were harmonious and constructive, and some cast members struck up firm friendships. All those involved in the ritual of spirit-possession came to terms with their initial unease with apparently irrational behaviour, and felt enriched by immersion in traditional culture and exposure to a different belief-system. In interviews nine months later, attitudes appeared to have shifted on this issue. Students who had been initially reluctant to admit to a background of ancestor reverence now claimed to feel comfortable with the practices of their elderly relatives and were able to participate in some rituals without compromising their own Christianity. They felt that aspects of the two belief-systems are compatible, but they were unwilling to be involved with witchcraft.[17]

---

[16] *Lobola* is the paying of a bride-price in cattle (traditionally) or in money.
[17] Beatrice Motene, Ntutu Spelman & Stellar Zulu (interviews conducted by the author, June 1996).

The issue of truth and reconciliation, pivotal within the play, is seen by some as controversial and even divisive. One of the black students in the production, who comes from a politicized family who suffered imprisonment during apartheid, perceived the Truth and Reconciliation Commission as futile. In her view, it only aroused pain and anger: the pain of reliving the past, and anger that blacks were being asked once again to forgive and forget. This minority opinion was an important one shared by the Biko and Mxenge families, who experienced notorious human rights abuses.[18] However, the Truth and Reconciliation Commission was regarded by most South Africans as a crucial instrument of demystification.

Working on *Desire* was a valuable process for the students involved, since it served to open up discussion about numerous issues of importance to all cultures in South Africa and provided a multiracial group with the opportunity to work together on equal terms. It demonstrated that the nature of the rehearsal process allows for the detailed and layered investigation of text, issues and relationships, which can be an ideal medium for building understanding. The ritualistic and symbolic processes involved in the creation of theatre enabled this group to find a common purpose and a shared humanity.

Clearly, this experience of community-building occurred within a very particular environment, at a particular point in history, when the enforced separation of cultures in South Africa had been peacefully ended; many people were willing and curious to find out about each other. Future student productions need to build on this awareness and reflect an emerging integrated culture which will be created out of the meeting of formerly separated peoples and will engage with current social conditions and problems.[19]

---

18 The *Natal Witness* (13 June 1996) reported that five people are to be arrested in connection with the murder of Griffith Mxenge. Mxenge's brother, Fumbatha is quoted as follows, "We are not interested in compensation, we are interested in justice in this case" and in response to prime suspect Dirk Coetzee's plea for forgiveness, "We will never forget him for what he did [...] It impacted heavily on us."

19 A version of this paper has been published in *Theatre Journal* 49.1 (March 1997): 41–52.

The Rise and Fall of Mbongeni Ngema
The AIDS Play

❧ Bernth Lindfors

1 996 WAS NOT A GOOD YEAR FOR MBONGENI NGEMA. Since early January he had been assailed in the South African media not only by scores of journalists, television and radio commentators, news analysts and cartoonists, but also by numerous members of parliament, medical practitioners, fellow theatre directors, drama critics, outspoken ordinary citizens, and a Public Protector appointed by the government. The fuss was largely over money, but it also had to do with art, government, and disease – a volatile combination that kept the story on the front pages because it had real life-and-death implications. No one actually went so far as to call Ngema a murderer, but his manner of responding to the charges levelled against him, which ranged from rapacious greed and financial mismanagement to artistic incompetence and egomania, may have so alienated his national audience that he may unwittingly have put a premature end to his own spectacular career as a showman. He may have committed a form of professional suicide.

This is a pity, for he is clearly a talented actor, musician and director who, through his own abundant energy and enterprise, has made a major contribution to the development of black theatre in South Africa. His life, recounted sympathetically by Laura Jones,[1] is a classic rags-to-riches saga, replete with the usual mixture of archetypal ingredients: hard work, perseverance, self-reliance, resourcefulness, skill, a pinch of good luck and, in the end, a pot of gold.

Success on the stage has been his hallmark. In the past fifteen years no other South African has won so many prestigious local and international awards in the performing arts – more than fifty in all, including the Edinburgh Festival's Fringe First Award, the Los Angeles Drama Critics Award, and an Obie Award Special Citation for *Woza Albert!*; a Tony nomination and several AA Mutual Life Vita Awards for *Asinamali!*; five Tony nominations and a Hollywood contract for *Sara-*

---

[1] Laura Jones, *Nothing Except Ourselves: The Harsh Times and Bold Theater of South Africa's Mbongeni Ngema* (New York: Penguin, 1994).

final; a Drama Desk Award nomination for *Township Fever!*; and a share of a Grammy Award for producing part of the sound-track on Disney's *The Lion King*.[2] One would have thought that, with a track record like this, Ngema was destined to succeed in whatever theatrical enterprise he undertook. What, then, went wrong? Why did his most recent venture into musical drama fail so abysmally? What ultimately brought him down?

The failure in South Africa of his latest musical, which was a sequel to *Sarafina!*, may be attributed in part to Ngema's improvisional working methods and in part to his concept of himself as the equivalent of a Broadway or Hollywood producer. But *Sarafina 2* really flopped because it grew far too large, its expansion encouraged and augmented by procedural errors made by officials in the government's Department of Health, who approved a gargantuan budget of 14,247,600 rands (ca. £2.5 million or nearly $4 million then) for the musical out of funds donated by the European Union to combat the spread of AIDS in South Africa.[3] Indeed, most of the attacks on the production have been directed not at Ngema himself but at Health Minister Dr Nkosazana Zuma, whose supervision of the tendering procedure that won Ngema such a lucrative contract appears to have been characterized by another type of oversight – negligence.

No one denies that her intentions were good. Her idea was to use theatre as a means of educating young South Africans, especially those in the townships and rural areas, about the serious dangers posed today by casual, unprotected sexual intercourse – specifically the mortal danger of contracting HIV/AIDS. What better way to do this than to employ South Africa's most successful and most popular black director to mount a musical on this theme, a show that could travel on a year-long bus and truck tour to township halls, cinemas, shopping centres, schools and rural communities in all corners of the country? On her own initiative, she approached Ngema about this in June 1995, suggesting that the production be launched on 1 December, World AIDS Day.[4]

Ngema was keen on the idea, and "gave an off-the-cuff estimate of R800,000; Zuma subsequently set the ceiling at R5 million, but Health Department officials ultimately signed a R14.2 million contract with Ngema."[5] Worse yet, these officials skirted regulations governing standard bidding procedures on state contracts.

---

[2] Ngema ultimately was declared ineligible for this award due to a technicality; see Carl Coleman, "No Grammy Shock for Ngema," *Daily News* (March 9, 1995): 1.

[3] Stephen Coan, "*Sarafina*: There's Never Been a Theatrical Budget Like It," *Natal Witness* (March 5, 1996): 9.

[4] Gaye Davis, "Star Players in the Financial Flop," *Weekly Mail and Guardian* (June 7–13, 1996): 4.

[5] Chiarra Carter, "Comedy of Bungles," *City Press* (June 9, 1966): 4.

There may have been some urgency about getting the show on the road, but their carelessness in following established guidelines was to cost Dr Zuma many subsequent headaches. When the story hit the press, there were calls for her dismissal or immediate resignation, and the ANC-led government was faulted for its lack of transparency in accounting for expenditures made from funds donated by the European Union to improve public health in South Africa. *Sarafina 2* rapidly became a scandal.

Ngema himself had ambitious plans for this sequel to his most famous show. A month before it opened, he said:

> We will touch the people in every corner, and all colours of the nation [...] We are speaking to all of South Africa this time. Although *Sarafina!* [1] played on Broadway, and in Europe and Britain, the majority of South Africans didn't see the first *Sarafina!* It ran in Durban for three weeks – after playing five years in the rest of the world! This time we are aiming to reach 10 percent of the South African population. Perhaps in a few years time we will take the show to Broadway, but at this point in my life, my Broadway is my people. We need to perform to them [...] Many people have been craving to see the live production of *Sarafina!*, but I was not comfortable to bring back theatre that related to fighting for freedom – when we are actually free! So the idea of a sequel was born [...] it is no longer the fight for freedom, it is the fight for human survival.[6]

Big words, big ambitions, big show; extremely big budget. Ngema had set about assembling a company of between seventy and eighty singers, dancers, musicians, and crew, many of them veterans from his previous shows, some of them his relatives and friends. To play the lead role he selected the original Sarafina, Leleti Khumalo, who by then was his second wife. According to early reports, "The updated story sees Sarafina now a social worker but still very much in touch with school children who look upon her as a role model. She gives inspiration to students who are trying to get a concert together at a school in rural Zululand."[7] Does this recycled plot sound familiar? To provide further continuity, Ngema repeated several songs from the first *Sarafina!* even though these had nothing to do with the theme of the new show.[8]

But there was new material, too, some of it very explicitly concerned with AIDS. Part of the story-line focuses on "a popular high school girl who contracts the disease, sparking off an intense debate between pupils, the teacher, the nurse,

---

[6] Anon., "Bus-truck Tour for *Sarafina 2*," *Citizen* (November 3, 1995): 23.

[7] Anon., "*Sarafina 2*," *D'Arts* (December 1995–January 1996): 21.

[8] Abbey Makoe, "*Sarafina* Not a Total Sham, But Waste of R14-m," *Argus* (March 11, 1996): 3.

the social worker and traditional healers on how to deal with this situation."⁹ Some reviewers felt that the play was too didactic and said too much too stridently about AIDS; others felt that it did not provide enough basic information about the transmission of the disease; still others claimed that a good deal of the information offered was inaccurate and potentially dangerous to teenagers. Ngema was accused of confusing "the use of words like AIDS, HIV and *Ngculazi*. He uses all these words as though they mean the same thing. According to the play, the only way a person can get AIDS is by sleeping with many partners, which in real life is not true."¹⁰ There were complaints that some of the messages about AIDS, besides being "confusing and ineffective [...] were definitely degrading to women."¹¹ One distraught viewer who was HIV-positive walked out of the show in anger and disappointment, saying he could not cope with "such a blatant downplaying of this serious disease [...] They've taken a topic of genocidal proportions for a musical, thus making a joke of it. It's equivalent to making a musical of the Holocaust [...] By interval the only thing I [had] learned about AIDS was that once diagnosed as positive, you have to go to church and trust in God."¹²

Ngema clearly had not properly researched the problem *Sarafina 2* was exploring and exploiting. He was operating from a set of vague concepts – that promiscuity leads to AIDS, that young people are especially at risk, that condoms are the answer to the problem – but he seems to have been less concerned with articulating a responsible social message than he was with expressing a rhythmic song-and-dance medium. He once said:

> First and foremost, I'm an entertainer. And when I have entertained you, then I want to inform you, in that way I move you [...] My theatre must enlighten. The audiences must walk out of the theatre having learnt something [...] I direct as a musician. I see my theatre pieces as one song, as a whole, as a piece of jazz which changes beat, changes colours [...] What excites me is when the script and music become one, when a performance comes together [...] People must walk out and say "WOW!"¹³

In the case of *Sarafina 2*, people were walking out unenlightened and saying "WOW!" for all the wrong reasons.

Some, including a few who were most critical of the show, applauded its "dazzling brilliance" and "flawless" music and choreography,¹⁴ its "precision

⁹ Vusi Ngema, "Musical Which Tackles AIDS But Desperately Seeks a Story," *Natal Witness* (January 6, 1996): 7.

¹⁰ Reginald Khumalo, "Sloppy Show Disappoints," *Natal Witness* (January 11, 1996): 7.

¹¹ David Robbins, "Experts slam AIDS play," *The Star* (March 11, 1966): 1 [Tonight].

¹² Anon., "AIDS Message 'Not Effective,'" *Cape Times* (March 11, 1996): 1.

¹³ Delores Mendel, "Mbongeni Ngema," *Club* (April 1990): 19.

¹⁴ Ngema, "Musical Which Tackles AIDS," 7.

lighting, dance routines and beautiful faces,"[15] its "grand scale [...] ineluctable magnetism [...] disciplined energy [and] magnificent assault on the senses,"[16] its "glitz and glamour."[17] But despite such virtues, the general consensus among spectators was that *Sarafina 2* was "a loose, uncontrolled musical desperately looking for a story to tell,"[18] that there was "no drama in the entire play,"[19] that "it was the same old vague outline of nubile, nay, fat slags, with breasts and a great love for shaking their bottoms about," who moved awkwardly from "swing-your-pants stuff to straight lecturing to the audience,"[20] and that the show was far too long and needed trimming "by as much as half an hour."[21] Obviously *Sarafina 2* had failed not only to enlighten but also to entertain.

What drew most criticism, however, was the show's stupendous cost. As more and more budgetary details leaked out in the press, public fury grew. Taxpayers were shocked to learn

- that Ngema was receiving a salary of R300,000 for the production – this on top of his normal salary of R90,000 as Musical Director of the Natal Playhouse;
- that R1.1 million had been spent on a luxury bus for the cast, a bus equipped with a private toilet;
- that monthly salaries for administrative staff included R10,000 for an administrator, R8,000 for a company manager, R6,000 for an assistant director, R5,000 for a senior secretary, and R4,000 each for two additional secretaries – salaries considered excessive for such work;
- that the five principal members of the cast received R2,000 each per week, and the eight sub-principals R1,200 each per week, whereas professional AIDS workers in South Africa were paid only R2,000 per month;
- that fourteen musicians received R1,500 each per week, members of the chorus R700 each per week, and two bus drivers and two truck drivers R2,000 each per month;
- that everyone involved in the production also received a subsistence allowance of R50 per day for 365 days;

---

[15] Betsy Spratt, "The Kids Liked It But Did It Teach Them Anything About AIDS?," *Sunday Independent* (March 10, 1996): 1.

[16] Garalt MacLiam, "It's rock, roll and bop as *Sarafina 2* celebrates people power in Soweto," *The Star* (March 11, 1996): 1 [Tonight].

[17] MacLiam, "It's better than a poke in the eye with a sharp stick," *The Star* (March 13, 1996: 7 [Tonight].

[18] Ngema, "Musical Which Tackles AIDS," 7.

[19] Khumalo, "Sloppy Show Disappoints," 7.

[20] Annesh Ramklown, "Ngema's Latest *Sarafina* a Dismal Failure," *Natal Witness Echo* (January 11, 1996): 5.

[21] MacLiam, "It's rock, roll and bop," 1.

— that other budget categories seemed unusually inflated: R32,000 for two cellular phones, R50,000 for programmes; R50,000 for scenery, R100,000 for costumes, R200,000 for security equipment, R300,000 for four security guards, R1.2 million for lighting and sound equipment, R1.4 million for office rentals and equipment.[22]

Worse still, it came out that, in the first three months that *Sarafina 2* was on stage, R1.1 million had disappeared in unauthorized expenditures, that book-keeping was not up to scratch, and that there was no control over petty cash.[23] Money simply vanished without a trace.

On top of all this, Ngema was being allowed to charge R20 for admission to this government-sponsored show, a fee much too high for most of its intended audience. In its first hundred days in KwaZulu–Natal, only 5,868 people had seen the 36 performances of *Sarafina 2*, an average of 163 per night.[24] The numbers picked up dramatically in March when the show moved to Soweto's Eyethu Cinema and the admission fee for schoolchildren was dropped; 1300 people flocked to the opening night,[25] but within a few weeks only 80 spectators were turning up for a Saturday afternoon performance.[26] It was by now clear that this expensive vehicle would never succeed in reaching a tenth of the South African population.

However, the show might have gone on to the end of the year had Ngema kept his mouth shut. Stung by the negative press he was receiving, he responded by thumping his chest and talking back. He claimed that

> When the minister had this idea [of spreading information about AIDS through a theatrical production], it was clear in her mind she wanted me to do the play. There is no one else with an international track record and there was no one else who could produce this kind of play and draw in crowds of black people to the theatre.[27]

In a later interview he boldly asserted: "I am the best artist in the country. That's the reason why they contracted me."[28] The play had received bad reviews, he said,

22 Sapa & Brian Stuart, "Call for *Sarafina II* Probe," *Citizen* (February 29, 1996): 1; Kaizer Nyatsumba, "They Take the Cake," *Argus* (March 13, 1996): 18; repr. as "The Truth Will Soon Out," *Daily News* (March 14, 1996): 18; Anon., "Parties Claim It's a Cover-up," *City Press* (March 3, 1996): 2.

23 Davis, "Star Players in the Financial Flop," 5.

24 Thami Ngidi, "'The Show Will Go On'," *Saturday Paper* (March 9, 1996): 4.

25 Fiona Chisholm, "Reviewers' Thumbs-down for Zuma Play," *Cape Times* (March 11, 1996): 1.

26 Mark Gevisser, "Sarafina of the Health System," *Weekly Mail and Guardian* (March 22–28, 1996): 14.

27 Terry van der Walt & Sam Sole, "Ngema's Tender Touch," *Sunday Tribune* (February 11, 1996): 1.

28 John Scott, "*Sarafina 2*'s New Wisecracking Star," *Cape Times* (March 13, 1996): 16.

"because 'my people' cannot appreciate a 'Broadway class' production."[29] Furthermore, the attitude of South African journalists had been: "Let's find another famous black man and shoot him down."[30]

He expanded on these views in a lengthy interview, recorded as follows:

> About the bus he says, "Yes! It's about time our artists were transported in dignity. Why must we be transported in luxury buses in the United States, but come to our own country to be put in the back of Kombis? No way! I'm proud of our bus."
>
> Are his own services worth R300,000, particularly given the fact that he is paid another full-time salary, worth R90,000, by the state through his position as musical director of the Natal Playhouse? "No, they are not. I should be earning at least a million." But does any director in this country earn those figures? "I don't think you can compare me to anyone in this country."
>
> He is unrepentant about the cost of the production, putting a race-spin on it: "I'm not prepared to do a second-class production. Why should whites get state-funded first-class productions in the State Theatre, while blacks in the townships get flatbed trucks? No. Blacks deserve Broadway standards [...]
>
> What I'm doing with *Sarafina II* is an exact continuation of what I was doing with the original *Sarafina!* The only difference is that when we were doing freedom theatre, the government wouldn't pay for it. Now we are free, we are shifting to other stories, and the government is finally paying."[31]

The public reaction to these remarks was swift and censorious. Ngema was condemned for his "stupendous arrogance,"[32] for knowing "next to nothing about the discipline of educating through drama,"[33] for having "woven a slight and trivial message through a production which he was going to mount anyway, in order to secure funding which should have been deployed elsewhere."[34] One journalist wanted to know

> How much [...] has Ngema paid his actors in his other plays? Seeing that he has been immensely successful as a playwright, why is it that he has not previously used his not inconsiderable resources to buy his cast the R1-million luxury bus so that it could indeed travel "in dignity"? Could it be that it was only when the R14,27-million was made available to him to produce an AIDS play that he suddenly realized that the "dignity" of his cast was important?[35]

---

[29] Anon., "*Sarafina O*," *Daily Dispatch* (March 8, 1996): 14.

[30] Scott, "*Sarafina 2*'s New Wisecracking Star," 16.

[31] Mark Gevisser, "'I Should Be Paid a Million Rands'," *Mail and Guardian* (March 8–14, 1996): 16.

[32] Nyatsumba, "They Take the Cake," 18.

[33] Joseph Mondear, "'Slight and trivial message' woven into *Sarafina 2* production," *The Star* (March 26, 1996): 16 [Tonight].

[34] Mondear, "'Slight and trivial message'," 16.

[35] Nyatsumba, "They Take the Cake," 18.

Another journalist pointed out that

> Apart from the fact that [Ngema] is now a senior official at one of these "white" state
> institutions [he criticizes], where he has successfully produced three of his own plays
> using state money, the problem here is that he – as a creative artist – is dealing with
> the Health Department's budget as if it were funding for the arts rather than funding
> for health education [...] He was frequently slammed, in the 1980s, for capitalizing
> on the struggle. Is he now capitalizing on another?[36]

Even fellow playwrights began to speak out against Ngema's squandering of
state resources. Gibson Kente, Ngema's mentor, said, "The play carries an important message. It is beautifully presented but I think the money is a bit too much [...]
For that money, you can produce about 90 dramatic episodes [in a television se-
ries]. That could draw many more viewers and the message would reach many
people [...] I think the play should have been dramatized (instead of being a musical)." Matsemela Manaka agreed about the extravagant budget, maintaining, "It is
shocking that so much money could be given to an individual when there is such a
big need to fund the arts." Jerry Skosana suggested, "We have institutions rendering [AIDS education] services. The money should have gone to them. And some of
the money should, at least, have gone to schools, where sex education must be implemented." Another KwaZulu–Natal playwright, who asked to remain anonymous, put forward the view that "the money should have been given to directors in
all nine provinces. In that way, the message would reach people quicker."[37]

It was also pointed out that other theatre groups in the country had been carrying out very effective AIDS education work for some time with little or no official
sponsorship; among these were the Tivoneleni Vavasati AIDS Awareness Project, a
women's theatre group operating since 1991 in rural areas of the Northern Province;[38] the African Research and Education Puppetry Programme (Arepp) which
had been running for nine years a popular "Puppets Against AIDS" play that was
now reaching about 200,000 people each year in a countrywide network of clinics, schools, community centres, AIDS groups and civic associations;[39] and
Aidslink, another non-governmental organization that had developed an educational drama on AIDS to tour Gauteng informal settlements for four months.[40] All
these organizations were doing their work on very small budgets and without ac-

---

36 Gevisser, "'I should be paid a million Rands'," 16.
37 All quotations here from Mojalefa Mashego, "Sarafina II not the best medium for AIDS Issue," Sowetan (March 11, 1996): 15.
38 Tivoneleni Vavasati AIDS Awareness Project. "Ministry's Musical Should Sing a New Song,"
Mail & Guardian (February 23–29, 1996): 28.
39 Janine Simon, "Puppet players query Sarafina costs," The Star (March 1, 1996): 1 [Tonight].
40 Simon, "Puppet players query Sarafina costs," 2.

cess to luxury buses, expensive lighting and sound equipment, or lavish salaries. Asked if he had seen *Sarafina 2*, Gary Friedman, creator of Puppets Against AIDS, replied, "I can't afford it at R20."[41]

Faced with a relentless daily barrage of criticism in the press, the ANC-led government had to do something about *Sarafina 2*. At first they stood loyally behind Minister Zuma, leaving the matter to be investigated impartially by a newly appointed National Public Protector, Selby Baqwa. But the Department of Health also sought to control the damage by carpeting Ngema and asking him to make substantial changes in the play. When it was learned in May that one option they were considering was issuing a videotape of the musical so that more people could see it, a video that might cost the government at least another R2 million, of which Ngema was to receive an undisclosed sum, the clamour grew louder, with most opponents insisting that this would be throwing more good money after bad.[42] A month later, after the Public Protector published his report documenting serious administrative bungling in the *Sarafina 2* affair, the Department of Health finally pulled the plug on the play, Dr Zuma announcing it would no longer be funded by her Department but "by the private sector, although she did not give details."[43] Cancelling the contract would save the government about R5 million of the R14.27 million allocation.

This resolution of the matter did not satisfy all commentators. A columnist for the *Natal Witness* remarked that

> one of the most shameful aspects of the *Sarafina* saga is that Mbongeni Ngema will remain not only unscathed but richer for his involvement with "AIDS education." A disciple of KZN Premier Frank Mdlalose's dictum that "extravagance is a relative term," Ngema's response to the controversy has been to welcome the publicity it brought to the play. Relieved of the obligation actually to promote AIDS education, the government's withdrawal from the project "is just perfect for me." Now he can go ahead and con audiences with a piece of work that months after its launch was still so shoddy that he would not let the press review it. As for the money: "Maybe R14 million is a lot of money to us South Africans but it is not to everyone in the world."
>
> More important to Ngema than AIDS education, wasted money, unprofessional work, fraudulent tenders and government accountability, is what it has all done for Ngema. "My only competition for the front pages was Nelson Mandela [...] I have seen Ngema on the front page and Mandela on the inside pages some days." So much for humility. Maybe he'll be offered a post as minister of maladministration. For the moment, how-

---

41 Coan, "*Sarafina*: There's Never Been a Theatrical Budget Like It," 9.
42 Troye Lund, "*Sarafina 2* video goes on despite row," *The Star* (June 5, 1996): 1–2 [Tonight]; Anon., "*Sarafina 2* – Next: The Video?," *Eastern Province Herald* (June 4, 1996): 4.
43 Patrick Cull, "*Sarafina 2* Terminated by SA Government," *Eastern Province Herald* (June 6, 1996): 2.

ever, he's looking forward to *Sarafina* making so much money that R14 million will
seem more insignificant to him than it already appears now. "If you have the numbers you have the power," he says of the audiences he hopes will attend his show. He
could have taken the words right out of the government's mouth. Ruling by numbers
means never having to say Sorryfina.[44]

One gets the impression from Ngema's bemused and insensitive remarks that he is
still supremely self-confident about his abilities and unapologetic about his behaviour, that in fact he is treating the whole *Sarafina 2* fiasco as a huge joke and
laughing his way to the bank. But it is difficult to believe that he will "remain not
only unscathed but richer for his involvement with 'AIDS education'." Granted, he
may have made a considerable amount of money in 1995–96, but no one is likely
to forget in the years to come how he made it: by trying to bring a bit of Broadway
– bloated budgets, tinsel and all – to the back streets and backwaters of South Africa; by singing and dancing his way through a medical pandemic without being
fully aware that he was toying (or *toyi*-toying) with people's lives; by blithely and
brazenly profiteering from his own people's present and future misery.

AIDS is already a devastating phenomenon in South Africa. No one knows how
many South Africans have been infected with the HIV virus, but conservative estimates from July 1996 range as high as seven million, or one-seventh of a total
population of forty-nine million.[45] In March 1995 the *Daily News* reported that an
average of 20.13 percent of pregnant women at Durban's King Edward VIII hospital tested HIV positive. By July 1996 the rate had gone up to twenty-five
percent.[46] At the Pietermaritzburg Boom Street Clinic, the HIV infection-rate for
men and women treated for sexually transmitted diseases is even higher, ranging
between 54 percent and 62 percent in April, May and June of 1996.[47] All these
statistics come from KwaZulu–Natal, the province thought to have the highest incidence of HIV in South Africa. This is Ngema's home territory, so it is more than a
little disconcerting to learn that his funding for *Sarafina 2* was double the
KwaZulu–Natal AIDS budget for the year ending March 1996.[48]

The World Bank estimates that "by the year 2005, 600,000 South Africans will
have contracted [full-blown] AIDS, and between 300 and 500 people would be
dying daily from the disease."[49] However, the European Union, which had con-
tributed R100 million to the South African Health Department, "just under half of

---

44 Yves Vanderhaeghen, "The Play that Shamed the ANC," *Natal Witness* (July 11, 1996): 6.
45 Duncan du Bois, "Distorted AIDS Factor," *Natal Witness* (July 19, 1996): 10.
46 Anon., "Rise in HIV-positive Cases," *Natal Witness* (July 30, 1996): 4.
47 Anon., "Rise in HIV-Positive Cases," 4.
48 Pamela Sherriffs, "AIDS: It's Too Costly to Play Around," *Natal Witness* (March 1, 1966): 15.
49 Sapa & Brian Stuart, "Call for *Sarafina II* Probe," 2.

it specifically earmarked for AIDS programmes,"[50] was recently reported to be considering withdrawing its funding in the wake of the *Sarafina 2* scandal.[51] Ngema's legacy to his countrymen could thus translate very quickly into an accelerated AIDS death-rate in the next decade. And it may be this morbid fact that South Africans will remember best about *Sarafina 2* – not the dancing, not the singing, not all the glitz and glamour, but the flagrantly wasted opportunity to save and protect human life through effective theatrical intervention in a national health crisis. Mbongeni Ngema, the carefree, cavalier, Broadway-spoiled villain in this drama, by then may have been hissed off the South African stage.[52]

—— ℰℴ ℭℛ ——

[50] Anon., "*Sarafina* Shocker," *Saturday Paper* (March 30, 1996): 1.
[51] Pat Sidley, "AIDS Spreads as Money Lies Idle," *Sunday Times* (June 9, 1996): 4.
[52] I wish to thank Malcolm Hacksley and his staff at the National English Literary Museum in Grahamstown for providing me with numerous photocopies from their newspaper cuttings files on *Sarafina 2* and Mbongeni Ngema.

Theatre Festivals ∞

"The arts festival as healing force" (Athol Fugard)

The Role of the Two Major Arts Festivals and a Possible Resurgence in South African Drama

☙ Annette I. Combrink

Introduction

"A MODEST PROPOSAL, OR: Slouching towards Grahamstown":[1] this is the title of an article on the resurgence of South African theatre at the Grahamstown Festival, and the carefully allusive comments tie in with my own very cautious disclaimers, disclaimers intended not as a coy allusive hedge behind which I could take refuge if the idea boomerangs – but which describe the way in which this development is regarded. In view of the potentially lethal consequences of large claims in a field as uncharted as post-liberation South African arts and culture, it is therefore only right that any large or definitive proposals should be regarded with the contempt they (ought to) inspire.

The first impetus for this paper came from a statement made by Athol Fugard on the eve of the second Klein Karoo Kunstefees (The Little Karoo Arts Festival). In an interview in *Beeld*, the major Afrikaans daily in South Africa, Fugard said, among other things, that theatre is part of the healing forces beginning to work in the country; "*met die teater slaan ons brue. Dis in hierdie land die medium wat 'n nasie kan help bou.*"[2] This sentiment was unequivocally echoed by Deon Opperman, the dramatist regarded by many critics nowadays as the foremost Afrikaans playwright, who maintains that the future of theatre in South Africa lies with the arts festivals. He bases his statement on the impact made on the national psyche by the two major arts festivals – the Grahamstown Festival and the Klein Karoo Festival at Oudtshoorn. He claims that the enormous growth of the Klein Karoo in one year

[1] Humphrey Tyler, "Slouching towards Grahamstown," *Sunday Tribune* (June 4, 1996): 17 [Sunday Magazine].

[2] "The theatre helps us to build bridges. It is through this medium that we can help build a nation in this country"; Athol Fugard, "The Arts Festival as healing force," *Beeld* (April 2, 1996): 2 [Kalender].

and the impressive figures relating to the Grahamstown Festival (as released by the Grahamstown Chamber of Commerce) over the years both point to an important and indispensable financial base for the continuing growth of theatre – he goes so far as to predict that in a few years' time, there will probably be five or six such festivals, and the spin-off from that will be more audiences, and more audiences (hence more money and infrastructure) will mean more theatre will be created.

So much for fairly optimistic and confident predictions by two prominent and influential playwrights in Afrikaans and English. It might seem that confidence is not misplaced in the case of the KKK in particular – attendance grew in one year from roughly ten thousand to roughly one hundred thousand – and, as has been said, "What originally started as a manifestation of Afrikaner *angst* about its future has ended as a resignation: Afrikaans is not only here to stay, it is here to make a contribution."[3] It can be reasonably expected that these commentators are aware of what is happening in the field of theatre and would be able to make authoritative predictions. What, however, has been intriguing is that the same kind of statement has been made by other players in the field (who might or might not have been primed to make this kind of comment, but who just might have thought of it independently).

A similar sentiment has been heard in a quite different arena, where there is a great deal of interest in the creation of a unified, if rainbow-hued nation. Nelson Mandela, in a speech made at the 1995 opening of the new 1820 Monument ('new' after the fire that destroyed large parts of the Settlers' Monument in Grahamstown), referred to the Monument and the activities associated with it (most notably the Arts Festival) as "a national resource centre for the arts and culture which has to be forcefully identified with change and the reconstruction of our country." This was rather fulsomely echoed by the Minister of Arts, Culture, Science and Technology, Dr Ben Ngubane, when he visited the Grahamstown Festival in July 1995, when he maintained that "The Festival [is] a force for national reconciliation comparable to the recent Rugby World Cup – this event is terribly important. It's the only thing that really brings the whole country together nationally in the arena of arts."[4]

It would perhaps be apposite here to give a capping word to Pieter–Dirk Uys. He asserts, with sweeping panache and hyperbole, that

> The Grahamstown Festival is no longer just a celebration of a nation's theatre, music and art. In most instances, it is all that's left of what once was a nation's culture. Yes, the cities still do have their nuclei of expression. Brave art galleries and theatres and

---

³ G. Strauss, "Die Klein Karoo Kunstefees," *Beeld* (2 April 1996): 4 [Kalender].
⁴ Brendan Boyle, "Ngubane Backs Festival," *Cue* (8 July 1995): 1.

areas of music survive, but only just ... they are only the small pinpricks of light in a murky landscape [...] The new South Africa. A democratic wasteland of thump and thud, of shoot and shit. A Mad Max homeland where hijacking is the only public transport, and crime an investment for the future. [...] The Grahamstown festival can become the Supermarket of the Arts. The Bafana Bafana of Theatre. Amadrama-drama! Then bring in the impresarios from Edinburgh, Montreal, Sydney and the world. Invite the cities to plan their seasons from what they see. A new generation of supporters will rally to the flag. The community will become part of culture again, not just a tax-paying contributor. We'll be ready for anything with more experience. At the moment, too often, we're not even ready for a first audience.[5]

More importantly and disquietingly, he argues that

the cities don't allow experimentation any more. The cities are too tired to play nursemaid. There are not enough places where a new work can grow. There are a few bitter critics always prowling for the kill [...] let us move into the platteland [where the festivals are] where the people wait hungrily for what city-dwellers ignore. A national festival circuit might solve a cluster of problems. If there are three, four, festivals per month throughout South Africa, entertainment can grow and be shared. The performer/ musician/project can travel from one to the other. Stay employed, and live off the income while developing their show/cabaret/project.[6]

This is more soberly supported by the influential theatre critic Paul Boekkooi, who maintains that "Arts festivals will become the future life blood of smaller theatrical companies and individual performers when the new South African arts dispensation gets going."[7] Following these seemingly highly provocative statements from a range of speakers, what can one decide about the Festival(s)?

The major arts festivals: overview and assessment

For the purpose of this discussion, I will provide a brief historical overview of the festivals, concentrating on a selection. It is important to remember that Kampustoneel, a venture to promote Afrikaans drama on the campuses, has now to all intents and purposes been subsumed under the Klein Karoo Kunstefees. Supporting the cautious hope expressed about the role of organizational support and infrastructure in the writing and performance of drama, Deon Opperman said in his regular column in *Beeld*[8] that a very real word of thanks should be expressed to the ATKV (Afrikaanse Taal- en Kultuurvereniging/Afrikaans Language and Cultural Society) for having sponsored and supported Kampustoneel through the crucial

---

[5] Pieter–Dirk Uys, "On a penny and a poep," *Weekly Mail and Guardian* (10 July 1996): 4–5.
[6] Uys, "On a penny and a poep," 5.
[7] Paul Boekkooi, "Nostalgia and progression pull Karoo crowds," *The Star* (8 April 1996): 10 [Tonight].
[8] Deon Opperman, *Beeld* (24 September 1996): 3 [Kalender].

Eighties. He points out that he himself, and other prominent playwrights like Reza de Wet (*Diepe Grond*), also used Kampustoneel as a springboard for their professional careers as playwrights. He refers to the renowned poet and playwright N.P. van Wyk Louw, who maintained that on the one hand artists needed organizations, while on the other hand they felt themselves to be smothered by these same organizations. This is the kind of double awareness that one finds in the notion of a redevelopment of drama through the structures provided by festivals. How might the very nature of the festival structure be more constructive in terms of what is needed to revitalize the theatre, and nurture that which is already growing?

While important events and changes have occurred over a fairly long period of time, my discussion will concentrate on the period following the election of 1994, with a view to isolating a few trends.

The Grahamstown Arts Festival

This Festival has seen a number of name changes in the course of its history. It has also reached a momentous milestone, with the result that a number of luminaries have written longer or shorter commemorative pieces, some of which I will refer to here to evoke a sense of what the festival is all about.

An anonymous writer stated that the Festival started out in 1974 "in a very modest way as a celebration of specifically British and European culture [...] the Festival has grown across cultural, social and political borders to become an important shaping influence on South African arts and culture."[9] This somewhat bland statement finds a great deal of resonance in a solid and informative publication on the politics of the Grahamstown Festival by Kenneth Grundy.[10] Some remarks by Grundy will be helpful in understanding the ideological underpinnings and undercurrents of the Festival – notably his assessment of the relative importance of the range of sponsors that the Festival has had. Until the mid-Seventies, the organizers sought to finance the Festival through its own (admittedly very limited) resources, but gradually sponsors came forward to an extent large enough to have their names associated with the venue. From 1979, it was initially Five Roses Tea (for five years), and while minor sponsors remained in place, the Festival was then already called the National Arts Festival. From 1984 onwards, Standard Bank has, through generous sponsorship, played a substantial role. Market considerations played an important role in the early years, and the market was still dominated by conservative cultural forces.

---

9 Anon., "20 years' National Arts Festival," *Lantern* 43.3 (1996): 16.
10 Kenneth Grundy, "The Politics of the National Arts Festival," Occasional Paper 34, Institute of Social and Economic Research, Rhodes University, Grahamstown, South Africa (1993).

It is not the place here to go into detail about the way in which the Grahamstown Festival was gradually forced to emerge from cultural isolation and to come
to grips with reality:

> until [...] the 1980s, the Festival seemed to operate in a political cocoon [...] consider-
> ing that the NAF was supposed to be national, that the arts can be positioned at the
> cutting edge of social and political expression, and that South Africa itself was in
> turmoil and at the threshold of transition, the Festival was unnaturally bland and
> aloof.[11]

The Standard Bank involvement has been instrumental in widening the base and
impact of the Festival. Grundy goes on to document the development of the Festival
against the background of increasingly vociferous voices; his examination of the
negotiations between the Festival committee and various interested parties in the
late Eighties offers a good if somewhat wry and rueful generic description of the
way in which negotiations work in South Africa today. The history of the NAF, interestingly if ironically, has been strongly linked to the process of development in
South Africa generally, and it is notable that in the midst of the more raucous
voices demanding radical change some more temperate statements can be discerned. In 1989 both Albie Sachs and Barbara Masekela went against certain
popular demands for 'intervention'; in what would seem to be an endorsement of
the developments perceived to be occurring at the Festival, Masekela declared that,
while the ANC would insist on the transformation of the Festival at all levels before
it would endorse it fully, she also said that "[the ANC] regarded both English and
Afrikaans-based cultures as a valid part of the whole rich tapestry of South African
culture – *but a part, not the sun around which the whole universe revolves.*"[12]

Grundy further documents the development of the Festival from an event
largely English, and with a particular kind of English agenda, to one where material from a variety of language and cultural groups would begin to be included
in the programme. This process, however, is still far from fully developed, and
statements made during the 1995 and 1996 Festivals render pessimistic those who
would like to see the NAF as the specific site for a "demographically accurate and
politically correct" microcosm of change in South African art and culture. Mphah-
lele's impassioned statement about white appropriation of control over culture,
against the background of "the vicious economies of theatre and publishing, of the
art market and sponsored cultural activity which hold the artist to ransom,"[13] still
resonates in a 1996 statement by Mfundo Ndebele ("The festival is still largely

---

[11] Grundy, "The Politics of the National Arts Festival," 15.
[12] Quoted in Grundy, "The Politics of the National Arts Festival," 13 (my emphasis).
[13] Quoted in Grundy, "The Politics of the National Arts Festival," 17.

viewed as a forum for English culture"), where Maponya is also quoted: "One only needs to look at its programme to see that the event is basically a platform for the English culture. This gives the impression that the few black participants are a mere camouflage."[14]

Other commentators, including the minister Dr Ngubane, are somewhat more sanguine; Albert Wertheim, who has been chronicling the event and mapping trends, said that "A genuine rejoicing in a new society free from the old bars that separated not only races but people from people is what this year's Grahamstown Festival seems to be all about."[15] It remains disquieting, however, that perceptions about freeing up the Fest come from white writers, while black writers are still fairly uniformly critical of the ideological base of the venue.

The issues which remain troubling are those dogging the entire cultural and artistic debate in South Africa: inclusiveness and exclusiveness, eurocentrism and afrocentrism, and the ever-vexed issue of 'standards.' It is, of course, within drama that this debate is most acutely felt – and Grundy underlines the difficulty when he refers to the fact that the establishment (that is, the organizing committee) freely admits that it does not understand the purposes and standards of, for example, participatory peoples' theatre.

In 1995 this problem was given an interesting airing in the comments made by Duma kaNdlovu about the "forgettable" production that Ledwaba, the winner of the Young Artist Award, brought to the stage. The production in question took quite a battering from critics (for example: "[nevertheless,] flagrant bad craft is not excusable"[16]) and kaNdlovu referred in caustic terms to the fact that "the problem is, the black cultural broederbond in the arts desperately needs a think-tank that will meet the white artistic community head on in terms of ideas and innovations [...] let us use each other to improve our work before we take it to the stage for the world to see our nakedness."[17] The honest confrontation of nakedness of this kind should be part of the healing process which has to take place – and then perhaps the festivals can really make the contribution that so many prominent commentators clearly want them to.

∝

---

[14] Mfundo Ndebele, "Festival still the same," *Sunday Tribune* (14 July 1996): 11.

[15] Albert Wertheim, "Fest frees up South Africa," *Cue* (12 July 1996): 7.

[16] Allan Munro, "Reflections on South African theatre and performance: Commentary on the Standard Bank Arts Festival Grahamstown, 1995," *Word and Action* (Potchefstroom) 353 (Spring 1995): 24.

[17] Duma kaNdlovu, "Let's use each other to improve," *Sowetan* (17 July 1995): 11.

Klein Karoo Kunstefees

The Klein Karoo Kunstefees evolved as a family festival. In contrast to the National Arts Festival at Grahamstown, which is more generally an event for young people although it also draws older audiences from among those interested in theatre and music, the Kunstefees set out to draw families – although, as it turned out, it also has a significant audience among those who would generally visit the NAF. It began in 1995 at Oudtshoorn, and seems to be on an upward curve. In 1995 it was described as a "total onslaught of the arts,"[18] and while the contributor was cautiously optimistic, he still harboured many dark fears; but these would seem to have been exorcized by the end of the 1996 Fees. The presentation at this one Festival of important (and new) works by Harry Kalmer, Athol Fugard, and Kramer and Petersen's *Kat and the Kings* lent status and substance to the Festival. A cross-section of responses from reviews gives the following range: "Shouts of delight echo across the Klein Karoo";[19] "Culture blooms and grows in the desert"; "the festival is an Afrikaans-driven event, and yet, while the odd old Afrikaner rears his head once in a while, there's a determined effort not to allow this element any platform."[20] Adam Small, the prominent Afrikaans poet, could therefore say that at the Klein Karoo Festival of Reconciliation the past was faced squarely, and dealt with[21] – and this is very well exemplified by the impact of Opperman's monumental play, *Donkerland* – no less than Fugard's important play *Valley Song* (the performance of these two plays during the same festival is, to my mind, of great symbolic significance). It is also of high import, I think, that Lieske Bester could say of the Kunstefees:

> on leaving this friendly town, after a week of stimulation and enjoyment, I'm left with a final thought: the strength of this festival definitely lies in its women. As writers, directors and performers, they seem to outnumber the men in quantity and quality.[22]

The road ahead

Clearly, both drama and the festivals have a role to play in the development of a cultural identity for the "rainbow nation." If the context of reconciliation has rendered many areas problematic for a wide variety of reasons, this can only be to the good for all the people of the country. How to create this good, however, might

[18] Guy Willoughby, "Total onslaught of the arts," *Weekly Mail & Guardian* (—, 1995): —.

[19] Jill Fletcher, "Shouts of delight echo across the Klein Karoo," *The Star* (April 2, 1996): 13 [Tonight].

[20] Diane de Beer, "Culture blooms and grows in the desert," *The Star* (April 2, 1996): 1–2 [Tonight].

[21] Adam Small, "Interview," *Beeld* (April 2, 1996): 23 [Kalender].

[22] Lieske Bester, "New look at SA history," *Cape Times* (April 8, 1996): 11.

prove a very difficult enterprise. Grundy makes some profoundly sensible obser-
vations:

> In contemporary South Africa hundreds of issues are being addressed at local as well
> as national levels, in diverse forums, among a multiplicity of groups and interests.
> Some of these negotiations are highly structured. Some are ad hoc, impromptu ses-
> sions. Taken together they cover a significant part of the political fabric of South Af-
> rica. Unfortunately the outside world hears mostly about the high profile meetings
> between the most celebrated political actors. Terms like the Pretoria Minute, the
> Groote Schuur Agreement, and the National Peace Accord have become part of our
> national language. Yet it is arguable that in order for these larger activities to suc-
> ceed, a cumulative record of repeated agreement, compliance and implementation
> must contribute to a mood of trust, collaboration and creative adventure.[23]

If one could (begin to) create the atmosphere of compromise, tolerance and flexi-
bility clearly needed for this process, it might begin to work, and Uys's rather large
claims might indeed come to fruition. It is not possible to have big, visible change –
diffuse, multifaceted, slow development is more likely.

And how are we faring in these terms?

The highly enthusiastic responses to the 1996 Kunstefees have been hinted at.
These would seem to be warranted when one looks at a brief sampling of the
shows on offer, for, apart from the rich and varied offerings in terms of music and
cabaret, drama itself has played the major role so far. In 1995 some of the plays
were: *Braaivleis* (Charles Fourie), *Luc* (Marc Hosten), *Bobaas van die Boendoe* (André
Brink's reworking of *A Comedy of Errors*), *Die jaar toe my ma begin sing het* (Engemie
Ferreira), *'n Seder val in Waterkloof* (P.G. du Plessis) – these plays were all on at the
main festival and included some seasoned and safe works (those by Brink and du
Plessis). Exciting new plays by Fourie and Hosten brought in a note of novelty. This
was all still very Afrikaans, however. In 1996 the emphasis shifted somewhat to-
wards a more open linguistic basis: seven new cabarets were offered by the top
South African cabaret artists, including Pieter–Dirk Uys, Casper de Vries, Nataniel,
Amanda Strydom and Antoinette Pienaar, as well as the Dutch cabaret maestro,
Herman Van Veen. Five of the twelve plays presented were new: Opperman's
Donkerland, Adam Small's *Reiklanke van die Kaap*, Lizz Meiring's *Boom*, Harry
Kalmer's *Toe ons by Alice geslaap het*, and *Die Pakkamer* (Marga van Rooy). Of great
importance was the performance of Athol Fugard's *Valley Song* at this Festival. A
programme of words and song based on the work of the renowned Afrikaans poet
Eugène Marais provided one of the highlights of the Festival. The appearance of
the superb mime-artist Andrew Buckland was also significant.

---

[23] Grundy, "The Politics of the National Arts Festival," 6.

All of the difficulties associated with festivals are still there (sometimes in abundance), from technical difficulties to the exigencies and vagaries of the weather; but they can be addressed. The Klein Karoo festival as it stands represents a triumph in terms of its reception to date. The dates announced for the 1997 Festival indicated an extended festival, with a longer pilot festival provided for try-outs – the Klein Karoo Kunstefees is equivalent to the Fringe at Grahamstown. For the moment, the Klein Karoo has not been overtly political; as it is running on sponsorships from the business sector, it might continue for some time to escape the sort of (narrowly) political hamstringing that has been prevalent in Grahamstown. It also has the undeniable attraction and aura of newness.

What of the Grahamstown festival? That which has been offered here since 1994 has been very stimulating and wide-ranging. 1994 saw the presentation of Tom Stoppard's *Arcadia*, and the vintage *Travels With My Aunt*. Barney Simon's production of Can Themba's *The Suit* was considered outstanding. Von Klemperer picked as her winner of the Festival *Take the Floor* by Sue Pam–Grant; she also commended Slabolepszy's new *Victoria Almost Falls*, and Reza de Wet's *Drif* (all these at the main festival, not the Fringe).[24] The inclusion of works by international playwrights is a stronger feature at Grahamstown than at the Kunstefees, and this was evidenced again at the NAF in 1995, when Fugard (*The Island*) and Kentridge (*Faustus in Africa*) were joined at the main festival by Arthur Miller (*Broken Glass*). A reworking of *Medea* was also performed, transferred from its Cape Town airing by Mark Fleishman and Jennie Reznek. A great deal that was considered exciting appeared on the Fringe, including work by some of the foremost South African actors and improvisers, from Tobie Cronjé to Andrew Buckland (*Feedback*). In 1996 there came a shift, with a strong comedy focus on the Fringe ("...largely owing to South Africa's break with its self-conscious political past and subsequent desire to embrace the vibrancy of intermingled culture with all its attendant hiccups"[25]). This shift was also represented by vintage producer Nicholas Ellenbogen's *Raiders of the Broken Heart*. Iain MacDonald summed up by referring to a strong focus on plays dealing with prostitution, and commented that township drama, "now no longer focused on the struggle, seems to be milling around in some confusion, and has come up with sociological mirrors, largely educational and meaningful, about the lives of people in squatter camps, jail, shebeens and barber shops, mostly done in the usual semi-traditional singing and dancing formats."[26] Serious drama in-

[24] Margaret von Klemperer, "A score of Festival successes," *Natal Witness* (11 July 1994): 7.

[25] Iain MacDonald, "Comedy set to take centre stage at Grahamstown," *Argus* (27 June 1996): 8.

[26] MacDonald, "Comedy set to take centre stage at Grahamstown," 8.

cluded Terrence McNally's *Love! Valor! Compassion!*, August Wilson's *Piano Lesson*, and Deon Opperman's *Donkerland*. Another hit at the Festival and subsequently elsewhere was Terrence McNally's *Master Class*. An important local offering was Nicky Rebelo and David Butler's acerbic *What Annette said in her sleep last night*, which later transferred to Johannesburg.

In his thorough overview of the 1995 Festival, Allan Munro comments on the quality and the scope of the theatre presented and draws some conclusions about general trends within what he perceives as a movement in South Africa from a "culture of contest to a culture of consensus."[27] He notes that

> the Festival is beginning to create circles of focus. There is a strong Gay and Lesbian contingent, a strong Feminist contingent, but very little Black Consciousness. There are the mainstream aficionados (Rattigan, Slabolepszy at this Festival, Fugard and so on), a strong cabaret movement (Zietsman, Blacher, Uys, Cutt Glass, etc.) and a powerful jazz movement. (28)

He further points out that technical expertise is still woefully inadequate, that there is a strong movement to layer the political with the personal, that the boundaries between performance and reality will have to be investigated more rigorously, that there is a strong move toward ever smaller casts (for artistic but perhaps more for economic reasons? – whichever it is, it is generally accepted as a firm trend), that South African theatre relies increasingly on the musical component in it – and concludes with the view that theatre, and the demand for the theatrical, is flourishing, because "so many have realized the malleability and pliability of the medium, as well as its (relatively) low expense" (28).

After a range of very enthusiastic responses to the scope and impact of the National Arts Festival in 1994 and 1995, one might have misgivings about thinking that a renaissance had occurred, seeing as the Festival seemed to have toned down (perhaps ominously) in 1996. Typical responses included: "Spirit has gone out of the fest,"[28] "*Woema kort om aarde te skud*" (Oomph needed to shake the earth),[29] "Better weather, smaller crowd," and "Fun while it lasted – but did it really have a point? [...] there was a sense this year of a festival marking time,"[30] "They say it has no soul – what's happened to the Fest?"[31] The chief executive director of the Grahamstown Foundation commented on the fact that there were good ticket sales but a drop in numbers, and he also said that "Grahamstown is a mirror of SA art, [...] there are winds of change in South African art, but we still have a long way to

27 Munro, "Reflections on South African theatre and performance," 23.
28 S. Memela, "Comment on the Fest," *Sunday Tribune* (14 July 1996): 22.
29 P. Norval, "Woema Kort," *Beeld* (14 July 1996): 11.
30 von Klemperer, "Fun while it lasted," *Natal Witness* (18 July 1996): 7.
31 Willoughby, "They say it has no soul," 11.

go."[32] It is to be hoped that this is a temporary phase, and that the general atmosphere of rapprochement within the country, created in the context of the Truth and Reconciliation Commission, will help produce change.

After all, "to survive, we must tell stories"; and where better to tell them than on stage, where South African stories must find a local habitation and a (theatrical) space, and where local talent can be honed by interventionary structures such as festivals.[33]

———— ℰℴ ℒℬ ————

[32] Richard Chernis, "Grahamstown is a mirror of SA art," *Natal Witness* (18 July 1996): 11.

[33] It is a great pleasure for me to acknowledge the valuable and unstinting help of the staff of the National English Literary Museum (NELM) in Grahamstown in my gathering of material for this paper. Ann Dry (Chief Curator) and her team were always willing, informed, and incredibly efficient.

The German Presence
in New South African Theatre

∞ Eckhard Breitinger

Grahamstown 1996:
The marginalization of South African drama?

THE PROGRAMME OF THE 1996 GRAHAMSTOWN FESTIVAL re-
vealed a significant dominance of foreign plays, albeit in South African
productions. There was August Wilson's *Piano Lesson* (directed by Jerry
Mofokeng), Terrence McNally's *Master Class* and *Love! Valor! Compassion!* (both
directed by Mark Graham), Arthur Miller's *The Crucible* (directed by Lara Foot–
Newton), the stage adaptation of Dickens's *A Tale of Two Cities* (directed by Janice
Honeyman), Marthinus Basson's production of *Macbeth*, and Angelo Gobbato's of
Porgy and Bess. Only Ronnie Govender's *1949*, and *Donkerland*, written and directed
by Deon Opperman, were fully South African in origin, theme and setting,
authorship and production. The *Mail & Guardian* critic Hazel Friedman remarked
the lack of works "Made in the RSA."[1] For the outside observer, it was surprising
how far the political situation was minimalized. Ronnie Govender's main theme in
1949, the "race riots" between Indians and Africans, was presented and perceived
as if there were no parallels with the present ethnic tension in KwaZulu–Natal.[2]
Similarly, Arthur Miller's play about the McCarthy 'investigations' in the USA of
the late Forties was left in a twilight of indeterminate time and space. One of the
most topical South African plays of the 1996 festival, the adaptation of Ariel Dorfman's *Death and the Maiden*, was nonetheless based on a foreign play. Dorfman's
piece about how to deal with past human-rights violations was systematically
adapted to the South African setting, with such stereotypes as the new black elite,

---

[1] Hazel Friedman, "Tested, and oh so tired," *Mail & Guardian* (19–25 July 1996): 30. She also
complained that 'The festival is affordable only for the mainstream theatre and dance companies
fresh from or destined for the national rounds, the Sharkvilles, the Crucibles, the Greeks, the Kat
and Kings; those fortunate enough to have been paid their dues."

[2] Margaret von Klemperer remarked in her review for *Cue* (12 July 1996): "it is good to see a
home-grown play which throws a spotlight onto part of the past and recreates a world which
was to vanish with the forced removals of 1958 without drowning in either nostalgia or guilt."

the old Anglo-liberals, and the old Afrikaner *Verkramptes* [narrow-minded conser-vatives]. In the debate about the Truth Commission's dealings with the past, Latin American models of general amnesty had been discussed and rejected. But the lo-cal production of *Death and the Maiden* represented a re-opening of that debate. None of the other productions successfully relocated action within a distinctly South African setting. Neither the geographical nor the sociocultural space was anywhere convincingly reconstructed.

To this outside observer, it remained unclear what the open or implied mean-ings of the prevalence of foreign plays might signify. If directors and producers were looking for examples that could reflect their own situation, it was hard to see how the use of a foreign model was constructive in the present. On the other hand, looking outside for plays that could be staged inside the country after so many years of cultural boycott may be understood to represent an attempt to reintegrate and reposition South African theatre internationally.

The prevalence of foreign plays may be related to the intellectual and aesthetic climate of the transitional period, in which the only certainty has been the rejec-tion of old views. Ronnie Govender has said that "If you want to tell a story, even if it is about grief, get away from one-dimensional sloganeering. It is only by laying to rest the ghosts of the pasts, that we can look squarely at the future."[3] The pre-dominant mood was one of testing, exploring, and gauging which cultural import could be of relevance to the internal cultural market, and how home-grown cul-tural products could relate to or compete with foreign imports.[4] My impression is confirmed by the critic Adrienne Sichel, who diagnosed "a bad dose of transition-itis."[5] Mary Jordan explained the low political impact of the festival offerings in terms of the "apparently random connections and arbitrary associations between overseas playwrights and local directors," with the inevitable result that "Because we live in a society that has already shown its boiling hatreds and revealed its in-ner torment, audiences want to relax and peer at the facade only."[6]

♋

[3] Ronnie Govender, "Interview," *Cue* (13 July 1996): 7.

[4] The *South African Theatre Journal* 9.2 (September 1995) carried a number of articles on the transformation of the canon (Peter Ukpokodu: "'Lest one good custom should corrupt the world': African Theatre and the 'Holy' Canon;" 3–25; Marcia Blumberg, "Re-evaluating Otherness, Building for Difference: South African Theatre Beyond the Interregnum," 27–37; Jeanne Colleran, "Re-Situating Fugard: Re-Thinking Revolutionary Theatre," 39–49).

[5] Adrienne Sichel, "African artists draw on their heritage to break barriers," *The Star* (17 July 1996): 3 [Tonight].

[6] Mary Jordan, "Seeking out the summer time of easy living," *Business Day* (9 July 1996).

Dealing with plays of the classical canon:
Relocate or re-invent?

Local rewritings of foreign classics have attracted much critical attention. William Kentridge and the Handspring Puppet Company made a tremendous impact with *Woyzeck on the Highveld* at the Theater der Welt festival in Munich in 1993,[7] and the impact of their *Faustus in Africa* was even greater. This play was performed at the Africa 95 festival in Britain, in the USA, at the Avignon festival and in Sydney and Perth (Australia), as well as touring Western Europe. It became the ambassador of South African theatre in the Nineties, like *Woza Albert!* in the Eighties. Renate Klett concluded that "South Africa has found a new voice – and everybody all over the world is keen to listen to it."[8] With full-page reviews in *Die Zeit* and the *Süddeutsche Zeitung* and a full-page interview in the *Frankfurter Allgemeine Zeitung*, Kentridge had received maximum media coverage in the German dailies and weeklies that shape public and critical opinion in matters artistic.[9] Janet Suzman's adaptation of Bertolt Brecht's *The Good Person of Sechuan* was widely reported in the British press, in part because of her reputation as a director and actress. The production was intended as a watershed in the theatre of the new South Africa. It was described as at the most costly, lavish production ever mounted at the Market Theatre.[10]

In talking about the relocation and rewriting of 'classic plays,' one runs the risk of over-emphasizing the specificities of national cultures and literary tradition. Care is required when ascribing specific national/cultural properties to a source-text, properties that originate in the customary handling of a national theatrical tradition and a nationally oriented canon. From the perspective of an institutionalized national culture, the process of rewriting could be described in terms of disappropriation, piracy, or even plagiarism. It is easy to overlook those features of play-texts which induce a relocation to different cultural, spacial and temporal contexts. One should avoid talking about national cultural property in terms of ownership by one particular culture.

---

[7] Benjamin Henrichs, "Im Tal des Erstaunens" (In the Valley of Amazement), *Die Zeit* 27 (2 July 1993): 45–46.

[8] "Südafrika hat eine neue Stimme, und alle Welt will sie hören"; Renate Klett, "The Voice of Africa – The Handspring Puppet Company liest deutsche Klassiker anders: *Woyzeck on the Highveld* und *Faustus in Africa*," *Theater heute* 36.9 (September 1995): 10.

[9] Marion Ammicht, "Doktor Faustus im Aufwind des Propellers" (Doktor Faustus in the slipstream), *Süddeutsche Zeitung* (19 Sept. 1995): 16; Bartholomäus Grill, "Weimar, Soweto und zurück" (From Weimar to Soweto and back), *Die Zeit* (8 September 1995): 54; Wolfgang Press (interview), "Was sucht Faust eigentlich in Afrika?" (What's Faust doing in Africa?), *Frankfurter Allgemeine Zeitung* (November 21 1995): B3.

[10] Charlotte Bauer, "Cleopatra's reign," *Sunday Times* (23 July 1996): 17.

In analyzing three German plays in their South African rewritings, I wish to show how the specifics of the situation vary. Büchner's *Woyzeck*, which formed the source-text of Kentridge's and the Handspring Puppet Company's *Woyzeck on the Highveld*, is of course a German classic. As a nineteenth-century revolutionary play that anticipates many aspects of twentieth-century drama, *Woyzeck* figures regularly on the German stage – and, in recent years, abroad as well. *Faust*, on the other hand, presents a theme long familiar throughout European literature, from popular theatre and puppet theatre to the sixteenth-century *Volksbuch* [chapbook] and twentieth-century novels. Although *Faust*, even in Goethe's version, is an international literary presence, it is also a quintessentially German text. No German secondary-school student leaves school without being treated to at least Part I of *Faust*. Part II, however, is little-known and rarely performed. Goethe's *Faust* is generally considered the German national play, and every educated German has at least a dozen quotations from *Faust* to hand. Brecht's *The Good Person of Sechuan* is a very different case. The play was written while Brecht was in exile during World War II, and with a non-specific, Chinese, allegorical setting. Brecht had been banned by the Nazis, so there was no immediate German audience, and the play premiered in Switzerland. The setting of this parable-play does, however, travel easily to distant locations – for example, I recall seeing a version in francophone Cameroon.

In the Janet Suzman/Gcina Mhlophe adaptation of *The Good Person of Sechuan* as *The Good Woman of Sharkville*, the modern classic is relocated to a culturally, socially and politically specific setting, thereby giving the parable a more direct and contemporary meaning. The allegorical "Sharkville," suggesting rapaciousness as the dominant theme, is almost a homophone with Sharpeville, a place-name with very distinct political and historical connotations. But this naming evoked political expectations that were not and perhaps could not be realized by the parable play. The rewrite of a classic play-text is always caught by the difficulty of standing in its own right as an independent and original vision of the time and place into which it has been reset. That is to say, the new play has to be functional and effective in and of itself.

Illustrating the coloniality of Hegel's *Weltgeist*

William Kentridge's point of departure was not the play-text, but his multimedia mode of presentation – a mode partly derived from his art as creator of sophisticated animated films. His *Felix* films, for example, shown at the 1995 Grahamstown Festival, were strongly influenced by Expressionist drawings and design, and by silent-film dramaturgy. Equally important in Kentridge's creative process has been his work with puppets, and the puppeteers of the Handspring Company, which also communicates through image and movement. It is significant here that the types of image created by Kentridge – visual or facial expression, movements on the projection screen, and the manipulation of puppets at centre-stage – are stylized, *verfremdet* (alienated), each in its own specific way. There is a clear distinction between images and movements on the two-dimensional projection screen, and the three-dimensional presentation of puppets and their movements in and through the performance space. The similarity and the dissimilarity of the two forms of presentation construct a new level of meanings or responses from the audience, independent of thematic issues and content, which are determined primarily by the presentational style.

Another source of inspiration that was developed into a distinctive stylistic feature with *leitmotiv* functions in *Faustus in Africa* was circumstantial. Kentridge witnessed West African military and police brass bands while accompanying Nelson Mandela's state visit to Ghana; along with the mainly impressionistic musical idiom, this style of syncretic music became a useful signifier of the colonial heritage and post-colonial atmosphere of *Faustus in Africa*. A further indicator of the importance of visual effect and visual communication is Kentridge's archival research for graphic materials representing colonialism – architecture, institutions, personalities, and advertising. The design of *Faustus in Africa* was based on a photograph of the telephone exchange, newly established in the early Twenties, in Lourenço Marques (Maputo). The play's animated film projects maps from World War I colonial campaigns, illustrating, for example, the British and French pincer strategy against the Germans in Cameroon. The puppets strangely combine historical and invented heroic figures of the colonial imagination. Faust was modelled on the French explorer Brazza (1852–1905), and Helena's image was taken from a popular advertisement for Juno cigarettes. This female figure embodied the dreams of white male smokers sitting in their offices throughout the Empire. Gretchen was based on a photograph of a laboratory assistant at a malaria research station. And the face of Johnston/Wagner represents Patrice Lumumba. All the main characters reflect the historical function of their originals during the days of colonialism. This re-creation of new dramatic characters from historical personae suggests the process of the overall project of rewriting Goethe's *Faust* into an African context.

The different weight given to written/textual communications is evident from the passages where Gretchen's monologue is projected onto the screen in English translation. The text itself is spoken in hesitant German, with Faust as a pedantic teacher, with the result that the emotional resonance of Goethe's well-known *"Meine Ruh' ist hin…"* ["My peace is gone"] monologue is deflated, the spectators' attention having been diverted by the script projection and the teacher–pupil/ Faust–Gretchen dialogue. In Goethe's text, Gretchen's spinning-wheel monologue reveals the end-result of the imbalance of power between Faust and Gretchen; here it is transformed into a display and critique of the continuing processes of their power-relationship. The scene discloses most aptly Kentridge's technique of 'writing back' – or, rather, 'performing back' – to Goethe's metropolitan version. In the original, *"Meine Ruh'ist hin..."* is Gretchen's soliloquy, spoken while she is sitting at the spinning-wheel and revealing her reaction to her encounter with Faust. Her place at the spinning-wheel manifests her social and gender role, and marks her as lower-middle-class. She is presented performing a typical female task, one that binds her within the house, both in the domestic work she is doing and in the product she is delivering. In Kentridge's version, the eighteenth-century specifics of female gender roles are present only as a literary reminiscence, through the addition of the teacher–pupil and North–South relationships to the male–female imbalance. In yet another variation on the Prospero–Caliban or Crusoe–Friday constellation, Faust here teaches Gretchen *his* language. He prioritizes the master tongue, thereby marginalizing or even erasing Gretchen's language. Gretchen's reaction to Faust is reduced to the parroting of a prefabricated text, loaded with associations which are not really her own. The colonial Gretchen is thus silenced, disempowered, and linguistically disabled. The changing of *"Meine Ruh' ist hin"* from a confessional to a linguistic/cultural construction signifies the mental reconditioning of the 'mimic men' (and women) who live in a borrowed, not yet fully appropriate or appropriated, cultural, linguistic and emotional framework.

Kentridge's easy – not to say casual – relationship with the canonical text becomes particularly clear from what he does with the second part of the play. *Faust II* is a complex and mystifying philosophical work, in which the many scenes and themes do not correspond to any easily stageable dramatic structure. Goethe himself pondered staging *Faust II* with the help of a *laterna magica*, to extend its limitations – an idea adopted in the form of Kentridge's projections of animated film. The Kentridge version ties the whole concept of *Faustus in Africa* to a brief passage in *Faust II* in which Faust, old, blind, in the very last moment before his death, has visions of opening up new terrain through labouring serfs:

> *Arbeiter schaffe Meng' auf Menge,*
> *Ermuntre durch Genuss und Strenge,*
> *Bezahle, locke, presse bei!* [...]
> *Eröffn' ich Räume vielen Millionen...*[11]

---

[11] "Produce vast numbers of workers, / Enthuse them by profit and control, / Pay, entice, press-gang! / [...] I create spaces for many millions"; *Faust*, Part Two, V.11552–24, 11563.

Kentridge redefines this Faustian principle of the unconditional, expansionist search for wisdom and power in colonial terms, by inventing correlatives with key scenes in *Faust*, Part II. He teamed up with the Soweto rap poet Lesego Rampolokeng (not a writer to be overawed by the weight of tradition or canonized texts), merging the rhythmical pattern of *Knüttelvers* (doggerel) with his own speech-rhythms while retaining a clear emphasis upon the difference between the colonial Faustus and the philosophical wizard of the early-nineteenth century.

With *Faustus*, says Kentridge, "we wanted something that relates to our situation, but which is geographically broader then *Woyzeck*, something that at the same time celebrates and comments, presents and criticizes the original vision."[12] The ending, where Faust is pardoned for the crimes he committed, again relates directly to the present situation in South Africa. Kentridge's decision to relocate Faust in Africa may be understood as a Hegelian conception of the *Weltgeist* that deserted Africa with the decline of the Pharaonic empire, never to return. For Kentridge, another type of *Weltgeist* developed in Europe in close relation to Hegel's and was reimported into Africa through colonialism. Goethe's version of *Faust* is one of the key texts of the European tradition representing the Hegelian *Weltgeist*. The intention to open a new discourse, a dialogic alternative reading, of that spirit now becomes obvious.

However, a number of purely pragmatic considerations entered Kentridge's production on various levels. Puppeteers cannot hold and manipulate puppets in scenes of more than three to five minutes, with the result that the play has to be loosely structured in a sequence of short scenes, or the plot has to be cut up into short takes. Puppeteering also determined the construction of the Kentridge set, with its different levels for the full appearance of the puppets in the front, for partial 'American' framing of the puppets on the higher middle level, and open wings for the actors to appear at the sides. The set is thus constructed like a triptych, a winged altar, with the projection screen as its centrepiece.

The multiple presence of the actors-cum-puppet manipulators and the puppets has become one of the trademarks of the Handspring Company and William Kentridge's theatrical style.[13] This, too, is based on an essentially pragmatic decision. When Kentridge and Handspring were first experimenting for the production of *Woyzeck*, they decided to operate more in the traditional style of puppeteering, where the puppet carries the full weight of the entire physical and vocal repre-

---

[12] William Kentridge, interview with the present author, Johannesburg (July 1996).
[13] Handspring Puppets were part of the Junction Avenue production of *Tooth and Nail* (directed by Malcolm Purkey), which also experimented with the double presence of actors and life-size puppets. Similarly, Mavis Taylor in Cape Town experimented with life-size puppets in her play *Tina Bantu*.

sentation, while the puppeteer, lending voice to the puppet-character, remains invisible. The troupe first experimented with lighting designs that spotlight the puppets and leave the puppeteers almost invisible. A related concept was also tested, in which the puppeteers wore hoods that disguised the actors' presence and allowed the puppet manipulator to be only vaguely visible. This idea was also rejected, because it created the wrong associations – such as the Ku Klux Klan, or medieval plague figures. Once the group decided in favour of the double presence of puppet and puppeteer, they developed this into a positive theatrical idiom, signifying ambiguity, multi-dimensionality, and *Verfremdung* (alienation).

Kentridge takes his spectators on a triangular tour through different media with their specific forms of perception – the animated film on the projection screen, the puppets, the actors – each of which relates to the others, comments on them, and interacts with the events and the presentation in the other two media. All three media involve critical discourses on the other two, while also being self-reflexive. *Faustus in Africa* thus becomes a play about Faust, about Euro-African relations, about colonialism, about the semiotics of colonials, about theatre, media, performance, and about past and present.

Parable play – *Lehrstück* – social reportage?

Suzman and Mhlophe's adaptation of Brecht's parable-play *The Good Person of Sechuan* reportedly marked the first occasion on which the Brecht heirs gave permission to make changes to the original text. According to Eric Bentley, who first translated and performed the two *Parables for the Theatre*, *The Good Person of Sechuan* and *The Caucasian Chalk Circle*, Brecht was highly conscious of the difference between script and performance, between original, adaptation, and translation: "Brecht toyed with the idea of his plays always being literally translated for publication and freely adapted for performance."[14] Inspired by the discovery of Asian theatrical forms, he wrote dialogue for *The Good Person* in a highly formulaic, stylized and abstract language that was meant to reflect the alien cultural milieu of the parable. He also created the symbolic and allegorical town of Sechuan, situated in a cultural no-man's-land, China. Where Suzman/Mhlophe's Sharkville and Brecht's Sechuan are closest to each other is in the conception of the setting as a space in transition. Suzman herself was convinced that relocating "the play to South Africa now would give it a fresh light."[15] Her changes occur mainly in the

---

[14] Eric Bentley, ed., tr. & intro., *Parables for the Theatre: Two Plays by Bertolt Brecht* (New York: Grove, 1961): 15.

[15] Quoted in Gillian Anstey, "Suzman to do *Sharkville* in SA," *Sunday Times* (28 January 1996): 18.

second part of the play, and concentrate on two aspects: the songs, and the socio-economic setting.

The music for the songs in *The Good Person of Sechuan* was originally written by Paul Dessau (not by Kurt Weill, as most critics have assumed). It is difficult to tell how far song-lyrics like those of the pilot's song *"Das Lied vom Sankt Nimmerleins-tag"* [The Song of Saint Never-On-Your-Nellie's Day] can be easily translated into a different musical idiom, since there are so many sociocultural and political associations connected with the Brecht/Weill song-style. For the Suzman/Mhlophe production, Didi Kriel wrote a new musical score, which was praised as an ideal fusion of African rhythms and European lyric diction.[16] For me, the satirical edge of the original songs was blunted without fully acquiring the punch of the African song-tradition. But it was not only the musical idiom that was changed; new tunes were set for new lyrics. Drastic change came with the unemployed worker's song. The Brecht original, *"Das Lied vom achten Elefanten"* (Song of the Eighth Elephant), tells in ballad-like fashion how one tame elephant in a herd of eight is sufficient to undermine the independent spirit and to betray the whole gang to their master and to capitalist exploitation. The eighth elephant, the capitalist slave-driver, reflects the unemployed pilot's betrayal of his comrades (he is appointed overseer in the tobacco factory). Brecht's song is a parable within the parable-play. The issue of relations between labour and capital, however, was discarded for *Sharkville*, so that the song took on an entirely different quality: instead of the subtle subversiveness of Brecht's original parable, it became a forcefully presented protest song. If the punch was there, the direction of attack was lost.

It is particularly in the second part of the script that Suzman/Mhlophe altered the tone of the play. In the Brecht version, the prostitute Shen Te sets up business as a tobacconist, investing the money given to her by the gods. In the Suzman/Mhlophe version, Sizakele goes into dope-peddling. Shen Te illustrates entrepreneurial behaviour, making her money work for her instead of her body. But Sizakele embarks on a crooked deal, embezzling the goods with which her friends entrust her. This quite alters the tone and message, changing the relationship between the characters of Sizakele and Vuyani (Shen Te and Yang Sun). In Brecht, the tobacconist signifies the bottom rank of the capitalist class, the level where mimicry of bourgeois and petty-capitalist entrepreneurship begins. Brecht singled out his kind of behaviour as the decisive shift from proletarian prostitute Shen Te to her alter ego and businessman-cousin Shui Ta. The transition from Sizakele, the

---

[16] See, for example, Paul Boekkooi, "Brecht work patchy, despite its splendour and vitality," *The Star* (10 July 1996): 2 [Tonight], and Garalt MacLiam, "*Sharkville* gleams with jewels," *The Star* (18 July 1996): 2 [Tonight].

happy hooker, to the nasty dope-peddler Suduka in *Good Woman of Sharkville* seems much less sophisticated. In Brecht, Yang Sun, the unemployed pilot, is made over-seer in Shui Ta's tobacco factory – he is the mean exploiter, the slave-driver; he is Shui Ta's willing executioner and, as such, part of the exploitative capitalist sys-tem. Yang Sun is the accomplice, not the victim, of Shui Ta. This makes his relation to Shen Te, the prostitute, much more complex, because as overseer he is helping to exploit the class to which Shen Te belongs, while, as Shen Te's lover, he is bent on exploiting the exploiter. In Suzman's *Good Woman of Sharkville*, there is no longer an ideological battle, no longer a class conflict. For Brecht, it is the class conflict, the overriding presence of economic exploitation, that prevents the ex-ploited as well as the exploiter from remaining good. In *Sharkville*, conflict is reduced to the alternative of making a lifetime career of crime, or remaining an honest failure. As Robert Greig has said,

> Invoking the anti drug-crusade is glib and trendy […] it blurs the moral development of the good woman who moves from selling her body to selling others. Similarly, the role of Sizakele's suitor is rewritten […] he is written off as a junkie. That finger-wagging is too easy: it forces us to take the easy route of moral judgement rather than moral understanding.[17]

Changing the economic and social conflict to a merely criminal issue reveals the limitations of this way of looking abroad and attempting to rewrite a classic Euro-pean drama for South Africa; whereas Kentridge's example demonstrates the positive potential of such a dramaturgical strategy.

———

17 Robert Greig, "This black Brecht…," *Sunday Independent* (21 July 1996): 20.

Interviews ❧

A Voice for the Afrikaner?

An Interview with Athol Fugard
by Dennis Walder

❧   London, 20 February 1996

A THOL FUGARD is South Africa's most important and prolific playwright, and was the first to have an international reputation. His plays – now numbering some twenty in print – command audiences the world over, despite (or in some respects because of) their local origins and idiom. He has transformed the ordinary people of his corner of the Eastern Cape into dramatic images of profound significance. His collaborative work with performers across racial divisions during the apartheid years helped legitimate black experience as a form of cultural expression, and he has remained a powerful influence upon all South African dramatists. His commitment to the theatre is total; his moral concern undeniable. His first theatrical production after the 1994 elections was *My Life*, an orchestration of the voices of five young women. His play *Valley Song*, set in the small Karoo town of Nieu-Bethesda, where the Fugards have a house, premiered at the Market Theatre, Johannesburg, in August 1995. The American opening at the McCarter Theater, Princeton, in October 1995, was followed by a run at the Manhattan Theatre Club in November 1995, with the role of Veronica played by Lisa–Gay Hamilton. The South African cast (the author and Esmeralda Bihl) appeared at the Royal Court Theatre in London in February 1996.

DW *I wanted to ask you first of all, Athol, some general questions, and then go on to* Valley Song. *Do you still think of yourself as a "dissident voice" – a phrase you used about yourself during the apartheid years?*

AF No. I think that, even given some pretty rough scenarios for the new South Africa, I would not ever see myself in that role. Too much has happened. I would like to believe that, once our new constitution is finally negotiated, there will be in place enough safeguards to prevent there ever being a situation in which one finds oneself in such stark opposition to the system, to the establishment, as was the case in the old South Africa. There are a lot of scenarios I know that I would not be happy with, so one could speak of possibly trying to maintain a certain vigilance. But "dissident" in the sense that there was this stark, energizing polarity in the apartheid years, when it was so easy to identify the enemy, so easy to use those two unremarkable little words, "yes" or "no" – in no sense could I ever see myself back in that position.

The other aspect of that phrase that I liked was the idea of you as a voice of some kind. Are you still a voice, and if you are, who are you speaking for?

I've got to feel my way into my answer to that question. The first thing I must say is that I think one of the consequences of the huge political drama that has played itself out over the past five years – and which is ongoing; we don't know where it's going to take us – is that it is very liberating. One of the things that I've been liberated from – maybe dangerously so – is a sense of having to speak for a silenced majority; of having to try and break a conspiracy of silence that was abroad in South Africa. Maybe there's been a dangerous liberation from that responsibility, and now the voice is only my own. I speak for myself, except that – something I became conscious of in the writing of *Valley Song* – one of the wonderfully liberating aspects of the experience that I've gone through as a new South African – I'm now free to be a total Afrikaner, and that maybe I could even conceive of a scenario where I am a voice for the Afrikaner.

I mean, old Buks is Afrikaans, you know, in the original version of the play in South Africa, or as I will do it down in Oudtshoorn, where I will do the play for four days at this beautiful Karoo Festival, the Afrikaans-language festival. We are taking the play down there, and some of the things – the psalms, for example – I'm going to put into Afrikaans. We're going to make it really Afrikaans, and in that context, I think Buks is going to refer, as Afrikaners would, to the author as the *skruiwer*, as an *Engelsman* – which is the way I've always thought of him; and then I've had to translate it on paper. Because once you say "Englishman," it's not the same thing. But you know the way an Afrikaner uses that word, *Engelsman* – it is somebody who speaks English.

So, yes, maybe I can, unashamedly and with a huge sense of relief, just be an Afrikaner. I don't think that in any sense the Afrikaner is ever remotely going to need a voice in the way that the silenced majority of the apartheid years needed a voice. They're not going to be persecuted. When I think of myself as being an Afrikaans voice in the future, maybe it is just finally that, without any sense of guilt or any problems connected with it, I can celebrate – celebrate being an Afrikaner.

Yes, and it is there in Valley Song ...

Buks and his talk about what the land means to him, and the Author trying to understand what Buks and the land together mean: that's really an Afrikaner reality,
do you know what I mean? Buks is quite simply an Afrikaner – finish, *en klaar*.

One of the things about it is that the play represents a more inclusive notion of the Afri-
kaner –
Absolutely.

Because it's including black people, as coloured people in South Africa would be called here.
Absolutely. You see, that is the wonderful thing that is happening – that the sense
of being Afrikaans has suddenly gone from this narrow exclusive vision to something that is much more generous and/or bigger. *Ja*, and that is what this Karoo
Festival is about as well – all the Afrikaners mixing it and challenging each other.

I can always remember – and this was prior to de Klerk's historic February
1991 speech – one of the most incredible pieces of political drama that I saw, was
a series of interviews, of confrontations, on Afrikaans television, and Allan Boesak
[Cape Coloured moderator of the Dutch Reformed Mission Church], who was
talking in Afrikaans, was asked about forgiveness and reconciliation, and it was
put to him that he was also an Afrikaner, and he said, "No! No, not until we can
vote in a democracy." It was absolutely gripping stuff, and it is at the heart of what
we are looking at.

Breyten Breytenbach as a writer and Albie Sachs as an ANC spokesperson asked us to re-
member that Afrikaans, and many of the people who speak it, should not be equated with the
apartheid regime. So this is also being rendered concrete in your actual performance in the
play?
It's also fairly established that the roots of Afrikaans don't lie actually with the so-
called Afrikaans ancestors, the Dutch, but that we come from the kitchens and the
servants ... That is where the roots of Afrikaans started.

It's a much more polyglot language than the Afrikaner Nationalist movement suggested,
with this whole purity notion which went along with it. It's a language that comes from
English, from German, from French; and, as you say, it is also a language from below.
Absolutely. And you talk to Veronica – when we work together, Veronica and myself, we don't speak English.

You mean Esmeralda, of course?
[*Laughter together*]
Yes. Our entire rehearsal process, and now our sort of private life as we work to-
gether and look after each other on stage, it's all in Afrikaans.

Is that new for you, then, too?

With Marius Weyers – who, interestingly enough, is going to be replacing me in New York on *Valley Song* – with Marius, when I directed him in *A Lesson from Aloes*, we had an Afrikaans thing going as well. But Shelagh Holliday in *Aloes* couldn't speak Afrikaans, so one had to be very discreet about using it – because you're going to exclude people. But Esmeralda has no hesitation in excluding everybody; she's going to talk Afrikaans!

We were talking about this after the production at the Royal Court. It seemed an Afrikaans play in many ways – from the start, there was a lot of Afrikaans which wasn't translated. There's the hymn "Ek sal die Here loof" ["I shall praise the Lord"] that's not translated, and the audience, if they're not Afrikaans-speaking, has to pick that up.

There's no way you can translate that. The great danger I share with a lot of Afrikaners – a degree of terrible apprehension, at one level, and one little part of myself – as we approached nearer and nearer the arrival of the new South Africa, was about the future of the language and the culture. What I never actually realized or never imagined was that the language, effortlessly or relatively effortlessly, escaped the association with apartheid as the language of the oppressor, and therefore to be denied, therefore to be negated, therefore to be put down. I don't doubt that there is a lot of feeling along those lines in South Africa. But it is obviously not going to win. The ANC on the one side and the Nats on the other are really fighting for the soul of the coloured people, for example. "What are you? Are you a black man or are you an Afrikaner?" And the coloureds say, "I'm a black Afrikaner."

I wanted to ask you who you saw being your own presence in this play. You've spoken about yourself before in terms of a particular figure who represents you in some sort of deep way, as in Road to Mecca, for example, in which (you said) the Miss Helen Martins figure represented you.

Look at the fact that I play both Buks and the Author; that's the answer to that question. Those two characters are the two sides of the same coin. You flip the coin, and you get heads for Athol Fugard, born with a white skin, born into privilege, a good education; finally, money and all the securities that go with being a white man in South Africa in those years. You flip the same coin, and you get tails, and you're Buks, you're Abraam Jonkers – no land, no ownership, no education, no security, living on the edge of desperation all your life. They're the two faces of the same reality. I feel very passionately that Abraam Jonkers with his handful of pumpkin seeds is Athol Fugard with his handful of words. For our opening night at the Manhattan Theatre Club I looked around for a little gesture towards my wonderful stage manager there [Sandra Lee], and I found a book of Seamus Heaney's poetry. And I just opened it before I parcelled it up to give to her and I saw a poem that I hadn't registered before. He's sitting with his pen in his hand and a sheet of blank paper in front of him, and he looks through the window, and there's his father with a spade out in the garden, digging potatoes, and sort of beyond his father he sees his grandfather, and that's what I'm also thinking, except that I've got a fountain pen and this piece of paper; and that profound empathy I felt for Abraam Jonkers; which is why those two men, I insist, are played by the same man. I will not allow a production of this play with three actors. I would go so far as to accept a black actor playing those roles, but only one.

I wanted to ask you about that. Can a black actor play both Author and Buks, as you do?
I think you're going to lose out on some very interesting overtones, because, by virtue of it being a white actor, you make a point, when you see a white actor suddenly say "I'm a coloured man." You're making a point about a common humanity. "I'm a coloured man, I'm a white man, now I'm a coloured man, now I'm a white man." You're doing the one-coin act; these are the two faces of that one human reality.

But you don't lose that if you have a black performer, do you?
No – well, you wouldn't lose that, but what you would then lose out on is the image of an old or aging white man coming together with a young black woman and making a family that you must believe in; and that's a challenge to your perceptions, a challenge to the audience. I've often thought the key word for me in this play is "challenge." Challenge is what Veronica's life is about as she moves through this play, as she takes on its journey through the challenges – the challenge to confront her Oupa, the challenge to confront an uncertain future; or, conversely, the challenge on the part of old Buks, the challenge on the part of the Author, to understand actually who owns the land. So you miss out on a point there, and then the same point when, later on – and this time it's not her grandfather – she confronts the white man and she says, "You will never see me scrubbing." There the political point receives a completely clear statement by virtue of the white man and this young girl. There's a production of *Valley Song* coming up at the La Jolla Playhouse outside San Diego (a theatre I have worked a couple of times), and the director of that production phoned me and said, "Let's talk about a black actor playing the two roles"; and I said, "I wouldn't stop you if you wanted to go along that route, but, just understand what you would be losing, and what you won't have on stage in front of that retirement world of very rich Americans. Just understand that, in an area where also Mexican poverty is just a stone's throw

down the road. Just understand what you want to have on the stage if you do that." .... Actually, I think an element of timidity and cowardice informed me in saying "the same actor," not "the same *white* actor." I think I was trying to avoid political flak. I think I should have gone the whole hog. I don't mind making that absolutely honest admission.

If we think of your word "challenge," and the land issue, and also the idea of you as a sower of words with your pen, can't we think of your theatre as being interventionary, of making a difference? I know it can entertain; but for me it does very much more.
Well, it has to entertain in order to make a difference.

You say very explicitly in the play that this land belongs more to Buks than it will ever belong to me, the white man, but I have the title deeds. Now, nobody is asking you to have a political discussion in the play. But you've limited Buks even so; you've given him just a Standard One education, and a certain way of thinking about the world. What about taking it further?
Let me first of all say that, after Veronica has left the play and I have a moment alone with the audience, I tried to have it as part of the play to examine that issue. It was the only moment where I could do it without interrupting the dramatic movement. I was going to sit down and say, "Okay, now listen, I've raised this land issue, what's it about?" The material that I actually had in the play and then slashed out during the rehearsal period raised the question: does that land belong to Buks, or does it belong to Landman, who was there before Buks's father came to work on it? If you're going to say it wasn't Landman's, then whose was it? How far back do we go? Do we talk then about the first Dutch settlers, who came into this valley and created the village? What about the Bushmen and the Hottentot who were here grazing? Where do you draw the line? What it finally came down to was that I don't know how to deal with that. What I do know is that there is him, and there is me, and this is our reality. And rather than get involved in a self-glorifying exercise in which I indicated that as far as I was concerned he was a partner on my land, and his family will be a partner on this land, I just used the metaphor of finding him in his poverty; which is virtually the way it happened.

What I found in the rehearsal room and then through a first couple of previews in Johannesburg was that the play is really an emotional journey, and to suddenly stop, break an emotional experience, and serve up a chunk of that issue (although maybe I just wasn't doing it well enough) damaged the chemistry. I can remember that after making that little attempt at an excursion into "what is this question of owning the land really about?" – after having done that in front of an audience, and then coming back to what is now the ending, where you've got to imagine that he's following me out onto the land, and the audience clapped – I can't tell you how startling the difference was. It happens every night in the Court theatre, it happened every night in the American theatres, it happened every night in the Market Theatre. When I finally say, "Come!," I hear people go, "Aaah," yes, and, you know what I mean, " Come, that's it! COME."

It would have been too didactic at that point.
I accept as a valid observation, not a criticism, that "Listen, the issue of land is raised, but you don't really come up with an answer to it, do you?" No, of course I don't bloody well come up with an answer to it; the new government hasn't come up with an answer to it yet. My responsibility to you is to make you ask yourself: "Who owns it, do I own it? I got it from my father, my father worked hard, and I work hard, so is it mine? is my responsibility now in this new world to give it away? Is that the way I become a citizen?" You know what I mean?

What you've just said about the process of rehearsal interests me as well because your plays develop quite a lot after the first time they are written down, so that in the case of The Blood Knot, *for instance, the play had developed so far that you allowed me to publish a new script [as* Blood Knot*] in my Oxford edition. I wondered if something similar had been going on with this play. I noticed that Veronica says to her Oupa "You listen to me," after he's criticizing her for fabricating the contents of her letter – a phrase that really shook me with its power – but when I looked at the text, I couldn't find it. Instead, she says, rather plaintively, "You're not listening to me, Oupa."*
Yes, but that is what is played. And now I'll tell you where it came from. This is a very interesting development in terms of the play, and as an example also of how much an author can learn, not knowing what he's got down there on paper, how he needs the experience of both the rehearsal room and the audience exposure to find out. If you had seen the South African production, you would have been startled to see how submissive Veronica was. I don't think you would have heard that line in the South African production. I'm not talking about text, I'm talking about interpretation of the role. The startling experience waiting for me in America was to be in a rehearsal room, with an actress who is really powerful, powerfully equipped, superbly trained and a drivingly ambitious young talent, who dug into that role, and brought to that role questions which showed the limitation of the craft, the limitations of the life experience, of Esmeralda. The American put Veronica on a new level of political awareness. She was as passionate about the new South Africa and about freedom as about her own personal ambition to be a singer. In the South African production, the sense was almost that Veronica's one ambition was to be a good singer, with a few sort of related little questions and

thoughts about what's going on in the country. But what Lisa–Gay Hamilton showed me was how there was this other incredibly energizing and passionate level to Veronica. And now people have said to me, people that have seen both productions, by virtue of what Lisa–Gay did with that role the play became about Veronica. Whereas here it's not a play about her alone, but about the old men as well.

I thought it was a debate. I mean, there were images which moved me one way, and there were images which moved me another.
There is no question about it; that is what I think I was doing. I mean, why did I write those two bloody characters in, why didn't I just have a monologue? It's very challenging for the Veronica character because it's so hugely weighted on the other side.

But she is making the demands. Buks is, too, but they're not nearly as strong, and he's locked in the past, he's got his memories, he's been worrying about them. We are talking about the balance between the characters, and how that is different in different productions. Another thing, though, is the South Africanness. That is something Esmeralda seems to bring to the part herself – the nuances, the gestures; they are very special. You, of course, bring that too ... would you like to say something about yourself as the framing character?
Firstly, it is a story that comes from my life, my experience. Also, I'm actually up there telling the story – I start off telling a story. A lot of people have said, in a very nice way, that it was so marvellous to be told this story – just to be told a story in which my language and my imagination did the work. I start off by saying to you, "Once upon a time, there was ...," and now I've got to end it; no matter what, I've got to end up finally by saying, "They lived happily ever after."

Your theatre work is moving more towards narrative. You always said that what you're doing is telling stories, but you have also been saying that the safest place I can be is inside a story. Is it such a safe place?
What I mean by "safe" is that all the ontological securities come into play when I'm there. I know who I am, because I have mastered a set of tools and I know what I'm doing. The story might itself, at another level, involve me taking dangerous journeys into asking myself questions. When I'm talking to young would-be actors or students, particularly about the rehearsal process, the point I make is that what they must know about the rehearsal room, for it to be creative, is that they must make it – or the director must make it – a safe, dangerous place. They must feel free – sufficiently secure, and trusting of the director's presence and his or her observation and ability to guide – to be able to go in really dangerous directions. It's a strange paradox; like the one in which freedom is found within limits.

This reminds me of what you used to say about working with Yvonne Bryceland. I know you have said that you feel that there's a creative future perhaps with Esmeralda, but is this how you felt with Yvonne?
Absolutely – in the sense that the one quality one just immediately associated with Yvonne, in addition, obviously, to all the craft and skill and talent she had, was the courage. She was brave; and certainly a great actor has to be brave. You've got to be prepared to go to that edge, and camp there, and Yvonne would do it. It's not easy to find the edge, and getting there can sometimes be very, very hard; and your responsibility as a director is to help the brave ones find a route to the edge, so that they can live there.

Esmeralda definitely has that potential. But it's going to depend – and this is where one holds one's breath. I'll certainly look after her as long as she's with me in *Valley Song*. But I know that *Valley Song*'s going to come to an end in June, because I want to return to my life, and then what is there for Esmeralda? Are people back in South Africa going to have the sense and the passion to nurture this young talent? Because it still needs to be nurtured. Are they going to see beyond those pronounced and really exquisitely beautiful Khoi features? Are they going to say: "There's a beautiful Juliet!"? That's the terrible thing about woman actors; it's a life of dependence.

Do you think there's an environment in South African now for more opportunities?
Less so now that Barney [Simon]'s gone, I'm afraid. Because he was the sort of man who could spot a talent like that and then, by virtue of his place in the Market Theatre, would try and nurture and create opportunities. Now there's Mannie Manim; he might go back to the Market, but he's at Wits. If he were to return I'd feel easier about Esmeralda's future, and not just Esmeralda's. He understands what his responsibility in that position would be. Mannie has the vision – he has always had it, that's why I have had a relationship with him. When he was eighteen years old, he pulled the curtain at the Brian Brooke Theatre for the one-and-only performance of *No Good Friday* there. He pulled the curtain at a theatre where it had all been *Irma La Douce* and *Two for the Seesaw*, and then suddenly Brooke made a concession and gave us the theatre one Sunday night. Suddenly, for the first time in his life, Mannie saw South Africa on the stage, and that started him off. That's why our friendship has survived for so long. Mannie has a passion, and a vision.

Are there any other directors and playwrights working [in South Africa] now who make you feel there's a future growing there?

It's very incoherent and muddled and a bit confused at the moment. From having a relatively easy ride on the basis of just being a black writer crying out in pain, suddenly it's come down to good theatre. If you're going to get anywhere in the new South Africa, if you're going to deliver, and get abroad, it's about good theatre. The days of protest theatre have had it; people don't want to know about that any more. So, a lot of young talent in South Africa has been caught on the wrong foot, and they've got to re-adjust their position. If they want a life in theatre, it's still there, but now they've got to start writing plays, not just crying out in anger or pain.

What about women writers?

Well, of course, there are wonderful people like Gcina Mhlophe. And at one point there was the wonderful Fats Dike; but Fats is still part of the old work, like me. I am not aware of any one young woman's voice. But when I'm in the country, unless I'm directing a play, I'm hiding in Port Elizabeth or in the Karoo. I'm a little bit out of touch with the real scene in Johannesburg, although Mannie tries to keep me informed.

What do you think about all these plays and productions that have become available in South Africa, now that the boycott's gone? They won't make people feel: "we can't do this"?

That is why we need them. We've got to understand what good theatre's about. One of the legacies of those years of isolation is that standards in South African theatre are very low. I've found making theatre in South Africa frustrating, because I've been spoilt by the low standards. There have got to be standards. It's a fine young craft in America, it's an even more finely honed craft here in London, where your audiences, having grown up, come to the theatre and, by their very presence, their awareness of theatre, challenge the writer. Writers try to get away with rubbish, but they get found out pretty quickly, and we need South African audiences to start saying "No – this is rubbish." Educating South African audiences is as important as educating our writers, our actors, our technicians and our designers.

When we were playing in *Valley Song* in Johannesburg there was a period of two weeks during which the annual Highveld Schools Festival arranged a series of matinee performances at the Market Theatre, and that coincided with Lisa–Gay being in the country and going down to Nieu-Bethesda to see what that world was all about. So I said to her and to Esmeralda, let's try and go to see some theatre in the evening. We went along to the Civic Theatre, to see one of the early Pieter–Dirk Uys plays, which had got good reviews, and I was so embarrassed. Pieter–Dirk's writing wasn't really so bad – it was the appalling level of crude caricature that was being served up by the actors, in terms of "Capie" accents; and, Christ, the vulgarity of the design! Sitting next to me was Lisa–Gay, and I had spoken very lovingly about Pieter–Dirk .... The rest of the audience was loving it. *Standards.*

The notion of a standard is important, but it can also be limiting. Is it a question of perspective, too – for example, to enable a response to theatre by and about women?
I would like to believe that, independent of one's perspective or where you come from, in assessing the significance of a piece of writing there are certain objective standards in terms of craft and skill.

Take Fats Dike's So What's New?, *where you have four women watching soap operas in the township. These domestic scenes are rated as being less important, less worthy of our attention, because of the subject. Maybe there should be a notion of standards that is more inclusive. In London, the craft is such that even something that's quite a weak script gets such performers, such designs, such theatres, that you feel that, although this play hasn't quite made it yet, it works because of the craft that goes into it. When I first saw David Hare's* A Map of the World *[1983] I thought what's working here is the performers, the design, the theatre technology, but the play itself needs more written into it. On the other hand, of course, a brilliant production can make something work which hasn't been working as well as it might, like your* Place with the Pigs, *done last year in Edinburgh. It was incredible.*
Yes, people have come to me in New York, friends who've seen it, and have just raved about that production by Communicado. Where they used, for the pigs, a little brass ensemble. The young director of that play was in one of our audiences about ten days ago; he introduced himself, and I suddenly realized he was the director of this apparently extraordinary production.

This is interesting to me because, as I see it, Pigs *is the end of a line through your work, an allegorical line from plays like* Dimetos, *in which the internal dynamic is very personal.*
Yes, that's right.

Would you also therefore say that Dimetos, *for example, could also be done again, perhaps in some exciting new way?*
Oh, I would like to think so. I would never return to it myself – but, oh yes; I think *Dimetos* is standing in the wings waiting for its moment. And it's very interesting that one of the thoughts or sets of images that I am mulling over, that I am living with, in terms of what might well be new writing now, involves picking up on that very, very personal thread.

You're obviously brimming with new plays, and it's an amazing thing. But in Valley Song, *the Author says: I don't have the courage to move on in the new world coming ...*

Just being in that village, I know that the new South Africa is going to eventually impact on the lives of those absolutely at the bottom; people in the little location attached to the village. I know that ultimately they're going to be delving into opportunities. At the same time, I can remember when I first came to the village, and there they were playing in the streets, in this incredibly beautiful, almost idyllic little village. But where do you find them now – in the brigadier's shop (because the brigadier is a reality in the village)? No – in front of the video-game machines, and you know what that's doing [to them]; or sitting in front of television. That wonderful oral tradition in the village is passing. The world is changing, and it is a part of me, too.

And yet the changes come, in fact, with the elections, the possibility of more Veronicas leaving that village and doing whatever they want to do, if only they had the material wherewithal to be able to support themselves to leave.

Yes, but I don't know about the world Veronica's going into – I mean, she wants to be Whitney Houston ... well, I know that is reality, and I know there's no stopping the clock. But I cannot avoid, in all honesty to myself, lamenting the passing of what has been very beautiful, very simple, informed with a natural piety. In the last five, six, seven years, having never known about it before, things are coming in ... there were forty years of vicious censorship but also, in terms of one of those incredible paradoxes, a thriving literature – underground sometimes, but a literature. And what is the first thing that happens when censorship goes? Every piece of pornographic filth in the world, and on the Internet, flies into South Africa.

It's a poisoned chalice, the future, isn't it? That's one of the strong things in Valley Song – *this feeling of fear, fear of change, because of what it brings.*

Well, that bloody machine, which I refuse to turn on, is doing terrible damage. People go on about the good things that it does as well, but the harm it does outweighs the good. I know about your world as well, Dennis, and you are feeding everything in that you need to, to neutralize it. But you're not representative of the great majority out there, my friend; neither am I. And what it's going to end up doing is making people powerless, because it's taking away their imaginations. It's making them illiterate – it's becoming a verbal culture instead of a literate culture; and what that means is that power in the world is going to belong to an elite, the elite that reads books. That's the political future, I think.

––––– ᘒ ᘒ –––––

Fatima Dike and the Struggle
An Interview by Marcia Blumberg

ᐊᑳ   London, May 1996

F ATIMA DIKE has written poetry since the early Seventies, when she became involved with the Black Consciousness Movement. In 1975 she was appointed
Assistant Stage Manager at the Space Theatre in Cape Town, and the following year, with
the encouragement of Rob Amato, wrote her first play, *The Sacrifice of Kreli*, which tackled
a significant event in the history of her Xhosa people. The next play, *The First South African* (1977), exposed the pain of racial classification and the inhumanity of the apartheid
system. In 1990, her all-female comedy *So What's New?* offered new possibilities for independent single black South African women. Her 1997 play *Street Walking and Co.*
continued her engagement with gender issues by exploring the dilemmas of young black
women in post-election South Africa. Dike's third play, *Glass House*, premiered in Cape
Town in 1979 and was also staged that year in New York at La Mama Theatre and at the
White Barn Theatre in Connecticut. It places the spotlight on two South African women,
Phumla and Linda, who regard each other as sisters during a period when the political
realities of apartheid set the scene for the tensions that play themselves out in their lives.
Since Phumla's parents work as the maid and chauffeur for Linda's parents, the power-
differentials within the domestic locale and, more importantly, their racial and class
differences within the wider societal structures form sites of struggle. The play is set in the
present, with interstitial flashbacks staging the past and their developing friendship.
During Dike's five-month tenure as Writer-in-Residence at the Open University in 1996,
she revised her original manuscript of *Glass House* and directed this version in Milton
Keynes, with further performances in London at the King's Head and at the Centre for
English Studies, University of London, during the conference. Dike acted Phumla while
Libby Anson performed the role of Linda. This dialogue occurred prior to the perform-
ances while Dike was revising the text, and focuses on the historical and political context
out of which the play emerged.

MB   *Over the years when we have spoken about your work I have been struck
by the way that you write very much from your life. You have lived so
many different aspects of life that you must have an unbelievable bank of experience to draw
on. Is that how you approach your work?*

FD My work is based on truth, but what makes a story more interesting is the mixture of fiction and truth. I manipulate these very same stories the way I want them to be. So that you never know where the fiction starts and where the fiction ends, where the truth starts and the truth ends. And this is the beauty of storytelling. Because when you were a child you grew up in your home and your mom used to tell you bedtime stories, African folklore. If you didn't say "*chosi,*" and so on, my mother wouldn't talk. But before the story begins, you have to say this one magic word, because if you don't you will grow horns. Especially if the story is told during the daytime, because you can't tell bedtime stories in the daytime. So you have got to say "*chosi,*" the magic word. In the daytime, it's the word that stops all the evil fairies from giving you horns because you are telling stories in the daytime. In the evening, you say "I am paying attention, please go on, I want to hear."

What about the truths and experiences that form the context for the play you are revising?
Glass House came out of anger. It was loss of faith in mankind, because, really, in South Africa in the beginning we didn't believe that the government would kill the children, and I feel that's why they used the children in the struggle, in the beginning, as a way to make the government impotent.

In what you thought was a safe way.
Yet the South African government did kill children.

Now you are talking about 1976 in Soweto.
Yes, I came out of that situation. If I was speaking in Xhosa I would say, "*Andinamagama Bandivale U Mlomo,*" "I had no words, I was speechless."

From anger, from bewilderment, or from disbelief?
All of them. At first it was anger; when the anger subsided it was bewilderment; when that went, it was total disbelief. I believed that inside every person there is goodness. And there is one element that God has put inside everyone, it's your conscience. Your conscience never sides with any part of you that is bad; if you do something, your conscience bites. And the things that were happening in South Africa, to me were conscience-killing in that sense.

Because they were so terrible?
Ja. And because I was angry, and I wanted to write Glass House at that moment. I didn't have time to really reflect on my words or the way I saw it. So, in a way, Glass House was a play that was born as a foetus, not a baby.

The Soweto riots occurred in 1976 and you wrote the play in 1979.

When the riots started I was doing *The Sacrifice of Kreli*, so I couldn't write *Glass House* .... I used to be an obsessive worker. I used to write a new play every year in the beginning. In '76, I wrote *The Sacrifice of Kreli*; in '77 I wrote *The First South African*. In '78 I did *The Crafty Tortoise*; in '79, *Glass House*. Then I left South Africa and went to live in America. When I came back from America in November 1983, South Africa was burning and there was just too much violence and what they called theatre was – phew! [*exhales*] for me; so I just sat down.

Can you qualify what you just said – "what they called theatre"? Do you mean protest theatre? Or, what kind of theatre are you talking about that wasn't theatre, in your view?

The kind of protest theatre that was going on at the time had been taken over totally by the struggle, and anybody and everybody just got on the stage and lifted their fists in many, many cases and called it a play. And I was very confused. I have a lot of white friends, and during the struggle it didn't sound right for me to stand on the stage and talk about hating white people, because not all white people were bad. I get upset, too, when people say "Black people are stupid," or "Black people breed." When a person opens his or her mouth and says that ... I don't understand people who talk like that. So it was difficult for me then, during the struggle, to stand on the stage and talk about hating white people and putting white people down. What was wrong was the system – the white system. The white government was wrong. What was wrong, to me, were all these white people who sat back and enjoyed what that system was doing; *that* was wrong.

Because that represents a silent complicity.

Yes. I couldn't stand up on stage and say all white people are bad, but I had problems at the same time, in that there was a system here that catered for white people and those people who were also my friends were gaining from that white system. But, again, those white friends of mine made certain things possible for me at that time which wouldn't have been possible – not that I wanted my life or the lives of black people to be like that. You understand me? No; I didn't want my life to be lived through a white person.

Or in the image of a white person.

Always having to have a white person to get things done – no. But I had those problems: as much as I did not want to stand up and put the white race down as bad, at the same time I had problems, in that there were people, the very same people who were my friends, who were sitting back and living under this system – they were saying that this system was not correct, but they were not doing anything to overthrow the system in any way. So those were my problems during the struggle.

To return to Glass House: *what made you revisit the play?*
When I went back to *Glass House* in 1996, it was very funny. I had read the play two years before, and the first thing that came to me was the writing: it was not right. Something was being said, but it was *not* being said. It was half-born.

You described it as a foetus, not a baby.
Right. You can't describe something that you don't understand to an audience. You see, when '76 happened, I did not understand why some things were happening. And it was close, very close.

And you were very angry. Then that doesn't make for informed writing.
No. I watched the struggle unfold and I understood certain things, the things that I didn't like about what was happening. OK – for instance, in the beginning, there was a very clear-cut and very noble ideal in the struggle. And then I went to live in America. When I came back, things had changed drastically. I remember one day suddenly thinking: "Where is so-and-so?" And I asked these kids at home: "Where's Patso?" You know why I remember Patso? Patso was in the front row on that day on the eleventh of August. I knew Patso when he was a baby. His aunt was my senior in boarding-school; she was the head prefect when I was in Standard Seven and she was in Standard Nine; I know that whole family. I was surprised to see Patso walking in the front row of the struggle on the eleventh of August be-cause he was just a *slapgat donner* of a child – a sweet child who obeyed his parents, went to school and was well behaved – a child like that you wouldn't ex-pect to be a revolutionary. But there was Patso that day, serious, walking, marching in the front row. He was, in fact, holding the banner: "Afrikaans does not educate. It oppresses." There was this sweet child saying, "Actually, I am politi-cized!" Then suddenly, again [*snaps fingers*], "Where's James?" "Who's James?" "James Magwaca was the son of a policeman who was murdered by unknown people in the township." "Ah, James. James left." "James left? Hmmmm." You know, like [*snaps fingers*] – do you understand?

Strange things were happening?
Where were these kids? Kids just disappeared. Then I go to America. One day, I remember, I was in one of these areas where the exiles live, and there was a con-cert and there were two children – I will call them kids because they were about sixteen, fifteen years old – playing bongo drums and singing freedom songs. And I just heard a murmur in the crowd that they had just arrived from home. I said "What do you mean?" So I called these kids and said, "Tell me, what are you doing

here?" They said, "We are in the struggle." *Ja!* I laughed. I said: "What do you know about the struggle?" They said, "No, don't be mistaken, there are kids younger than us, nine years old, we walked to the border with them on foot to Lesotho." Hey! – and then I began to realize: this thing is serious. But when I got back to South Africa, what had happened was totally different. They had skipped the country. Even their parents didn't know.

They were committed to doing whatever they could?
The children were not listening to us any more. My son was standing outside, alone, kicking a ball, in front of the house. As I was cooking, I would look through the window and he would be standing there. Then another boy came, and they were kicking the ball together. Thirty or forty minutes later, another one, and another one. In two hours time there was a whole crowd of them kicking this ball. I didn't take any notice, and then suddenly it was nine o'clock and I thought: "These kids can't be kicking a ball outside." I looked, and they had gone. I don't know when they left. Every time I looked they were kicking the ball. The phone rang at nine thirty and somebody said to me over the phone, "Can you come to Number 11 Mvambo?" And I said, "Why?" "Oh your son is here, he's injured, but don't worry, he is not dead."

So they had been were involved in some march or something ...
They weren't kicking the ball, they were talking about going to a meeting. They were kicking the ball –

– as a ruse?
They were standing in a circle and the ball was being controlled with their feet while they were talking. My problem then was the curfew. It was night-time; the township was in darkness, there were no lights. I had to go to number 11 Mvambo, past a police station, across a field. I put on my black pants, black polo shirt, my black woollen cap. And my mother said, "Who told you that Mpho was injured?" And when that happened, she just said, "Oh, my God!" and started singing a hymn. She was thinking; I was doing. As I left the house she started to shout, "Where are you going?" You know what she meant – "he's gone, you're going, both of you might not come back." I was running down the road. And there was nothing inside but fear and a prayer. I was running and chanting, "Please God, don't let them shoot me." I got to Mvambo. At the point where the two streets meet there was a Casspir with bright lights all over the street. My first instinct was to jump into someone's yard and hide behind the hedge. When I had already jumped and was already behind the hedge I suddenly remembered: "What if they've got dogs?" Finally, when they were gone, I went down Mvambo Street.

There were no lights anywhere. I was looking for number 11, and every time I came close to someone's gate the dogs barked. Suddenly I was in the darkness, frantic. And somebody came up behind me, grabbed me, and put his hand over my mouth. Suddenly a voice in my ear said: "Don't scream, come this way."

Was it somebody from the house looking for you?
Waiting for me. The room was lit with one candle and there were piles of bodies on the floor. I forgot my manners. I didn't say, "Hullo, where's my son?," I just saw the bodies and dived in there and started looking and calling for my son. Someone said: "Don't be mad, you're crazy, come out, your son is not there. Go home." How could I go home when I had just crossed the field with a prayer and fear in my heart? Those are the things I didn't like about the struggle.

How did the struggle develop?
Later on in the Eighties, after 1985, when things began to deteriorate in South Africa, the street-element entered the struggle. Some of them could have been working for the police. They hijacked the struggle. Now I know the comrades, the school-children, I also know the street-element. So when they came into my shop, I just looked at them and I could see: "Ah, so-and-so, since when have you become a comrade?" Because he was a tsotsi who had been pickpocketing and gambling on the street corner yesterday; today he was in the struggle. Those are the things I didn't like about the struggle. They were holding these kids at gunpoint, they would force them to go into all the shops and beg for food and money because they were going to a funeral in Paarl. Once the kids got outside, the street-element fought with the kids and took all the food as well as money to buy drugs and booze.

There were people genuinely involved in the struggle, but did you feel that others abused the struggle?
And this steadily grew so that if you were standing outside and people were marching to protest something – whether it was to the police station because somebody was detained, or whatever – the marchers had a new slogan: "You spectators, when we come back we will get you." You couldn't stand in your yard and watch. In other words, if you were black, you couldn't just be there and say, "No, I'm neutral now." You had to be involved.

Was it their own ground-rules that apparently had nothing to do with the struggle itself or with the right motives for the struggle?
No, the whole point was that you were sitting there watching others go out to fight and die. When freedom comes it is not going to choose those who fought, it is going to be for all.

You're not talking about the street kids now?
No, I'm talking about the whole thing. You had to do something for the struggle or else be known as a sellout. But if you were a person who was genuinely involved ...

You wanted to stand up and be counted.
Exactly. People who meted out punishment to those whom they felt were not part of the struggle were ruthless.

Was that the rash of necklacings?
Exactly. It was mostly the same element. The people were running around with the police at night and then they were holding these kids at gunpoint during the day. When you looked at the whole thing, you just saw the school-kids in the front and the hooligans behind. So, in a way, right through that period, we did not have freedom to do what we wanted. There were people who were artists and supported the struggle by writing banners and doing performances and were never paid. They themselves were compromised by continually being asked to contribute. But even those things were happening because of what the system, the government, was doing to the people. The end result: at the root of it all, the government was there. So, I look at *Glass House* then and now, and I find myself exploring things which perhaps then I could not have been free to explore. Because people would have regarded me as being negative or anti-black.

Or not whole-heartedly and uncritically supportive of the struggle in a way that you are able to be now, at a distance, when you look more objectively; there are always contradictions and complexities.
The same problems that I was experiencing personally are reflected in the characters' situations. Here is Phumla, who grew up with Linda, and you see all the reasons why she is happy that the kids have suddenly gone on the streets to strike, because she went through school and did certain subjects in Afrikaans and they just complained amongst themselves, but it ended there. Thirteen years later, these kids decide, enough is enough. She sits back and looks at herself, and what she sees nauseates her, because she sees herself and her generation as cowards. But then Linda says to her, "Now, wait a minute, you did two subjects in Afrikaans, they were made to do every single thing in Afrikaans, and at least, during your time, you had an education." They don't have an education now. There is nothing for black children in schools. Things have become so extreme that they have reached this point. But still, you look at yourself, being black; you look at these kids: they are black; and you feel nauseated that you didn't do what these kids have done. But then things escalated, got out of hand. And suddenly Phumla finds herself in a unimaginable situation. She lives with a white family. The white man is killed in

her presence. Now her world becomes a dangerous place. The black community are scared that she will tell the police who killed the white man. Nevertheless, the white community expects her to tell the truth. She says something very beautiful: "You know, when you are a sellout your community spits you out." You are like nothing, although you are something because you are a person with life. It's even worse when you know that you have done nothing wrong but, the way the truth about you has been presented to the people, it leaves them without a doubt that you are what they say you are. Everybody knows you, everybody has discussed you, people are even wondering why are you still living in this community after what you have done; why don't you leave? Even small children who are not old enough to join the struggle physically but who can lift their fist and shout "Black Power!" know what you have done. When they see you walking down the street, they say: "There goes sis Phumla, the *impimpi*."

The informer.

Ja. And when a stranger comes into your community and speaks about you this way, they ask: "Why is she still alive, why is she still here with you if she is what you say she is?" And people say, "No, she is no longer the person that she was. Her white masters used her and spat her out and this is what is left. She now lives with her conscience." And in the meantime, you are sitting there, knowing full well that your conscience is clean because truth has a very funny way about it. It may rob, but it will never save. Truth is like a body – you know you kill somebody in the middle of the night, you chuck his body in the river, next week the body rises and floats on top of the water and comes to the shore. You can't throw that body back to the bottom of the river. Truth is like that. So, what makes her survive is that she knows the truth is like that body; it's going to surface one day. And as long as she keeps that light burning inside – that she actually is not guilty – she is able to live with herself.

She can still believe in herself.

Ja. But then something very strange begins to happen to Linda. They were fighting about the way that her father died, and the fact that Phumla is unable to divulge who killed him. When the police decide finally they are sick and tired of this thing, they put her into solitary confinement, they make her go mad. I know people who have said to me, "When I was in solitary confinement a fly came into my cell and I felt good because there was some form of life. But the day the fly flew out of the window of my cell, I cried." So they sent this poor girl to the mental hospital and put her under hypnosis so that she could tell the whole story of how the white man died. And that is why the community said that she sold out. Because, unconsciously, the information was sucked out of her. Linda watches the system breaking Phumla again and she can't stand it, so she gets up and fights the system for Phumla. And now she finds herself being totally interested in the struggle. She meets up with a reporter and decides to go into the township with him. He knows a lot of comrades and he works with them in the townships. And what she sees there fucks her mind up. Sometimes it is surprising when they let an apparent "informer" live, and then suddenly an unlikely candidate is accused. More shocking is the speed with which that person is taken to a kangaroo court and sentenced to death by necklacing – "instant justice." For me, this is madness. Linda comes home and says "This is it. I am leaving. I've had enough of South Africa." And Phumla has one question: "If you leave, where will you go?" She says, "I am white, I can go anywhere I like. Tomorrow I can pack my bags, buy a ticket and get out of this hell-hole which is South Africa." Phumla asks: "But where will you go?" And she says "Anywhere in the world." She says: "When they ask you where do you come from, will you tell them? Will you tell them you come from South Africa? You with your white skin?"

So it never leaves her.

No, they are both prisoners [*laughs*]. Phumla says, "You know something, as long as I am oppressed, you will never be free." That's the real written version of *Glass House*.

Reworking it in 1996, post-election, post-apartheid – so-called – and I say that only because the laws have made it post-apartheid, but the conditions on the ground –

– are still the same. We are all still the same people. We've got racial prejudices like before.

Also, so many millions of people are still materially deprived because unemployment is so high and the gap between rich and poor is so enormous.

To put it nicely, we are now having tea with the aftermath of apartheid.

And the aftermath seems to be taking a long, long time; the contradictions and the problems and the oppressions may not be quite there in the same blatant way as they were under the old system but, in the reality of the everyday, a lot of this is still going on. The play is then as relevant as ever.

But now, because I have seen the full script played out to the end, I understand. I didn't understand – because the script was just being written in '76, '77, '78, '79 – when I wrote that play. But I have had the opportunity to go with South Africa from the beginning to the end.

[Dike's thoughts about future projects expressed at the Conference in August, 1996:]
I want to write about reconciliation. During the struggle, the times taught us how to do things. Now there's no one to teach us how to live with freedom. Many in South Africa don't understand freedom. Many of those black people who encouraged the struggle don't understand about reconciliation and why whites are not being killed. I am concerned about reconciliation. It is a fragile job for black writers. Change is an understanding; peace is here in the heart, and we as black South Africans can use the same power to understand. They wanted the country – they have the country. [But] they have to work to maintain the country. Now, what you fought for was the vote – use the vote; it is the first key. I feel there are basic things that writers should write for. If people feel the government is not giving what they want and worked for, we could be heading for disaster. I want to write a play about reconciliation and the Truth and Reconciliation Commission. Tolstoy wrote about a man who spoke to an angel. The angel said: "If you were not born, a lot of things would not have happened." The angel erased what he did. We have to show that we can make a difference.

More Realities
An Interview with Reza de Wet
by Marcia Blumberg

❧ London, 1 September 1996

P LAYWRIGHT/ACTOR/ACADEMIC REZA DE WET has written two trilogies of Afrikaans plays, the *Vrystaat Trilogie* and *Trits*, separated by two plays in English, *In a Different Light* and *Worm in the Bud*. Her recent plays, directed by Marthinus Basson to critical acclaim, engage in a dialogue with Chekhov: *Drie Susters Twee* [*Three Sisters: Two*] (1997) and *Yelena* (1998). The former won four Vita nominations, received four nominations for the Fleur de Cap, and won the Hertzog Prize, the most prestigious award in Afrikaans literature, for the best script. The State Theatre in Pretoria mounted a new production, directed by Marthinus Basson, of *Drie Susters Twee* [*Three Sisters: Two*]; this ran in tandem with his production of *Yelena* (Reza de Wet's response or sequel to *Uncle Vanya*), which premiered at the National Arts Festival in Grahamstown in July 1998.

MB *How did the idea of a sequel to Chekhov's* Three Sisters *evolve? Why are you writing* Drie Susters: Twee *now?*

RdW When I was about fifteen – I know, because it is written in the front of my collection of Chekhov's plays – I was astonished and deeply moved by it because it seemed so magical and evocative. At the same time, it seemed so familiar; it had the quality of a memory for me. Then later, under Robert Mohr, when I studied drama, I did a lot of Chekhov. He translated Chekhov and was the expert. He never allowed his students to do Chekhov for auditions for PACT [the Performing Arts Council of the Transvaal], but he allowed me to do two pieces and said I was the absolute Chekhovian actress. It seemed to be a total manifestation – in my body, my hands, and my feet. I seemed to feel Chekhov very, very deeply. At Rhodes University I started lecturing on Chekhov, and would become so ecstatic that the students would lose track and just gape at me open-mouthed.

You were transporting them to another world, to Russia at the end of the nineteenth century.
I hope so. More than three years ago, Marthinus Basson, who directed my play *Mirakel*, said by the way: "Why don't you write a sequel to the *Three Sisters?* Because we have lovely actresses here and they would be wonderful." Then we went on to other conversation, but it absolutely stuck in my mind and made complete sense – like an electric shock, in a way. It activated something and I couldn't stop it. Then I started manufacturing stories, but I realized that at all times they were only fictitious and that I would have to wait for the truth. I prepared myself by reading autobiographies by Russians who had survived the Revolution: Paustovsky, the most superb writer, Pasternak (there's a bit of *Dr Zhivago* in the play), a lot of Tolstoy, and everything of Chekhov. I begged Rhodes [University] to let me direct *The Cherry Orchard*, because it was an expensive production. I wanted to get into Chekhov's skin – particularly the last resounding echo of Chekhov. In getting to know that play as I directed it, I realized that it was much lighter than I had ever imagined, and also much sadder. He empathizes with his characters, he is never commenting on them – I understood that very well as I saw his characters in the flesh. Then I waited and nothing happened, and I was really going to give up when, there in the bath, Eureka! This really happened, as if someone came to tell me: "Do you know what happened to the three sisters?" I was told and I knew, all at once. It was such a simple story, and not really what I had wanted to write. There was nothing dramatic – it was matter-of-fact, but it was true. Then I had the best time of my life. The play, in a sense, wrote itself, but it was a matter of being terribly in tune. I didn't want to emulate Chekhov – no one can ever do that, because, I believe, his reality was so peculiarly his own and he never compromised. To write this play truthfully having heard the story, I had to listen to my own music, my own depths, to find my own truth. Then the play happened. It was a musical experience; suddenly I became deeply aware of orchestration. I empathized with the characters more and more deeply. I made no connection with South Africa.

In fact, you were in Russia. In your body and your mind.
By that time I was totally there, but I kept being very weepy about Russia. Suddenly I became very unhappy about the Afrikaans language, because there was talk about not having it in schools, not using it as a medium in Afrikaans schools. So I was weeping about all the people who had started the Afrikaans-language movement when it was not allowed under British rule. Then one day I suddenly made the connection, and I realized that, apart from the spirit of Chekhov, there is a force-field that we share. Beyond that, when I was fifteen I recognized in the for-

lorn quality of his characters that there was a sense that something was irrevocably going to change. At fifteen one is not politically that aware, but there was always talk that the old way of life was passing. I am not talking in political terms; I am talking about a more intimate way of life. For the Russians, their way was also not wrong – it was the way they had lived for such a long time.

For the bourgeoisie it wasn't wrong; but for the serfs it was a different story.
In my grandmother's house, the whole way of life – which goes beyond politics or, rather, is more intimate ... there was always a sense that we were in a period of transition and that even the most intimate, known, and cherished things would disappear. There was no sense of stability. Like the characters who were constantly in a state of flux and yearning for Moscow and something of ultimate value – in that way, I empathized with them. As I was writing the play, I became a little more conscious of it, because although the situation was entirely wrong they were born into it and they were having to go through a very painful process of renouncing the identity that they had been given. The pain of transition, confusion, loss, of being forlorn and everything fragmenting – Tim Huisamen [a colleague at Rhodes] said to me, "Today the Afrikaner is living Chekhov." The empathy I felt for the characters is possibly apparent in the play. I understand the ridiculousness – their obsessiveness; and they are such hypochondriacs – but I understand them because they are just like me. Apart from that, the way they behave, they are very temperamental – that is, in a more personal way, my family. I recognize them much more strongly than in the other plays I wrote.

I would like to return to the parallel with South Africa: things there are in flux?
Certainly they are disintegrating for the Afrikaners.

I think that it is disintegrating for everybody in terms of previous structures. For many black people, unfortunately, the promises and the changes have often not brought improved material conditions.
I know the same happened in the Russian Revolution.

As an Afrikaner, this is an important story for you. How do you see the place of the Afrikaner now?
There's a lot of dislocation and confusion. We are probably in a slight state of dementia or slightly psychotic. Think of the history – first the French [Huguenots] came to the Cape and, as Laurens van der Post has pointed out, the Dutch were not Afrikaners. They were the smallholders, and they were keeping a kitchen garden. The French fled from persecution under the Edict of Nantes and were persecuted at the Cape by the Dutch. Their language was eradicated and there was enormous discrimination against them. There was a slow fight towards establishing their

identity. Then the British came and drove the Afrikaner, who had been a mixture of French and Dutch, out of the Cape Colony, and they founded at last – through hell and damnation, suffering and death – two colonies. Then the British came and took that away. This schizoid state has been perpetuated. Then they started grabbing and holding onto whatever they could – I think that the past few decades have been the expression of a very scared rat-in-the-trap mentality. That's no way of excusing it, but I think that historically one can understand the level of trauma now that the Afrikaner suffers, because the worst nightmare has once again come true. They have been marginalized, they haven't got a place, and [have] been made to feel like fugitives, but there is nowhere to trek. There has been a history of paranoia.

For certain people in South Africa, in fact, the apparently miraculous changeover to the new democracy has been exhilarating. There was a euphoric sense about the process. Do you think there is a stocktaking? For example, as many black people are coming to terms with the continued lack of water and housing, so Afrikaners are realizing in effect what has happened.

There was a sense of euphoria. It was a bloodless revolution, but I think that the exhilaration is past, and the adrenalin rush – but now there is definitely a sense of delayed shock. Something has irrevocably happened. In many ways, everyone's worst fears are being realized. I am afraid to say that there's no sector of the population that is not in a sense traumatized. The black people are traumatized that at last this has happened and it is not good. Economically, they are already much worse off than they were. There is much more crime, and people in the townships are being robbed and killed and raped. Nothing has been gained from the Afrikaner perspective in terms of stabilizing the country and making people happy and giving them a greater sense of security for all the people. Everything has been lost for the Afrikaner – Afrikaans is marginalized, there's chaos, danger, people have lived behind fences, everyone's scared, and the money is worth nothing. All in all, it is really like the aftermath of the Revolution when everyone in Russia was suffering and starting to wonder whether it wasn't better before, even if it was atrociously wrong. That is why the writing of the play was enormously cathartic, because I could express those doubts and fears and the refusal quite to come to terms with it. A lot of Afrikaners do that – glossing over, and still talking the old lingo of being very liberal, being euphoric and looking at the inauguration over and over again.

Do you mean the subtext, what they are really feeling?
Yes, the subtext is really Chekhovian – loss, devastation.

There is another way of looking at it. Chekhov's characters yearn for what was. They don't actively try to find positives in change.
They are incapable of it, of course. But that is peculiarly Chekhov.

Obviously, you are talking about Afrikaners in general. I hear stories or meet people who say it is a new South Africa and who feel an enormous sense of liberation.
There was always social movement. The Afrikaner and the black people have always been terribly close. That is why the bloodless revolution, I believe, could happen. Laurens van der Post says that they are a African tribe. It was always a tribal situation.

Perhaps Afrikaners working on the farm regarded the black people working with them as extended family but they were never social equals.
On a very deep level, many Afrikaners have a 'black' psyche. For van der Post, Africa has seeped into the Afrikaner's soul in a way that no one can really understand who is not Afrikaans. They think these are white people, but it is a tribal situation and could perhaps be dealt with in a different manner. I think that the Afrikaner and the black people understand each other with a strange and immediate recognition. Not all Afrikaners, but the ones that I know well. There is an Africanness – after hundreds of years there is a spirit of the place that transforms your very chemistry. I do yearn back to my childhood, when, without knowing that it was wrong, we lived closely with black people – not only the woman who looked after me, whom I still regard as my mother and still see every year. All the people in my grandmother's house who were doing the ironing, cooking and cleaning – there was enormous love between all of us, immediate intimacy; it was a pre-Eden kind of existence when I wasn't aware and they weren't aware. There was an incredible sense of everyone accepting each other. Of course, my family were terribly kind and there was never abuse of power. I didn't understand it. There was this wonderful sense of safety and security of the rural existence. Going on a Sunday, always, to take Betty back to her house, and having tea with her – true love between all of us. As soon as consciousness came, it caused a rift between us and them. Then the country became more and more dangerous and more and more politicized. I have a yearning for that perfect, undifferentiated, complete equality in a very essential way.

You are speaking about your own situation, and you know how those people in your grandmother's house related to you?
Yes – that is my Chekhovian experience. How the serfs and the landowners were interconnected in a very organic way. From a so-called organic good life, the Russians became aware that there was a lot of injustice and ignorance.

There must have been many people working on farms unlike yours who suffered terrible oppression?
Oh, yes, but I was never aware of it. I write from the experience of that yearning for that idyllic warmth and total love in that house of my grandmother. Apart from the black/white thing, I was also not aware that families lived in torment. It was the Proustian thing, with his mother and him thinking that it was paradise and not being aware, because they were upper-middle-class, of the exploitation of the French peasants. I am, like Chekhov, yearning for a time of simplicity and beauty when there is no awareness. It is really an ancient and archetypal situation: a time of unity, the oneness of the universe. You can't retrospectively become conscious.

Can you tell me more about the play itself?
I wanted to write the four acts because I felt that I wanted to write within a Chekhovian structure. I read all the first acts of all his plays. Then all the second, third, and fourth acts. He actually wrote in a very musical, symphonic way. The first act is quite upbeat and fairly fast, the second act is more languid and slow, the third one is the cathartic act, the fourth is bringing all the strands together and resolving them in a musical way. So I was challenged to do that, and it happened almost by itself. I approached the first act as the beginnings, the arrivals. Then the rest of the play did follow that pattern. So that was very exciting – and the subtext, and the people doing things, two pages later, when they have been harbouring resentments while the other people have been talking. I had to follow, very delicately, the little characters, because Chekhov doesn't create grand complex characters. It was wonderful to understand why that one was quiet for a page – not because they have left the stage, but because they are resentful and it is suddenly going to burst out over nothing.

As spectators we have to work at the subtext.
Chekhov, above all, should be seen in performance.

When will your play be staged?
We are planning, but things are very dislocated in South Africa in those terms.

Do you have specific actors in mind?
Oh, most definitely yes; and I am worried. For the first time I want to be very sure. I feel that I haven't written the play at all – not that Chekhov has written the play, but because it was such a completely organic and joyous experience. This is the largest play I have ever written; it will run about two-and-a-half hours. It is more dense, more controlled. I feel that as a theatre artist I have achieved a greater measure of craft. I feel that I am starting to master it now, and that is so exciting.

I would like to change focus to 1990, when you wrote Worm in the Bud, *one of your English plays. In 1995 you told me stories about your grandmother that informed the play..*
My grandmother, in about 1920, was a teacher. She studied in Grahamstown at the Teaching College and went to teach on a small farm school in the Karoo – quite a desolate part, where *Worm in the Bud* is set. She was quite protected and very anglicized. Being of Afrikaans ancestry in the Eastern Cape, she and her mother and sisters spoke English to each other. She was very insulated, and then she was suddenly exposed to this raw Afrikaans rural life. She had to sleep with four children in the same bed together with bed-lice. She had to go with a donkey to school an hour away. The donkey fell off the bridge and the cart overturned and there were snakes in the schoolroom. She had what you would call a nervous breakdown. Later, her brother, who was a school inspector, encouraged her to sue the school board. She won her court-case and studied further. She was a primary-school teacher but after further education could then teach in a more civilized way. But that experience haunted her forever – how the older son used to peer through the window and look at her while she was undressing. I have never forgotten those stories, but I transposed them. The story [of the play] came to me very suddenly. Also, living in Grahamstown and being treated a bit like a savage. When I was in the English Department I remember the one English Senior Lecturer saying, "Oh, I know another Afrikaner. She is just like you – she is the salt of the earth." This was absolute bigotry.

You don't fit stereotypes of an Afrikaner. But it raises the question of otherness, which is so important to your play.
I experienced it very deeply. I was tolerated as an Afrikaner and regarded very oddly. This was in the 1980s. I was so angry. It is the only play that I have written in anger. I relished the destruction of this poor character, the philanthropist who goes to Africa and tries to enlighten the Boers. I have never been happy with the attitude from the outside world. – people who are not South African and have not had the South African experience and are very wise and very didactic about it, talking totally from outside. I am very deeply irritated by their simplification of the situation. Of course, Emma is typically that. To take her to Africa with her corset, her hat and her gloves, not wanting to touch anything and horrified by the dust. Yet she wants to comment on the Afrikaner, to uplift them. She has the audacity to want to understand them so that there will be lasting peace between the nations. To me this is a comment on all the philanthropists who come from elsewhere for a week or two and then become authorities on the South African situation – a black/white situation. A lot of those angers were expressed in that play but filtered

through a black comic gothic structure so that it doesn't become didactic or offensive. I think, personally, that it is very funny.

I haven't seen the play staged but have read material around it, such as the writings of Emily Hobhouse. You get her turns of phrase amazingly. We are moved back to another era in the mode of expression of the two sisters.

The sister in England is not enlightened. She is the Victorian doll in the gilded cage, constantly pregnant. What a ridiculous situation for her spinster sister to try and enlighten the Afrikaners when she should try and liberate her own sister! I believe that philanthropists are so often projecting their own inner trauma and repressions onto other people. They want to help people outside themselves because they are incapable of facing the dilemmas within themselves. Denial is what happens to this poor character. She can't cope at all.

Regarding the structure of Worm in the Bud *– you have letters and then diary entries, which are in fact letters to oneself.*

Oh, yes. My grandmother kept diaries for forty years. I kept them in a trunk. I can read back to when she was twenty-five. She confessed things in that diary that on the surface I was never aware of. It shocked me terribly when I first saw it. I thought: "Was every day a torment for her?" My grandmother had many nervous breakdowns; she was febrile and neurasthenic. She was almost, in a sense, like the American Southerner – a Blanche [Dubois] character, although a much more mysterious, more alluring woman. An amazing woman; her kind will never be seen again. But she maintained a beautifully harmonious exterior. I was nurtured, and everything worked beautifully. Everything was fragrant and had its place; her house was rich and nourishing. I wasn't aware of her personal sufferings, her doubts and her deep neuroses. She didn't allow them to impinge on us, but she expressed them in her diaries.

Was writing for her an immense process of catharsis?

For me the same. I inherited that from her and never knew, until after her death and after I found her diaries.

Do you keep diaries?

Never. My plays are my diaries.

You use a lot of intertexts in Worm in the Bud. *The title is obviously from* Twelfth Night, *but you also mentioned a book on Victorian sexuality by that name.*

It fascinated and enthralled me – the way the wives had to be like little dolls, and at the same time the men frequented children's brothels. There were hundreds of thousands of children from the age of three, and many brothels around London.

They had these child-wives with little waists and unknowing innocence. Society was very peculiar and repressed. Even the 1820 settlers [from England] and soldiers who came out to fight the border wars [in South Africa] embodied that repression. In fact, there are more lunatic asylums than block-houses or barracks in the Eastern Cape. The African experience shattered that entire repressed Victorian persona; they couldn't cope with it. My great-grandmother was a Welsh settler's daughter who married an Afrikaner. She always wore her corsets, but it was very hot in the Free State. In fact, she didn't want to hear Afrikaans, and called it "that language" and was terrified of it. She was also terrified of black people. She grew English flowers and had a Victorian house and afterwards she became rather demented. Then she started wearing her corsets outside her clothes. She couldn't cope with the African experience and withdrew into a pseudo-Victorian world, totally insulated, in the middle of this town. I have photographs of her house in the middle of the Orange Free State.

Both Worm in the Bud *and* Drie Susters: Twee *are set back in time. Did you purposely choose the Chekhov that inspired you, and the Boer War as a context for the other play, with the realization that they featured similar historical times?*
I was never aware of that, but it is quite true; I must have some form of empathy with that period. My grandmother's childhood was at the turn of the century and her stories about it evoke a complete Eden. She lived in Somerset East at the foot of a mountain. They used to slide down, and there were little springs in the forest. Then, at age sixteen, both her parents died, and the whole family were destroyed by that; but she always spoke to me about an Eden that existed before she was neurotic, before she was tormented, before the world came to an end. Maybe that stuck in my mind as a time when everything was coherent.

What about the other intertexts – the Robert Louis Stevenson and Shelley poems?
I wrote *Worm in the Bud* in a week. It poured out of me almost like a compulsion. About the Stevenson and Shelley poems: I knew at that stage of the play that it was necessary to embody the whole ethic of that time. It was more a musical thing, something for her to cling to almost as a ritual that she could repeat and repeat. Of course, it shows an obsessive, compulsive nature. She has to try and control everything, and she can't. The play was an outpouring – a lot of very deeply felt things that suddenly came out.

What issues were you addressing in particular?
I have never been treated by a black person as 'other' as much as I was treated [so] by the English.

To speak more broadly about your work, what does theatre mean to you?
Theatre, for me, should evoke a different world and transport the audience into a different reality, a heightened reality of some kind or another. From that standpoint, I think that you would view everything differently when you come out of that reality. It is like a cleansing process. Then you can see your own world in a different way. It is as though you have been to another country and then you go back home. The alternative world to which you are transported is the specific and unique vision of that writer or artist. It applies to looking at paintings or reading books. I mean, by "a different world," activating the dream, the imagination. For me, the only reality is the imaginative world, the world that each of us perceives totally differently. If I read Proust I can understand his world utterly – it reflects an incredibly strangely evoked imaginative world; but it is real in his terms.

What about plays that encourage the purging of emotion and a resultant calm – what does that do to spectators, especially in South Africa, a society that needs lots of change?
We are all encased in our own particular reality. The more realities you encounter, the more you expand as a human being, the more heightened your awareness becomes. All forms of art give us that – being released from our own narrow field of experience, from the prison of ourselves, and filling us with awe when we become deadened to the mysterious and the unknowable.

How do you relate as a writer to what is going on in society in terms of people's lives?
I see people as an entire world and am endlessly fascinated by them. I am as curious as a monkey, and people respond to me with stories. I am also filled with awe. I am blessed to have that quality.

There are certain writers – take Caryl Churchill as an example – who set out to write a play that focuses upon certain problems in society. Her plays are often structured in a way that reveals necessary areas of societal change. How do you approach your plays?
I agree with Sam Shepard that a play can never come from an idea, in the sense of: what is this play going to say? It grows from images, fragments, sounds, from your own inner world that you explore. He says that language is not only meaning but the sound that hits the air between the audience and the actor – there is a ritual quality about theatre. What I am exploring is: why is there something rather than nothing (a question that Heidegger asked himself); what is the mystery? I suppose that I have a strong mystical bent. What is the miracle of being, what is every moment revealing? Talking about what is wrong with society is never as interesting for me as: why are we alive? – as immoral as that may be.

You are obviously aware of what is happening in society – you spoke of flux, instability, the sense of loss. Is your approach to work with those feelings rather than to question ways of changing society?

For me, what the play ultimately is, is what Vershinin says when everyone he has ever known and loved is leaving: "It is still a beautiful day. Why am I still so joyous?" He says, "Maybe I will still find out." It is that question that he asks – "Why am I still happy?" – that informs me as a person. Where does the awe come from? In spite of some things, people find moments of pure joy. It is the hope, the capacity for joy, that makes people transcend all limitations. It is often said that Chekhov is negative and pessimistic, but if you see a production of his it always leaves you with a sense of exhilaration. That comes from the artistic structure he creates around the pessimistic givens that transcend those circumstances – it shows joy and creativity, musicality, and the hope without which Chekhov could not set out to write a play. He said when he wrote he enjoyed himself.

You have spoken about the joy you have found in writing this sequel to Chekhov's Three Sisters *and the positive and enthusiastic responses from people who have read the play. Do you know where the work is headed after this?*

I always have an idea of future projects, but I would rather not talk about it now, otherwise there will seem to be an obsessive fascination with Chekhov. I am still stuck with Chekhov, blessed to still have Chekhov around. I want to work now on a different play in a different way.

"God is in the details"
An Interview with Janet Suzman
by Dennis Walder

∞ London, 20 June 1997

P ROMINENT PERFORMER/DIRECTOR JANET SUZMAN has always main-
tained close links with South Africa, in particular with the Market Theatre, despite
having left the country in the late Fifties. Shortly before the Conference, her co-adaptation
(with Gcina Mhlophe) of a Market Theatre production of Brecht's *The Good Person of
Szechuan* with an all-black cast was premiered at the National Arts Festival in Grahamstown as *The Good Woman of Sharkville*. This updated and re-sited version of Brecht's play
marked another milestone in her long involvement with South African theatre: as a performer (in Fugard's *Hello and Goodbye* in 1973 and his *Boesman and Lena* in 1984, for
example), a director (of a South African *Othello*, with John Kani in the title role, in 1987),
and as an adaptor of classic European plays, such as the Brecht and, most recently, an acclaimed version of *The Cherry Orchard* set in the Free State (from an adaptation by Roger
Martin). She has said that she and Barney Simon had long ago discussed the possibility of
repointing the politics of Chekhov's play in the light of a new order in South Africa.

D W *I would like to ask you some general questions, and then turn to your
Chekhov production, currently on in Birmingham . Where do you see
South African theatre going today?*

J S I think the most important thing is that black writers should write, and
that whatever mode of theatre-making is the most attractive and suitable for South Africans today must be pursued, with vigour and enjoyment. It may
be improvisatory, as it has been in the past, as with most of the famous plays that
came out during the old regime, such as *Asinamali!*, and *Sizwe Bansi is Dead*, and
The Island most particularly, I suppose – but that had a very interesting other
agenda, based on *Antigone*, which is where my agenda also sneaks in. But the big
difficulty is the language. One of the reasons why Britain has this incomparable
dramatic tradition is that it has this elastic language, and it's the sole language.
From Chaucer onwards, its efflorescence has been the wonderful ingredient.

But English is used in South Africa, too, and used for the theatre as well, isn't it?
Obviously; but what I'm saying is that acting in a second language is a very, very difficult thing to do. English is the lingua franca, the language that can cross all the linguistic boundaries. But there might be a really major playwright lurking in the wings who will want to write his first play in Sotho or Tswana or Zulu, and then it'll have to be translated, rather as Chekhov has to be. But I think it's important that people should write in their own language first – as André Brink does; he writes in his language, and then translates it as he sees fit. But I think that is one of the conundrums of South African theatre: for theatre to flourish, it needs to be the expression of the nation, and since our nation is polyglot, up to now we've had polyglot theatre, and it doesn't give it a clear stream; it makes it very diverse and very interesting, but it also messes it up in some ways. With English, I think there's just no contest; it has to be the going language.

Do you think there's been any problem about the kind of tradition that English-language theatre has created for South African theatre-makers? It's actually quite a limited tradition, from, say, the 1830s, 1840s onwards, since when South African literature has always had to look abroad for quality. Isn't that a problem about using English – that English in South Africa has been infected by a kind of inferiority complex?
Not exactly. I don't want to sound snobbish, but when I grew up it was – apart from one visit I recall the old Old Vic Company making with Irene Worth, luminaries of that stature, who came and did *Midsummer Night's Dream* and work like that – apart from that, it was Brian Brooke and Toby Kushlick; staunchly middle-class companies, who imported English lower-brow stuff. It was left to campuses and to the curious to raise the level. Meanwhile, theatre never got to the black population; theatre is not endemic in South Africa. It's really different from the old Soviet Union, which had a very deeply embedded culture of some kind already. But the same sort of thing is happening today in Russia as in South Africa –once the enemy has gone, what the hell do you write about, how do you redirect your thoughts in order to address present-day problems? You have to look in your own back yard, rather in the way the Australian film industry did for its material: there was this wonderful burst of creative energy when they started looking at their own stories. So, I would say it's terribly crucial that South Africa looks at its own stories and stops importing. I don't think English theatre can teach us much. What I think *can* teach us something is the great classics; you can always learn from great art.

It's part of its definition. That's what makes it a classic: it continues to teach you something.

Yes, it continues to illuminate, wherever you are – not teach, so much as illuminate the human condition. Because, you know, human beings don't change, and probably the circumstances they find themselves in don't change, but the means by which you express human dilemmas and agonies do change.

Is it also a question of what one defines as theatre? I would say there has been theatre in South Africa for a long time, but it hasn't been theatre in a building with audiences in the European sense, which of course goes back a long way in Europe. But there are other forms, aren't there? Which can be and have been drawn on by many theatre-makers like Fugard, Ngema and others. Doesn't it depend on how one defines theatre in the first place?

I don't think it's definable. A visitor to the West End will understand it one way, and an experimental group in Brixton will understand it another way. Theatre is nothing but a forum where people gather, to have a lot of entertaining stuff thrown at them, and to participate in it. The point about theatre is that you go, at a specific time, to a specific space – whether it's outside or in a back yard doesn't matter – in order to participate in some live event, with words. That's all. Whatever form it takes.

There is also some kind of representation, isn't there? That is its agenda. One of the things about theatre that distinguishes it from TV, for example, is that it is metaphoric, it is representational in some way.

That's probably right – only, the words muck us up a bit. You could say that a sitcom represents a normal family at work and play, but it represents it without the other agenda; it represents it as a slice of life. What theatre does – and I think you're right in this – is that it's more emblematic and, indeed, metaphoric. Because, when you come out of a play, whatever form it has taken, the first thing you're trying to work out is: what was that really about? So it's almost as if the play is in code: you hear the words, they seem everyday, but they are emblematic of something else – some malaise, or some problem in society. Theatre represents something larger than itself. That's why theatre continues to fascinate people, because people like a little bit of a crossword puzzle. Real theatre-goers like sitting there thinking: what is it about? even if it's in iambic pentameters. What is *Hamlet* about? Well, it has puzzled people for the last four hundred and fifty years. The story-line on its own would be yawn-making; so would that of *The Cherry Orchard.*

What are the stories in South Africa that are waiting to be told? Are they for other people to tell? Or is that part of your agenda?

I'm in a funny interim period now, where the idea of transposing a couple of classics, a Brecht and a Chekhov, to a more local scenario has absolutely engrossed me. But this phase might pass [*laughter*], and were I to do something South African, I would really like to be there. I think you have to be there, and sniff around for those stories, which are lying about everywhere.

It is fascinating that in this phase, this moment of post-election, pre-revolution South Africa – as Roger Martin calls it, a moment in which he felt his version of Chekhov belonged – in this moment you have felt that the thing you want to do is to take the classics from the Western past and transpose them. What's very interesting is that other people have had exactly the same urge – William Kentridge, for example.

Yes, I'm by no means an original in this field. It stares you in the face that a great idea can be recycled, can be re-used and rethought.

But why now?

I think that after the shock of democracy, the shock of the removal of fear, and after the shock of not being able to bunch your fist at some fiend – that hand has to relax, and pick up a pen, and now what do you write about? The plays that I specifically have chosen seem to be a sort of interim measure, that's all. I'm just a sort of a stop-gap, and all I can bring is my passion for the theatre and my knowledge of the classics, because I've been engaged with them for so long, here. All that is useful, nothing more. I'm praying that, even as we speak, somebody sitting in Khayelitsha or Soweto is feverishly covering blank pieces of paper with his or her ideas, and they're coming out with dialogue, in characters' mouths – that would be thrilling. When Chekhov wrote *The Cherry Orchard*, he was dreaming of the new world-order at that time, and when his play first went on, people in the audience would have had the same secretive excitement in their bellies as they watched, that sense of forbidden dreaming, in 1901 or 1902, I would imagine – similar to what a South African audience might have felt when they watched our agitprop plays during the dark years. One of the reasons I did Chekhov is that when it is done in England it's all so bloody traditional, it all becomes a rather English, class-laden exercise; all the political philosophizing that Chekhov obviously felt really strongly about becomes quaint and distanced. We can view it with a certain sense of irony now, because not only did Chekhov dream of revolution, but that revolution came and then went; so there's a double somersault there. Those pre-revolutionary maunderings from Trofimov the eternal student are seen through a sort of historical prism. And I was so intrigued by the idea: what if Chekhov was bang in the present?

What role did the Roger Martin version have?

Roger Martin was a British actor, who, like a lot of people here with a kind of modicum of political sense, simply fell in love with the events taking place in South Africa, because it was so exciting, so thrilling. He conceived the idea, not knowing that it was very much in the forefront of a lot of other people's minds, and he came to me with his draft of *The Cherry Orchard* transposed to South Africa. He came to me because – remember how a good English teacher would say to you, "Write about what you know"? What Roger was finding was that, never having been to South Africa, not being a South African, he was in deep water. South African speech-patterns and nuances are quite beyond somebody who's not part of it. He instigated the idea, but it became absolutely clear to me that I had to take it on to make it speak. A play is dialogue, and therefore it speaks, it's a verbal medium, and unless the dialogue lifts off the page you don't have a play; what you have is a thesis. Roger wrote a very well-intentioned thesis, but it wasn't living. I was in the end forced to take it over and write the version that you saw. I have the greatest respect for him, but you can't expect somebody to reproduce on the page the expressions, the polyglottisms, the amusing things, when they haven't been there. And humour always gets to the core of a psyche, you know, or a national psyche.

So you wrote the dialogue, or at least much of it?
I wrote all of it.

Which means that, for example, you rewrote the remark that's made to Chekhov's Trofimov in Act Three, when Ranyevskaya says something like "Why haven't you got a mistress at your age?" You made it "Are you gay?" Why? Questioning his sexuality from another direction?
One mustn't get too ponderous about this. In the action of the play, it's an off-the-cuff tease, and, of course, baldly on the page you may say, yes, she's questioning his sexuality, but actually she's not. What she's doing is teasing him, she's playing the coquette. And whereas to have a mistress is an essentially sophisticated European question and therefore quite proper in the francophone upper-middle classes of Chekhov's Russia, I had to find an equivalent that would suit a young black radical. The young black radical would be really enraged if an older white woman teased him as lightly as a wasp sting. That was the aim: to get him off in a wild temper, because that's what the dynamic of the play requires. If she had said, "Haven't you got a mistress yet?," he would have said "What? What are you talking about – what does that mean?" African men have them, but that's not the right word, in South African Speak. It was necessary to allow that young man to storm off, so that he could be brought on with a lot of laughter and teasing by the two girls thereafter; so that there could be a reconciliation between them.

It is still a very interesting kind of tease in a context where attitudes towards sexuality are changing, as towards everything else. Traditional attitudes are not what they were, even if they are still there.

Well, remember this: this is the first play I've come across in South Africa which is entirely rural. All the other plays are cosmopolitan – *Faustus, Woyzeck*, and all the agitprop plays. Apart from *The Island*, which was set in a prison and therefore has its own special agenda, they're all urban, Jo'burg plays, or straight off the streets of Soweto or one of the other urban sprawls.

With a few exceptions like Fatima Dike's first play, The Sacrifice of Kreli.
Yes, but the point about this play is that it's set in this rural nowhere.

Well, it's a South African nowhere.
Chekhov always set his plays in Russia. There's that sense of isolation and space which allow certain agendas to be followed. This young man, Thekiso – he's been sent round the world, for MKZ [Umkhonto we Sizwe] or ANC (it's not quite speci-fied); that doesn't mean he's a cosmopolitan, it doesn't mean he's got the sophistication that Lebaka has acquired, so her throwing that it at him as a little *bonne bouche* [tasty morsel] means that his natural African manhood is suddenly insulted; whereas a young urban man who's used to the growing gay culture in urban Johannesburg/Soweto, would have taken it quite differently. "You joking, man," he might have said. There are some in-jokes too: in Act Four when he makes that wonderful little joke, "I even got to Moscow" – a direct quote from *Three Sisters* – he says that because he speaks Russian in the play. At the end of Act One, he speaks a little poem to Anna, in Russian, because he learnt Russian; and that hat of his – he says, "I need it like a hole in the head, but I like it, it brings back memo-ries," and obviously he had a Russian girlfriend when he was in Moscow; then in Act Four, he puts on the hat, and he says, in Russian, "Would you like to buy some filthy drugs?" – becoming a little mafioso for a second. It gives our Trofimov, our Thekiso, another dimension; a Russian dimension.

One of the wonderful things I noticed about the production (which I think also reflects on what Chekhov did) is the sense of it being a group play, not just focusing on one or even two or three characters.
The structure of the play is symphonic. The Chekhov is an overwhelming master-piece, quite awe-inspiring, when you start dissecting and refashioning it. He produces themes, and then another section of the orchestra comes in, and that theme is later picked up by another series of instruments and developed further, and then you come back to the dominant tune; and so it goes on, in an ever more symphonic way. In rewriting this, and finding my way through its complexities, I realized that Chekhov, like all very great playwrights, gives everybody a say. But the central starting-point for me was the bookcase. In Act One, he has Gayev making a speech to that bookcase, on how important it has been in all their lives,

because within it are works of literature which have inspired them over a hundred years. That bookcase became emblematic to me of a household in which freedom of speech and being able to pick up books was the order of the day – in other words, a place of inspiration as well as education. This was the device whereby everybody could be part of the very liberalizing influence in the house. I've cut out rather over-written speeches about the kind of books they had, but they would have been a pretty wide range – philosophy, economics, all the subjects that emerging minds would have been thrilled to pick up and dip into. If we remember it as a rural place, then here was this room in which anybody was welcome to pick up whatever book they wanted to, and to have it roundly discussed. You know that a lot of discussions took place in that room, till far into the night, and there are allusions to that, as when Thekiso comes back into the room and says he remembers the talks that went on into the early wee hours, with the dead Rademeyer (who I see almost in a dramatic sense as like a General Gabler in *Hedda*). His dead presence remains, a source of inspiration.

That's also a metaphor for South Africa as a place – isolated, but where there are certain people who have maintained the best from the past, from traditions which apartheid tried to stamp on and exclude, but which bring other problems in the present. Now there's a kind of freedom and yet, by the end of the play, the books are being packed up, taken away. What did that signal for you in terms of what was happening in South Africa?

The best of European literature might have been in those bookshelves, and that clearing away connects with what we were touching on before about how it's not necessarily the European way that is going to inspire people in South Africa. The empty bookshelves will fill up with their works. There's a point in Act Three when the young man says to Lulu, "Let's get rid of this nostalgia." In the end, they do feel the sense of a burden being taken off them, which I think white South Africa has felt, post-election. We felt that guilty burden of pedagogy and political consciousness being lifted from us. At the moment, an awful lot of white people just don't want to know any more; it's as if they've been traumatized, and it might take many years before they come outside their own front doors and sniff the air of South Africa and say, "Yes, I really want to be part of this new nation." But at the moment they're sort of closing off. And I think the decision that the white family takes brings relief. Chekhov actually has that in the original, too: once you make a decision there's a sense of relief about it. The clearing of that room of everything that made up that island of a household, wonderful though it was in its day and good though it did, it's past its sell-by date, and of course that is the central metaphor – the cherry orchard no longer bearing fruit; it has blossoms, and as Lebaka says, "You can't eat blossoms, damn it!" There has to be some pragmatism entering our lives now about what is useful rather than beautiful. The great collectors of Europe would collect things simply because they found them quite beautiful. Gardens were made simply because they were beautiful. Things in themselves – essentially an aristocratic European idea of what beauty is and how it should be cherished.

And that also implies a whole supporting social structure.
Right – and I think the the black element in the play is saying: that's gone now – let's see what works. There's a central debate about uselessness and usefulness.

My impression of the play's impact was that it made you think in a context of debates, not in terms of just one position that you then either accept or oppose, but in terms of debates going on. I think that is a very accurate reflection also of what's happening in South Africa at the moment.
Yes, I think so; it is a debating sort of a country. That's why I thought it important to put in that feeling of the restoration of the land being attempted now. That restoration is a very important element added to Chekhov's idea, which was simpler and therefore maybe better, I don't know, but which was for the peasant Lopakhin to achieve something he could never dream of achieving, and money gave him that power. This version addresses South Africa rather more directly. I think it also made it clear to a British audience that there were restorative feelings.

How might you want to revise it for the South African audience?
Well, I think a play like this is a living thing, and I will be fascinated to do it in South Africa, because there will be nuances that are picked up by a South African audience that couldn't possibly be picked up here. For instance, that tiny little encounter when the neighbour Pickford says, "Ah, a little bit of affirmative action," and Guyver says he hadn't thought of it in those "politically correct" terms, but that's in fact what he wanted to do: train up somebody to be able to manage an estate. A South African audience would immediately plug in to what affirmative action and its connotations are, while it is not something that a British person meets every day, it's not part of their life.

There are many little details like that in the play that will probably come more alive with a South African audience. Also, I can take shorter cuts: I think there are parts of Thekiso's speeches in Act Two which I can de-polemicize. It's a question of the audience's knowledge as much as the character's knowledge. In South Africa, the arrival of the stranger means something different, too – the sense of unease that comes on with him. That stranger was the one representative of the silent masses out there that walked into this almost fairy-tale place. Chekhov's invention was unbelievably useful – that passer-by upsets the apple cart, for a small moment. But, of course, that's also very African; Fugard always describes how you could be on an empty road in the middle of nowhere and there's always somebody walking by the side of the road. Where they've come from, and where they're going to, we will never know. That transposes well from the Russian scenario to an African one, because Russia too is full of wandering holy men who travel the length and breadth of the country. Distance is so gigantic, like at the end of *The Three Sisters*, when they say, "Goodbye, we'll never see you again," and you realize they're going from near Moscow to near Asia, a whole continent away, which is why they'll never see each other. That's when the play can't work in England, where you don't have that sense of terrestrial dimension, something Africa certainly has.... That stranger is a wonderful theatrical device: for a moment everything is uneased, nobody knows if he's drunk or he's serious, if he's going to attack them, if he's dangerous; but certainly he's frightening, he's a reminder of what's out there.

The crucial difference is that, in Russia, everybody spoke Russian. In that sense, there was no dysfunction between masters and servants. When you transpose it to South Africa, you have this instant problem of who speaks to whom in what; what language do the black people speak between themselves? On stage you have to find a device for them speaking English. Which is why I have Nyatso, the young valet, being the frightful snob he's turned into, refusing to speak anything else but English – "English is the language of technology, man." This is another South African problem – of people who have gone overseas and become changed by that, and find it almost impossible to go back. Going back is a very difficult thing anyway, and I think that's another theme among the exiles who want to return. Nyatso represents them; he has grown out of his home, doesn't even want to see his mother, and can't wait to get back to Europe. And so the maid Dikeledi has to speak to him in English. It's a very useful device, which allows all the black characters to speak English. But, in any case, English is the fashionable language now for young blacks.

You have them speaking Sotho at the beginning, though, don't you?
Well, on the basis that, when Dikeledi gets that fright because she doesn't know Lebaka is in the room, she lets forth a stream of invective in Sotho; and that immediately places her as a young country girl. It does several things; it places us as an audience in relation to her, we either understand her or we don't – and on the whole we don't. In South Africa as well as Britain.

Could I change gear and ask you about your work with the group, with the performers? I wondered first of all why you chose who you did. It's an extraordinary and interesting mixture of black British performers and South Africans of different races and origins.

Well, the black British performers – whom I greatly respect – were in a sense
foisted on me by the exigencies of British Equity. My dream has been to have an
all-South-African cast; and, of course, John Kani is born to play the part of the
butler – and he will be playing it in South Africa – the Burt Caesar part. I think the
most interesting thing for me was the yawning division between black British actors and black South African actors. As I saw the black British actors struggling to
re-africanize themselves, in the presence of youngsters from South Africa, it became a really fascinating tussle, as the British Caribbean actors tried to rediscover
their roots, in intonation and body-language. Although the black British actors
were as English – if you like – as the white actors, they felt this terrific pull towards their skin colour, and therefore towards the South African actors, so there
was some conflict, which the cast itself went through as well. This was inevitable,
because it is the kind of play that digs quite deep, into what it is you value and how
you'd like to say it vis-à-vis many things, but chiefly colour. The play became, in
its new context, an essay about colour; it crops up again and again. The daughter
Varya in the original, Chekhov simply says, is adopted, but he doesn't bother to
explain. No explanation belonged to genius, but since I'm not, a certain explanation became requisite. It seemed very important that coloureds were represented in
that rainbow array on stage, which provokes a series of arguments that of course
don't exist in the Chekhov. And so, in Act Two, when Lulu says "Come on, why
don't you marry Maria, she's a good girl, what's stopping you?" he says, "Well, I
don't know," and Lulu says, "You know you're of the same blood, her mother was
Sotho," and Lebaka says, "Not quite, her father was – " and Lulu says, "– Was
white, did you say?" and at the end of that speech she asks, "Does her colour matter to you, does it?" And there's silence. I thought that was legitimately bringing up
the all-pervading obsession with colour that exists in South Africa. Also, the Ro-
meo-and-Juliet element of the play seemed to me important, because it happens;
it's the going thing. I kept on bringing up Desdemona's deposition in the trial
scene in *Othello*, where she says "I saw Othello's visage in his mind," one of the
great lines of Shakespeare and one of the reasons why I did the play in 1987.
There are people who cannot bear to allow colour to be the arbiter of the way they
conduct their lives, and certainly for our young Anna, the fledgling student sitting
at the feet of this more sophisticated politico, there was no colour-problem. To her
it was an exciting gateway into the new South Africa, and a new life. But the
adopted Maria has a more contained, more cautious nature. The colour discussion
begins right in Act One with the conversation between the two girls – when she
says, "Maybe we're the rainbow nation, but people still have these problems with
colour" – and that somersaults into Act Three, when Khokoloho says to her: "What

are you? You're nothing. You're not black and you're not white. What are you? Maybe nothing," and she explodes, and says: "How dare you! Get out, get out! This is my father's house," and starts chasing him.

Did you also feel that the performers were coming from different acting traditions which were difficult to put together?

Yes, very much so. The British acting tradition is often very expert, but it is also rather stultifying. There's an expertise with words and the use of language, but there isn't the same untrammelled naturalism, and truthfulness, that you have with the South Africans. I frankly think that the South African actors taught the British actors quite a lot. The stage is at its most luminous when people are untrammelled by evident technique, and from that point of view the South African contingent, specifically those four youngsters, actually made the play happen. You know you could say to a British actor, "Use that word," and they'd know what you mean. With a young South African actor, you'd try a million ways to urge them to glow a word up for the meaning. But what they did have is absolute integrity, and that was terrific.

It reflects a poverty of drama schools and training, but it also reflects talent and drive and motivation. How did you choose them?

Three of those four had been to drama school. The Pretoria Technikon, UCT and Wits. Sello Motloung, though, has not, but he's an absolutely natural actor, the most instinctive actor I've come across in years. I auditioned in South Africa; I was there in October 1996 to revive the Brecht [*Sharkville*] which is coming over to the West Yorkshire Playhouse in October 1997, and certain replacements had to take place in the casting, so I auditioned for *The Cherry Orchard* at the same time. I knew Esmeralda Bihl because I'd seen her in *Valley Song* at the Royal Court, and I knew that she was going to be absolutely perfect for Maria. Moshidi Motshegwa [Dikeledi] was also known to me because I'd seen her in *Marabi*, here at Stratford East. Fana Mokoena [Thekiso] was quite new to me, and I think he's very impressive. So it was specifically those three I cast in the Chekhov. All of them have said at one time or another that there is not much choice in South Africa – there's the odd sitcom, plays here and plays there; but it's the same all over the world, good actors don't get that much good stuff to get their teeth into. The great reason for doing the classics is that it's the most expanding and exciting thing in the world to play something bigger than yourself. The whole idea of apprenticeship in acting is very unfashionable these days, but that's how actors grow – by being in plays that have been done by other people many times over in different ways. I remember one of my first days at drama school, the principal saying, "it's better to play *King Lear* in Scunthorpe than never to have played it at all."

Do you think there are no South African plays that have the stature for performers to learn from?

No, I'd never say that. We've been through an impoverishing time; the Windy Brow and the Civic, and the Baxter in Cape Town have had some lovely things, but they're few and far between. The Market is trying to find its feet again; it should be like the Royal Court, and encourage young writers and experimental productions. Thank God it has now got a subsidy. But it's thirty years behind when British theatre was subsidized. Subsidy is necessary: we have to have the right to fail. Theatre can grow only by failing.

You mentioned The Good Woman of Sharkville. *Did you feel it was successful in its politics?*

Bloody South Africans always talk in terms of politics, and it becomes a little irritating. Brecht wrote a parable-play. There's a fairy-tale element to theatre which has got to be grasped. The great mistake is to say it isn't like life. There's no such thing as authenticity on the stage: it's emblematic, metaphoric, and it's all the things we talked about at the beginning of our conversation. Unfortunately, because of the kind of diet that is mostly coughed up, all those poor plays that we saw during the dark years, with the tin shanty and the shitty clothes and the poverty – I thought if I saw another piece of corrugated iron, and another cracked enamel mug, I would scream. Theatre doesn't need that. Brecht chose Szechuan, in dim, distant, mythological, magical China. In 1938 we didn't know China, whereas of course China is now open to us, and we know that Szechuan exists. My production was deliberately non-realistic, deliberately fabled. You're not seeing realism, you're seeing a discussion about realism. A lot of incipient theatre-goers need to get their minds around the fact that the theatre is not simple representation, it is not realism; the best theatre is not realism. There was a whole period when we took kitchen-sink plays – you know, *Look Back in Anger* with real ironing-boards. All that makes you feel comfortable, because you recognize it. But I would say that the most achieved play of Athol Fugard's is *Boesman and Lena*, which is set nowhere.

There is corrugated iron   although, of course, it is also more than just a piece of realist design.

You can set *Boesman and Lena* just in a space; that's what it's about. But I think we have come to one of the most important things: the question of design, the visual fulfilment of a dramatic idea. I would like to see more young black designers, I would like to see the visual element of theatre being addressed – not just as a textual element, but how you visually make a metaphor. In Britain and Europe, they are immensely sophisticated about design. The impact of a visual on the stage is just as serviceable to a play as the verbal, and I think you have to be very visual, because you're competing with television and film. There's not a single person in Jo'burg who isn't addicted, as the rest of the world is, to the visuals that they switch on by the flick of a button every night.

Visuals are also a way of communicating across language, which in the South African situation is also very important.

And this is where modern art of the twentieth century is very important to us. I mean, Brecht was the first one to explode the idea that theatre was a place of realism. Fuck it, he said, let's show the lights! We're in the theatre, we're not pretending to be in somebody's drawing room. He couldn't bear all that *haut-bourgeois* feeling that you went to the theatre in tie and tails, and saw a representation of your own drawing-room on the stage. The theatre's great power is its non-literalness. If a South African audience falls into the trap of saying, "But we don't know these people, we don't recognize them," they're missing the point – the point is that these people are anomalous, they're not the two-dimensional sitcom people who live next door. In Chekhov's Russia they're unusual, so why shouldn't they be in the South African context?

That makes me think of how, when seeing the play today, you realize that although there are parallels there are also differences – differences which make you aware of the present.

This is one of the things we look at in updating. What is requisite is a newspaper in the rehearsal room. To see if certain absolutely current ideas can't be injected by a character, but only if it serves the play, not so that it becomes a *Sizwe Bansi* exercise, where the entire structure of the play rested on today's news, or like Pieter–Dirk Uys's work. There are certain universals which are addressed in the play, which I don't think are endangered by its non-currency. The ideas of stability, crime, colour, the fear a lot of whites have about change – all these things are discussed in the play and I think they'll still be current next year.

The past is present in very important ways in the play, too. The collective history – at the moment when everyone hears that sound, which they speculate is a collapsing mine-shaft. On one level, it does frighten you; the audience shares their fear of structural change, since mining was the basis of the whole economy.

And what it provokes is the great line from Chekhov, when the old retainer Firs (or Putswa in my version), says, "It was like that before the troubles," and Gayev says to him: "What troubles?" and he says: "The freedom." Chekhov's talking about the freedom of the serfs, but the phraseology works brilliantly in this play, where young Thekiso then says "Oh, God." Why? Because you can't change old people. What I like about the play is this generational feel, the age-spectrum is wide, and the attitudes to "the freedom" are all different. So I think that's quite embracing.

It also embraces the Afrikaner, in what you did with Karlotta, or Charlotta the half-German governess in the original – an oddity in Russia, which was very wary of German culture at the time, as you can see from Turgenev's work; but here you have her as an Afrikaans woman who does magic and seems odd, but then also very moving in that moment when she addresses her identity card; and the whole issue of identity in the politics of South Africa today is brought to the fore, particularly for Afrikaners now.

Absolutely. I thought she would represent the sense of a loss of identity now, culminating in her asking for a job from the black man at the end. The irony is there. And what a South African will pick up is that right at the end of the play Maria is asked where she's going, and she says to the Cape, and the response is: "Oh, I think you'll like it there, I think it'll suit you." That has a resonance which of course couldn't be picked up by a British audience; it is where the majority of coloureds would be. And the stranger also says: "Who's this little Hotnot cherrie?" – but the racial insult would be missed here. It is all in the detail; it is those details which count, since God is in the details.

———— ೞ ೦ ————

Works Cited

AFRICAN NATIONAL CONGRESS. *The Reconstruction and Development Programme: A Policy Framework.* Johannesburg: Umanya, 1994.

ALEXANDER, Neville. *Robben Island Prison Dossier: 1964–1974.* Rondebosch: U of the Cape P, 1996.

AMMICHT, Marion. "Doktor Faustus im Aufwind des Propellers," *Süddeutsche Zeitung* (September 19, 1995): 16.

ANGOVE, Colleen. "Alternative Theatre: Reflecting a Multi-Racial South African Society?," *Theatre Research International* 17 (1992): 39–45.

ANON. "AIDS Message 'Not Effective'," *Cape Times* (March 11, 1996): 1.

——. "Bus-truck Tour for *Sarafina 2*," *The Citizen* (November 3, 1995): 23.

——. "Fugard's Treaty for the Warring Sexes," *New York Times* (January 26, 1992): H 1, 23.

——. "Mbongeni Ngema, Director of Musical Theatre, NAPAC," *Tribute* (March 1996): 10.

——. "Parties Claim It's a Cover-up," *City Press* (March 3, 1996): 1–2.

——. "Plays not anti-SA-Fugard," *Eastern Province Herald* (February 5, 1974): 4.

——. "Rise in HIV-Positive Cases," *Natal Witness* (July 30, 1996): 4.

——. "*Sarafina 2* – Next: The Video?," *Eastern Province Herald* (June 4, 1996): 4.

——. "*Sarafina 2*," *D'Arts* (December 1995–January 1996): 21.

——. "*Sarafina O*," *Daily Dispatch* (March 8, 1996): 14.

——. "*Sarafina* Shocker," *Saturday Paper* (March 30, 1996): 1.

——. "Song of dissent never finds its note of passion," *Evening Standard* (February 6, 1996).

——. "20 years' National Arts Festival," *Lantern* 43.3 (1996): 16–18.

ANSTEY, Gillian. "Suzman to do *Sharkville* in SA," *Sunday Times* (January 28, 1996): 18.

APPIAH, Kwame Anthony. *In My Father's House: Africa in the Philosophy of Culture.* New York: Oxford UP, 1992.

ARTAUD, Antonin. *The Theatre and its Double.* London: John Calder, 1970.

ARTS AND CULTURE TASK GROUP (ACTAG). *Draft Report Prepared by the ACTAG for the Ministry of Arts, Culture, Science and Technology.* Pretoria: ACTAG, 1995.

ASANTE, Molefi. *Afrocentricity.* Trenton NJ: African World Press, 1986.

ASHCROFT, Bill, Gareth GRIFFITHS & Helen TIFFIN. *The Empire Writes Back: Theory and Practice in Post-Colonial Literatures.* London: Routledge, 1989.

AUGUST, Tyrone. "Interview with Gcina Mhlophe," *Journal of Southern African Studies* 16.2 (June 1990): 329–35.

——. "Interview with Gcina Mhlophe (1993)," in *Politics and Performance: Theatre, Poetry and Song in Southern Africa*, ed. Liz Gunner (Johannesburg: Witwatersrand UP, 1994): 280–84.

BAITZ, Jon Robin. *A Fair Country.* Johannesburg: Witwatersrand UP, 1992.

BARAKA, Amiri. "'Why I changed my ideology': Black Nationalism and Socialist Revolution," *Black World* 24 (1975): 30.

BARNETT, Ursula. *A Vision of Order: A Study of Black South African Literature in English 1914–1918.* London: Sinclair Browne, 1983.

BAUER, Charlotte. "Cleopatra's reign," *Sunday Times* (July 23, 1996): 17.

BECKERMANN, Bernard. *Theatrical Representations*. London: Routledge, 1990.

BECKETT, Samuel. *Waiting for Godot*. London: Faber & Faber, 1965.

——. *Waiting for Godot*. New York: Grove, 1954.

BEHR, Mark. *The Smell of Apples*. New York: St. Martin's, 1995.

BENEDETTI, Robert. *The Actor at Work*. Englewood Cliffs NJ: Prentice–Hall, 1976.

BENNETT, Susan. "Mother Tongue: Colonized Bodies and Performing Cultures," *Contemporary Theatre Review* 2:3 (1995): 101–109.

BENTLEY, Eric, ed., tr. & intro. *Parables for the Theatre: Two Plays by Bertolt Brecht*. New York: Grove, 1961.

BERESFORD, David. "Truth hearings beginning in South Africa," *Guardian* (April 16, 1996).

BESTER, Lieske. "New look at SA history," *Cape Times* (April 8, 1996): 11.

BHABHA, Homi K. *The Location of Culture*. London & New York: Routledge, 1994.

BHARUCHA, Rustom. *Theatre and the World: Performance and the Politics of Culture*. London: Routledge, 1993.

BILLINGTON, Michael. "'The frustration of dashed dreams," *Guardian* (February 6, 1996): 2.

——. Review of *Boesman and Lena*, *Plays and Players* (September 1971): 48–49.

BLUMBERG, Marcia. "Languages of Violence: Fugard's *Boesman and Lena*," in *Violence in Drama*, ed. James Redmond (Themes in Drama series; Cambridge: Cambridge UP, 1991): 239–49.

——. "Re-Evaluating Otherness, Building for Difference: South African Theatre Beyond the Interregnum," *South African Theatre Journal* 9.2 (September 1995): 27–37.

BOAL, Augusto. *Games for Actors and Non-Actors*, tr. Adrian Jackson. London: Routledge, 1992.

BOEHMER, Elleke. *Colonial and Postcolonial Literature: Migrant Metaphors*. Oxford: Oxford UP, 1995.

BOEKKOOI, Paul. "Brecht work patchy, despite its splendour and vitality," *The Star* (July 10, 1996): 2 [Tonight].

——. "Nostalgia and progression pull Karoo crowds," *The Star* (April 8, 1996): 10 [Tonight].

BOSMAN, F.C.L. *Drama en Toneel in Suid-Afrika*, vol. 1. Cape Town: J. Dusseau, 1928.

BOTHAM, Johann. "Afrikaans gee Kleur en Konteks and *Valley*," *Beeld* (April 2, 1996).

BOYLE, Brendan. "Ngubane Backs Festival," *Cue* (July 8, 1995): 1.

BRECHT, Bertolt. *Poems 1913–1956*, ed. John Willett & Ralph Manheim, with the co-operation of Erich Fried. London: Eyre Methuen, 1976.

BREINES, Wini. *Young, White and Miserable: Growing Up Female in the Fifties*. Boston MA: Beacon, 1992.

BREYTENBACH, Breyten. "Why are Writers Always the Last to Know?," *New York Times Review of Books* (March 28, 1993): 1; 15–17.

BRISTOWE, Andrea. "Beating the Wrong Drum," *The Star* (February 1, 1996).

BRODSKI, Bella, & Celeste SCHENCK, ed. "The Other Voice," *Life/Lines: Theorizing Women's Autobiography*. Ithaca NY: Cornell UP, 1988.

BUCKLAND, Andrew. "Bloodstream," "No Easy Walk," "Between the Teeth" (unpublished MSS).

——. "The Ugly Noo Noo," in *More Market Plays*, ed. John Kani (Johannesburg: Paper Books & Ad. Donker, 1994).

BUDICK, Sanford. "Crisis of Alterity: Cultural Untranslatability and the Experience of Secondary Otherness," in *The Translatability of Cultures*, ed. Sanford Budick & Wolfgang Iser (Stanford CA: Stanford UP, 1996): 1–22.

CARTER, Chiarra. "Comedy of Bungles," *City Press* (June 9, 1966): 4.

CARTER, Gary. "In The Plush Hush of the Mainstream," *Dance Theatre Journal* 10.4 (Autumn 1993): 7–9, 53.

CHAUDHURI, Una. *Staging Place: The Geography of Modern Drama*, Ann Arbor: U of Michigan P, 1996.

CHEKHOV, Anton. *The Seagull*. Oxford: Oxford UP, 1968.

CHERNIS, Richard. "Grahamstown is a mirror of SA art," *Natal Witness* (18 July 1996): 11.

CHISHOLM, Fiona. "Reviewers' Thumbs-Down for Zuma Play," *Cape Times* (March 11, 1996): 1, 3.

COAN, Stephen. "*Sarafina*: There's Never Been a Theatrical Budget Like It," *Natal Witness* (March 5, 1996): 9.

COHEN–CRUZ, Jan. "Notes Toward an Unwritten History of Anti-Apartheid Street Performance," in *Radical Street Performance*. ed. Jan Cohen–Cruz (London: Routledge, 1998): 282–87.

COLEMAN, Carl. "No Grammy Shock for Ngema," *Daily News* (March 9, 1995): 1.

COLLERAN, Jeanne. "Athol Fugard and the Problematics of the Liberal Critique," *Modern Drama* 38.3 (Fall 1995): 389–407.

———. "Re-Situating Fugard: Re-Thinking Revolutionary Theatre," *South African Theatre Journal* 9.2 (September 1995): 39–49.

COPLAN, David B. *In Township Tonight! South Africa's Black City Music and Theatre*. London & New York: Longman, 1985.

CRESSWELL, Ryan. "Harsh facts of a land still divided," *The Star* (October 20, 1998): 1 [Tonight].

CROW, Brian. "Athol Fugard," in *Post-Colonial English Drama: Commonwealth Drama Since 1960*, ed. Bruce King (New York: St. Martin's Press, 1992): 150–64.

CULL, Patrick. "*Sarafina 2* Terminated by SA Government," *Eastern Province Herald* (June 6, 1996): 2.

DALEY, Suzanne. "'I'll have to ask my Husband," *Mail & Guardian* (October 16–22, 1998): 5.

———. "Sitcom's Ticklish Idea: Will South Africa Laugh?," *New York Times* (December 5, 1995): A5.

DANIEL, Raeford. "Finest in Years," *The Citizen* (Johannesburg; August 17, 1985).

DAVIS, Gaye. "Star Players in the Financial Flop," *Mail & Guardian* (June 7–13, 1996): 4–5.

DE BEER, Diane. "Culture blooms and grows in the desert," *The Star* (April 2, 1996): 1–2 [Tonight].

DE JAGER, E.J. *Images of Man*. Alice, S.A.: Fort Hare UP, 1992.

DELGADO, Maria M., & Paul HERITAGE. *In Contact with the Gods? Directors Talk Theatre*. Manchester: Manchester UP, 1996.

DEPARTMENT OF EDUCATION (South Africa). *Curriculum 2005: Lifelong Learning for the 21st Century*. Pretoria: Department of Education, 1977.

DIKE, Fatima. "So What's New?" in *Four Plays*, compiled & intro. Zakes Mda (Florida Hills, S.A.: Vivlia, 1996).

DLAMINI, Moses. *Hell-Hole, Robben Island: Reminiscences of a Political Prisoner*. Nottingham: Spokesman, 1984.

DRAMAIDE EASTERN CAPE. *DramAidE Eastern Cape Pilot Project: Final Report*. Grahamstown: Rhodes University, 1996.

DREWAL, Margaret Thompson. *Yoruba Ritual: Rites and Ceremonies*. African Systems of Thought Series, Bloomington: Indiana UP, 1992.

DU BOIS, Duncan. "Distorted AIDS Factor," *Natal Witness* (July 19, 1996): 10.

DUBOIS, W.E.B. "The Drama among Black Folk," *The Crisis* (August 1916): 11–14.

DURBACH, Errol. "Surviving in Xanadu: Athol Fugard's *A Lesson from Aloes*," *ARIEL: A Review of International English Literature* 20.1 (January 1989), 5–21.

ELAHIL, Nushin. "Earthy Entertainment," *The Citizen* (March 20, 1992).

FEBRUARY, Vernon A. *Mind Your Colour: The 'Coloured' Stereotype in South African Literature.* London: Kegan Paul, 1981.

FLEISHMAN, Mark. "Workshop Theatre as Oppositional Form," *South African Theatre Journal* 4.1 (1990): 88–118.

FLETCHER, Jill. "Shouts of delight echo across the Klein Karoo," *The Star* (April 2, 1996): 5 [Tonight].

———. *Story of Theatre in South Africa 1780–1930.* Cape Town: Vleeburg, 1994.

———. "They are on a high in the Klein Karoo," *Cape Times* (April 3, 1996): 13.

FLOCKEMANN, Miki. *"Have You Seen Zandile?* English or english: An Approach to Teaching Literature in Postapartheid South Africa," *AUETSA [Association of University English Teachers of Southern Africa]* (Fort Hare/Potchefstroom, 1991): 509–23.

FONTYN, Yvonne. "The world is listening to Gcina's tales," *Weekly Mail & Guardian* 10.20 (May 20–26, 1994): 36.

FREDERIKSE, Julie. *None But Ourselves: Masses vs Media in the Making of Zimbabwe.* London: Heinemann Educational, 1982.

FREGE, Ilona. "An Interview with Gary Gordon, Rhodes University, October 1994," *South African Theatre Journal* 9.2 (September 1995): 97–102.

FRIEDMAN, Hazel. "Tested, and oh so tired," *Mail & Guardian* (July 19–25, 1996): 30.

———. "Two minds meet in *Medea,*" *Mail & Guardian* (February 3–10, 1996): 30.

FUCHS, Anne. "Re-Creation: One Aspect of Oral Tradition and the Theatre in South Africa," *Commonwealth* 9.2 (1987): 32–39.

FUGARD, Athol. "The Arts Festival as healing force," *Beeld* (2 April 1996): 2 [Kalender].

———. *The Blood Knot.* New York: Samuel French, 1984.

———. *Blood Knot* [rev.ed. of *The Blood Knot*], in *Selected Plays*, ed. Dennis Walder (Oxford: Oxford UP, 1987).

———. *Boesman and Lena.* London: Oxford UP, 1973.

———. "Graduation Address, Arts Faculty Graduation, University of the Witwatersrand, 20 March 1990," in *Playland ... and Other Words.* Pretoria: Witwatersrand UP, 1992.

———. *Hello and Goodbye.* New York: Samuel French, 1971.

———. *"My Children! My Africa!" and Selected Shorter Plays.* Johannesburg: Witwatersrand UP, 1990.

———. *Notebooks 1960–1977*, ed. Mary Benson. London: Faber & Faber, 1983.

———. *Playland ... and Other Words* Johannesburg: Witwatersrand UP, 1992.

———. *The Road to Mecca.* New York: Theatre Communications Group, 1984.

———. "Some Problems of a Playwright from South Africa," *Twentieth Century Literature* 39.4 (1993: Athol Fugard issue, ed. Jack Barbera): 381–94.

———. *Valley Song.* London: Faber & Faber, 1996.

———, John Kani & Winston Ntshona. *Statements: Three Plays.* London: Oxford UP, 1974.

GATES, Jr., Henry Louis. *Loose Canons: Notes on the Culture Wars.* New York: Oxford UP, 1992.

———. "The Trope of a New Negro and the Reconstruction of the Image of the Black," *Representations* 24 (1988): 129–55.

———. "'What's Love Got To Do With It?': Critical Theory, Integrity, and the Black Idiom," *New Literary History* 18.2 (1987): 345–62.

———, & Cornel West. *The Future of the Race.* New York: Alfred A. Knopf, 1996.

GEVISSER, Mark. "'I should be paid a million Rands'," *Mail & Guardian* (March 8–14, 1996): 1, 16.

———. "Sarafina of the health system," *Mail & Guardian* (March 22–28, 1996): 14.

———. "South African Theater Faces a New World," *New York Times* (August 14, 1994): H5.

———. "South African theatre: a crisis in faith," *Weekly Mail & Guardian* 10.51 (January 5, 1995): 30, 33.

———. "Truth and Consequence in Post-Apartheid Theatre," *Theatre* 35 (1995): 9–18.

———,& Edward Cameron, ed. *Defiant Desire: Gay and Lesbian Lives in South Africa.* New York: Routledge, 1995.

GILROY, Paul. *There Ain't no Black in the Union Jack: The Cultural Politics of Race and Nation.* Chicago: U of Chicago P, 1987.

GORDIMER, Nadine. "Blacks Apart," *New York Times Magazine* (June 8, 1997): 46; 48.

GOVENDER, Ronnie. "Interview," *Cue* (July 13, 1996): 7.

GRAY, Stephen. *Southern African Literature: An Introduction.* Cape Town: David Philip, 1979.

GREIG, Robert. "Fugard by Fugard suffocates the play and shields the audience," *Sunday Independent* (Johannesburg; August 20, 1995): 21.

———. "*Medea* creates a thrilling language of passion for a new order," *Sunday Independent* (Johannesburg; February 4, 1996): 21.

———. "This black Brecht…," *Sunday Independent* (Johannesburg; July 21, 1996): 20.

GRILL, Bartholomäus. "Weimar, Soweto und zurück," *Die Zeit* (September 8, 1995): 54.

GRUNDY, Kenneth. "The politics of the National Arts Festival," Occasional Paper 34, Institute of Social and Economic Research, Rhodes University, Grahamstown, South Africa (1993).

GZOWSKI, Peter. "Gcina Mhlophe interviewed on CBC," *Morningside* (May 8, 1995): 1–6.

HANDLEY, Patricia. "The First Physical Theatre Co," *ADA* 13 (Cape Town; 1995): 55.

HARE, Nathan. "Division and Confusion: What Happened to The Black Movement," *Black World* 25 (1976): 26.

HAUPTFLEISCH, Temple. "The History of South African Theatre: An Introductory Overview of Major Trends"; unpublished MS.

———. "Syncretism, Hybridism and Crossover Theatre In a Multicultural Community: Theatre-making in (a new) South Africa," *ASSAF: Studies in Theatre*, Section C, No 8 (1992): 161–76.

———. *Theatre and Society in South Africa: Reflections in a Fractured Mirror.* Pretoria: J.L. van Schaik, 1997.

———,& Ian STEADMAN, ed. *South African Theatre: Four Plays and an Introduction.* Pretoria: HAUM Educational, 1984.

HAY, Samuel A. *African–American Theatre: A Historical and Critical Analysis.* New York: Cambridge UP, 1994.

HENRICHS, Benjamin. "Im Tal des Erstaunens," *Die Zeit* 27 (July 2, 1993): 45–46.

HILLIS MILLER, J. *The Disappearance of God.* Cambridge MA: Belknap Press of Harvard UP, 1963.

HOBSBAWM, Eric. *The Age of Extremes: The Short Twentieth Century 1914–1991.* London: Michael Joseph, 1994.

HOFMEYR, Isabel. "'Wailing for Purity': Oral Studies in Southern African Studies," *African Studies* 54.2 (1995): 16–31.

HORN, Andrew. "South African Theatre: Ideology and Rebellion," *Research in African Literatures* 17 (1986): 211–33.

HOUGH, Barrie. "Afrikaanse kuns trek al hoër," *Rapport* (April 7, 1996): 7.

———. "*Out of the Blue*: A Celebration of Eugène Marais' Love of Life" (interview with Ilse van Hemert), *Vuka* 1.7 (1995): 58–59.

IBSEN, Henrik. "A Doll's House," *The Oxford Ibsen*, vol. 5, ed. J.W. McFarlane. London: Oxford UP, 1961.

———. "The Lady from the Sea," *The Oxford Ibsen*, vol. 7, ed. J.W. McFarlane. London: Oxford UP, 1966.

ILITHA ARTS EDUCATION PROJECT. *Ilitha Arts Education Project Conference Journal*. Grahamstown: Rhodes University, 1995.

JENKINS, Marilyn. "A *Medea* for today," *The Citizen* (February 1, 1996).

JONES, Laura. *Nothing Except Ourselves: The Harsh Times and Bold Theater of South Africa's Mbongeni Ngema*. New York: Penguin, 1994.

JORDAN, Mary. "Seeking out the summer time of easy living," *Business Day* (July 9, 1996).

JOYCE, Joyce Ann. "The Black Canon: Reconstructing Black American Literary Criticism," *New Literary History* 18.2 (1987): 335–44.

———. "'Who the Cap Fit': Unconsciousness and Unconscionableness in the Criticism of Houston A. Baker, Jr. and Henry Louis Gates, Jr.," *New Literary History* 18.2 (1987): 371–84.

———. *Warriors, Conjurers and Priests: Defining African-Centered Literary Criticism*. Chicago: Third World Press, 1994.

JUNCTION AVENUE THEATRE COMPANY. *Dikitsheneng*; unpublished, 1980.

———. *Marabi*; unpublished, 1982.

———. *Security*; unpublished, 1979.

———. *Will of a Rebel*; unpublished, 1979.

KAGAN–MOORE, Patrick. "The *Zandile* Project: A Collaboration Between UT, Carpetbag Theatre, and South African Playwright Gcina Mhlophe; An Interview," *Drama Review* 34.1 (Spring 1990): 115–30.

KANDLOVU, Duma. "Let's use each other to improve," *Sowetan* (July 17, 1995): 11.

KAVANAGH, Robert (Mshengu). "Art and Revolution in South Africa: The Theatre of Athol Fugard," *The African Communist* 88 (1981): 40–53.

———. "Political Theatre in South Africa and the Work of Athol Fugard," *Theatre Research International* 7.3 (1982): 160–79.

———. *Theatre and Cultural Struggle in South Africa*. London: Zed, 1985.

KHUMALO, Reginald. "Sloppy Show Disappoints," *Natal Witness* (January 11, 1996): 7.

KLEMPERER, Margaret von. "Fun while it lasted," *The Natal Witness* (July 18, 1996): 7.

———. "*1949*," *Cue* (July 12, 1996).

———. "A score of Festival successes," *The Natal Witness* (July 11, 1994): 7.

KLETT, Renate. "The Voice of Africa – The Handspring Puppet Company liest deutsche Klassiker anders: *Woyzeck on the Highveld* und *Faustus in Africa*," *Theater heute* 36.9 (September 1995): 8–10.

KOTZE, Astrid von. *Organize and Act*. Durban: Culture and Working Life Project, 1988.

KROG, Antjie. *Country of My Skull*. Johannesburg: Random House, 1998.

KROUSE, Matthew. "Bashing it out at the Market," *Mail & Guardian* (October 9–15, 1998): 14.

———. "Fugard's Fountain of Youth," *Mail & Guardian* (August, 11, 1995): 33.

———. "Looking back in nostalgia," *Mail & Guardian* (October 6, 1995): 29.

——, ed. *The Invisible Ghetto: Lesbian and Gay Writing from South Africa.* Johannesburg: COSAW, 1993.

KRUGER, Loren. "The Drama of Modernity: Plays, Pageants and Public Spheres in 20th Century South Africa," seminar presented at Northwestern University (April 12, 1995).

——. "The Uses of Nostalgia: Drama, History and Liminal Moments in South Africa," *Modern Drama* 38 (1995): 60–70.

KUZWAYO, Ellen. *Sit Down and Listen.* Claremont, S.A.: David Philip, 1990.

LAN, David. *"Desire" and Other Plays.* London: Faber & Faber, 1990.

——. *Guns and Rain: Guerrillas and Spirit Mediums in Zimbabwe.* London: James Currey, 1985.

——. "Spirit Mediums and the Authority to Resist in the Struggle for Zimbabwe," in *Collected Seminar Papers on the Societies of Southern Africa in the 19th and 20th Centuries* (University of London, Institute of Commonwealth Studies) 13 (1984): 152–61.

LANGELLIER, Kristen M., & Eric E. PETERSON. "Spinstorying: An Analysis of Women Storytelling." *Performance, Culture, and Identity,* ed. Elizabeth C. Fine & Jean Haskell Speer (Westport CT: Praeger, 1992): 157–79.

LAUTENBACH, Dale. "An Island of Dreams," *Weekend Argus* (Cape Town; November 2, 1985).

LEWIS, Desiree. "The Politics of FEMINISM in South Africa," *Staffrider* 10.3 (1992): 15–21.

LOCKE, Alain. "Steps toward the Negro Theatre," *The Crisis* (December 1922): 66–68.

LUND, Troye. "*Sarafina 2* video goes on despite row," *The Star* (June 5, 1996): 1–2 [Tonight].

MACDONALD, Iain. "Comedy set to take centre stage at Grahamstown," *The Argus* (June 27, 1996): 8.

MACLIAM, Garalt. "It's better than a poke in the eye with a sharp stick," *The Star* (March 13, 1996: 7–8 [Tonight].

——. "It's rock, roll and bop as *Sarafina 2* Celebrates People Power in Soweto," *The Star* (March 11, 1996): 1 [Tonight].

——. "*Sharkville* gleams with jewels," *The Star* (July 18, 1996): 2 [Tonight].

——. "*A Valley* of wonderful dreams," *The Star* (August 17, 1995): 2 [Tonight].

MACMILLAN, W.M. *Bantu, Boer and Briton: The Making of the South African Native Problem.* Oxford: Clarendon, 1963.

MAKOE, Abbey. "*Sarafina* Not a Total Sham, But Waste of R14-m," *The Argus* (March 11, 1996): 3.

MANAKA, Matsemela. *Egoli: City of Gold.* Johannesburg: Soyikwa–Ravan, 1990.

——. "Some Thoughts On Black Theatre," *English Academy Review* 2 (1984): 33–39.

MANDELA, Nelson. *Long Walk to Freedom: The Autobiography.* Boston MA & London: Little, Brown, 1994.

MAPONYA, Maishe. "The Hungry Earth," in *South African Theatre: Four Plays and an Introduction,* ed. Ian Steadman & Temple Hauptfleisch (Pretoria: HAUM Educational, 1984): 140–65.

——. "New Challenges Facing Theatre Practitioners in the New South Africa," in *Writing South Africa: Literature, Apartheid, and Democracy, 1970–1995.* ed. Derek Attridge & Rosemary Jolly (Cambridge: Cambridge UP, 1998): 249–56.

MASEKO, Sifiso. "Theatre to the people," *Electronic Mail & Guardian* (October 2, 1997).

MASHEGO, Mojalefa. "*Sarafina II* not the best medium for AIDS Issue," *Sowetan* (March 11, 1996): 15.

MCGANN, Jerome. *The Beauty of Inflections: Literary Investigations in Historical Method and Theory.* Oxford: Clarendon, 1988.

McLUCKIE, Craig W. "Power, Self and Other: The Absurd in *Boesman and Lena*," *Twentieth Century Literature* 39.4 (1993): 423–29.

MDA, Zakes. "Introduction: An Overview of Theatre in South Africa," in Zakes Mda, *Four Plays* (Florida Hills, S.A.: Vivlia, 1996): vi–xxvi.

——. "Theatre and Reconciliation in South Africa," *Theatre* 35 (1995): 38–45.

MEMELA, S. "Comment on the Fest," *Sunday Tribune* (July 14, 1996): 11, 22.

MENDEL, Delores. "Mbongeni Ngema," *Club* (April 1990): 18–19.

METSOAMERE, Victor. "Ngema Does it by Ear," *Sowetan* (February 10, 1995): 8.

MHLOPHE, Gcina, Maralin VANRENEN & Thembi MTSHALI. *Have You Seen Zandile?* London: Heinemann/Methuen, 1988.

MONDEAR, Joseph. "'Slight and trivial message' woven into *Sarafina 2* production," *The Star* (March 26, 1996): 16 [Tonight].

MTWA, Percy, Mbongeni NGEMA & Barney SIMON. *Woza Albert!*. London: Methuen Drama, 1983.

MUDIMBE, Valentin. *The Invention of Africa: Gnosis, Philosophy and the Order of Knowledge.* Bloomington & Indianapolis: Indiana UP, 1988.

MUIR, David. *Road to the Stamping Ground*. NOS–TV Holland & Polygon Pictures, RM ARTS, 1984.

MUNRO, Allan. "Reflections on South African theatre and performance: Commentary on the Standard Bank Arts Festival Grahamstown, 1995," *Word and Action* (Potchefstroom) 353 (Spring 1995): 23–28.

MURPHY, Mark. "A Conversation with Athol Fugard," Audience Guide, McCarter Theater, Princeton NJ, 1995.

NAIDOO, Jay. *Tracking Down Historical Myths: Eight South African Cases*. Johannesburg: Ad. Donker, 1989.

NATIONAL EDUCATION AND TRAINING FORUM. *Guide to Speech and Drama Syllabus: Standards 8, 9, 10 (Grades 10, 11, 12)*. Pretoria: NEFT, 1994.

NDEBELE, Mfundo. "Festival still the same," *Sunday Tribune* (July 14, 1996): 11.

NEAL, Larry. "The Black Arts Movement," *Drama Review* 12.4 (1968): 29–39.

——. "The Black Contribution to American Letters, Part II: The Writer as Activist – 1960 and After," in *The Black American Reference Book*, ed. Mabel M. Smythe (Englewood Cliffs NJ: Prentice–Hall, 1976): 783–84.

NGEMA, Mbongeni. *The Best of Mbongeni Ngema*. Braamfontein: Skotaville, 1995.

NGEMA, Vusi. "Musical Which Tackles AIDS But Desperately Seeks a Story," *Natal Witness* (January 6, 1996): 7.

NGIDI, Thami. "'The Show Will Go On'," *Saturday Paper* (March 9, 1996): 4.

NIETZSCHE, Friedrich. *On the Advantage and Disadvantage of History for Life*, tr. Peter Preuss. Indianapolis: Hackett, 1980.

NIXON, Rob. *Homelands, Harlem, and Hollywood*. New York: Routledge, 1995.

NOOTER, Mary H. *Secrecy: African Art that Conceals and Reveals*. New York: Museum of African Art, 1993.

NORVAL, P. "Woema Kort," *Beeld* (July 14, 1996): 11.

NYATSUMBA, Kaizer. "They Take the Cake," *Argus* (13 March 1996): 18; repr. as "The Truth Will Soon Out," *Daily News* (March 14, 1996): 18.

OPPERMAN, Deon. "Toekoms van die teater lê by die kunstefees," *Beeld* (April 2, 1996): 4 [Kalender].

ORKIN, Martin. *Drama and the South African State.* Manchester & New York: Manchester UP, 1991.

——. ed. & intro. *At the Junction: Four Plays by the Junction Avenue Theatre Company.* Johannesburg: Witwatersrand UP, 1995.

PARELES, Jon. "A Parable of Lovers' Quest In Today's South Africa," *New York Times* (April 22, 1996): C 11, 13.

PAVIS, Patrice. *L'analyse de spectacles.* Paris: Nathan, 1996.

——. *Theatre at the Crossroads of Culture.* London: Routledge, 1994.

PEARCE, Justin. "*Medea*'s angry resonant noise," *Weekly Mail & Guardian* (October 28–November 3, 1994).

——. "Visions of a rainbow culture," *Mail & Guardian* (July 21–27, 1995): 28.

PETERSON, Bhekizizwe. "'A rain a fall but the dirt it tough': Scholarship on African Theatre in South Africa," *Journal of Southern African Studies* 21.4 (1995): 573–84.

PHELAN, Peggy. *Unmarked: The Politics of Peformance.* London: Routledge, 1993.

PRESS, Wolfgang. "Was sucht Faust eigentlich in Afrika?" (interview with William Kentridge), *Frankfurter Allgemeine Zeitung* (November 21, 1995): B3.

PRIGGE, Lanon. "An Interview with Adrienne Sichel," *Physical Intelligence* 1 (June 1996): 4–5.

PURKEY, Malcolm. "*Tooth and Nail*: Rethinking Form for the South African Theatre," in *Theatre and Change in South Africa,* ed. Geoffrey V. Davis & Anne Fuchs (Amsterdam: Harwood Academic, 1996): 155–72.

——, & Pippa STEIN. *Sophiatown.* Johannesburg: Witwatersrand UP, 1988.

RAMKLOWN, Annesh. "Ngema's Latest *Sarafina* a Dismal Failure," *Natal Witness Echo* (January 11, 1996): 5.

RAYMOND, Gerrard. "A Lesson from Athol." *Stagebill: The Kennedy Center* (September 1998): 14, 21–23.

REPUBLIC OF SOUTH AFRICA. *White Paper on Education and Training, Government Gazette* 357.16312, Notice no. 196 of 1995. Pretoria: Department of Education, 1995.

RICCIO, Thomas. "Emandulo: Process and Performance in a Changing South Africa," *Theatre Research International* 19.3 (1994): 238–61.

ROBBINS, David. "Experts slam AIDS play," *The Star* (March 11, 1966): 1 [Tonight].

RODWELL, Bobby. "Gcina Mhlophe," *Speak* 37 (1991): 6–8.

ROSENWALD, Peter. "Separate Fables." *The Guardian* (January 8, 1974): 10.

ROY, Christopher. "Dance of the Spirits," in *Art and Death in Africa.* School of Art and Art History, U of Iowa P, 1988.

——. "Yaaba Soore: The Path of the Ancestors," in *Art and Death in Africa.* School of Art and Art History, U of Iowa P, 1986.

RUBADIRI, David, ed. *Growing Up with African Poetry: An Anthology for Secondary Schools.* Houghton, S.A.: Heinemann, 1989.

SACHS, Albie. "Preparing ourselves for freedom," in *Spring is Rebellious: Arguments About Cultural Freedom by Albie Sachs and Respondents,* ed. Ingrid de Kok & Karen Press (Cape Town: Buchu, 1990): 19–29.

SAID, Edward W. *Culture and Imperialism.* New York: Random House/Vintage, 1994.

SALTER, Dennis. "*When People Play People* in (Post) Apartheid South Africa: The Theories and Practices of Zakes Mda," *Brecht Yearbook/Das Brecht-Jahrbuch* 22 (1997): 283–303.

SCHMIDT, Klaus. *Inculturation in Malawi.* Munich: MISSIO München, 1994.

SCOTT, John. "*Sarafina 2*'s New Wisecracking Star," *Cape Times* (March 13, 1996): 16.

SEIDMAN, Gay, David MARTIN & Phyllis JOHNSON, ed. *Zimbabwe: A New History.* Harare: Zimbabwe Publishing House, 1982.

SEYMOUR, Hilary, "*Sizwe Bansi is Dead*: A Study of Artistic Ambivalence," *Race & Class* 21.3 (1980): 273–89.

SHERRIFFS, Pamela. "AIDS: It's Too Costly to Play Around," *Natal Witness* (March 1, 1966): 15.

SICHEL, Adrienne. "African artists draw on their heritage to break barriers," *The Star* (July 17, 1996): 3 [Tonight].

———. "Furious Fusions," *The Star* (February 1, 1996): 3 [Tonight].

———. "Getting physical with the classics," *The Star* (October 17, 1994) [Tonight].

SIDLEY, Pat. "AIDS Spreads as Money Lies Idle," *Sunday Times* (June 9, 1996): 4.

SIMON, Barney, et al. "Born in the RSA," in *Woza Africa*, ed. Duma Ndlovu (New York: George Braziller, 1986): 129–76.

SIMON, Janine. "Puppet players query *Sarafina* costs," *The Star* (March 1, 1996): 1–2 [Tonight].

SITHOLE, Nokwanda. "Once Upon a Time," *Tribute* (November 1989): 18–21.

SMALL, Adam. "Interview," *Beeld* (April 2, 1996): 23 [Kalender].

SNOWDEN, Jr., Frank M. "Bernal's 'Blacks,' Herodotus, and other Classical Evidence," *Arethusa* (Special Issue, 1989): 283–93.

SPARKS, Allister. *Tomorrow is Another Country: The Inside Story of South Africa's Negotiated Revolution.* London: Heinemann, 1995.

SPIVAK, Gayatri Chakravorty. *The Post-Colonial Critic: Interviews, Strategies, Dialogues*, ed. Sara Harasym. London & New York: Routledge, 1990.

SPRATT, Betsy. "The Kids Liked It But Did It Teach Them Anything About AIDS?," *Sunday Independent* (March 10, 1996): 1.

STAUNTON, Irene, ed. *Mothers of the Revolution.* Harare: Baobab, 1990.

STEADMAN, Ian, "Drama and Social Consciousness: Themes in Black Theatre on the Witwatersrand Until 1984." PhD dissertation, University of the Witwatersrand, 1985.

———. "Theatre Beyond Apartheid," *Research in African Literatures* 22.3 (1991): 77–90.

STEINBERG, Carol, & Malcolm PURKEY. "South African Theatre in Crisis," *Theatre* 35 (1995): 24–37.

STRAUSS, G. "Die Klein Karoo Kunstefees," *Beeld* (April 2, 1996): 4 [Kalender].

STUART, Sapa, & Brian STUART. "Call for *Sarafina II* Probe," *The Citizen* (February 29, 1996): 1–2.

SUBIOTTO, Arrigo. "Epic Theatre: A Theatre for the Scientific Age," in *Brecht in Perspective*, ed. Graham Bartram & Anthony Waine (London: Longman, 1987): 30–44.

TAYLOR, Paul. Review of Athol Fugard's *Valley Song*, *The Independent* (February 8, 1996).

TIVONELENI VAVASATI AIDS AWARENESS PROJECT. "Ministry's Musical Should Sing a New Song," *Mail & Guardian* (February 23–29, 1996): 28.

TREWIN, J.C. *Peter Brook: A Biography.* London: MacDonald, 1971.

TYLER, Humphrey. "Slouching towards Grahamstown," *Sunday Tribune* (June 4, 1996): 17 [Sunday Magazine].

UKPOKODU, Peter. "'Lest one good custom should corrupt the world': African Theatre and the 'Holy' Canon," *South African Theatre Journal* 9.2 (September 1995): 3–25.

UYS, Pieter–Dirk. "On a penny and a poep," *Mail & Guardian* (July 10, 1996): 4–5.

VAN DER WALT, Terry, & Sam SOLE. "Ngema's Tender Touch," *Sunday Tribune* (February 11, 1996): 1, 5.

VANDENBROUCKE, Russell. *Truths the Hand Can Touch: The Theatre of Athol Fugard.* New York: Theatre Communications Group, 1985.

VANDERHAEGHEN, Yves. "The Play that Shamed the ANC," *Natal Witness* (July 11, 1996): 6.

VOGEL, Susan, & Francine N'DIAYE. *African Masterpieces.* New York: Center for African Art, 1985.

WALDER, Dennis. *Athol Fugard.* Basingstoke: Macmillan, 1984.

——. *Athol Fugard: The Township Plays.* Oxford & Cape Town: Oxford UP, 1993.

——. "'My English Name is Patience': Mediating the Voice of the Other in South African Theatre Today" (1993); unpublished MS.

——. "Presentation of Gcina Mhlophe for an honorary degree of Doctor of the Open University" (April 1994); unpublished MS.

——. "Resituating Fugard: South African Drama as Witness," *New Theatre Quarterly* 32 (November 1992): 343–61.

——. "South African Drama and Ideology: The Case of Athol Fugard," in *Altered State? Writing and South Africa*, ed. Elleke Boehmer, Laura Chrisman & Kenneth Parker (Mundelstrup/ Sydney: Dangaroo, 1994): 121–35.

WATTS, Jane. *Black Writers from South Africa: Towards a Discourse of Liberation.* London: Macmillan, 1989.

WERTHEIM, Albert. "Fest frees up South Africa," *Cue* (July 12, 1996): 7.

WILLOUGHBY, Guy. "They say it has no soul: What's happened to the Fest?," *Sunday Tribune* (July 14, 1996): 11.

——. "Total onslaught of the arts," *Weekly Mail & Guardian* (—, 1995): —.

WORKSHOP '71. *Survival: South African People's Plays*, sel. & intro. Robert Kavanagh. London: Heinemann, 1981.

WRIGHT, Harrison M. *The Burden of the Present: Liberal–Radical Controversy over Southern African History.* Cape Town: David Philip, 1977.

ZAVIS, Alexandra. "South Africa's Post Apartheid," *Electronic Associated Press* (August 16, 1997).

—— ℬ ℭ ——

Contributors

David Alcock is an award-winning actor and director who also teaches – most recently as Guest Lecturer in the Drama Department, Rhodes University. He has performed extensively for the Baxter Theatre, and the former Cape Performing Arts Board, and has appeared at the Market Theatre. Since 1997 he has acted in many productions in England.

Michael Arthur is a doctoral candidate at the University of Texas at Austin, where he is completing a dissertation on "South African Theatre of Transition." He has published articles and presented conference papers on contemporary theatre, and is the immediate past editor of *Theatre InSight*.

Yvonne Banning is Lecturer in Drama at the University of Cape Town. Formerly a South African Broadcasting Company television producer, she is the author of several articles on contemporary South African theatre.

Hazel Barnes is Associate Professor in the Drama Studies Department of the University of Natal, Pietermaritzburg, where she has directed numerous student productions over the last twenty years. She has a particular interest in the use of educational drama in therapeutic situations, and is currently compiling an anthology of plays by South African women.

Marcia Blumberg is Visiting Research Fellow at the Open University, UK, attached to the Post-Colonial Literatures Research Group. In 1996 she organized the international conference "South African Theatre As/And Intervention," and is currently completing a book, *Engendering Intervention in Contemporary South African Theatre*. She has published widely on contemporary drama, in particular on representations of AIDS, and on South African theatre.

Eckhard Breitinger, Professor of African Studies at Bayreuth University, has taught at several African universities and is the author and editor of books on American radio drama, African literature, and African theatre.

Michael Carklin, who lectures in the Drama Department, Rhodes University, was chairperson of the Southern African Association for Drama and Youth Theatre during 1996–1997 and director of the Ilitha Arts Education project, 1995–1997. He has recently completed his second MA (at the School of Oriental and African Studies, University of London).

Jeanne Colleran is Chair of the English Department at John Carroll University, Cleveland, Ohio. In addition to writing numerous articles on contemporary theatre and fiction, she is co-editor, with Jenny Spencer, of *Staging Resistance: Essays on Political Theatre* (U of Michigan P, 1998).

Annette Combrinck is Professor and Head of the Department of English Language and Literature at Potchefstroom University. She has completed a major research project on South African English drama, and has published articles on contemporary South African theatre.

Errol Durbach is Associate Dean of Arts and Professor of Theatre and English at the University of British Columbia, where he teaches theatre history and comparative drama. His publications include *Ibsen the Romantic, A Doll's House: Ibsen's Myth of Transformation*, and numerous articles, including several on Athol Fugard.

Anne Fuchs was Senior Lecturer and Head of the Drama Department at the University of Nice–Sophia Antipolis. Her publications include *Playing the Market: The Market Theatre Johannesburg 1976–1986* (1992), and *Theatre and Change in South Africa* (co-edited with Geoffrey V. Davis, 1996). She now divides her time between Nice and her home town of Birmingham, England; she is currently preparing a revised edition of *Playing the Market*, and a book on Indian theatre in Britain.

Robert Leyshon has taught in London and Cambridge, and is currently Lecturer in Drama and Theatre Arts at the University of the West Indies (Barbados) and Artistic Director of Cave Hill Theatre Workshop. Directorial credits include Ibsen's *An Enemy of the People*, Ariel Dorfman's *Death and the Maiden*, and the world premiere of *Ja Ja: King of Opobo*, by Alvin Cummins.

Bernth Lindfors is a Professor of English and African Literatures at the University of Texas at Austin. He has written and edited numerous books on African writing, the latest being *Conversations with Chinua Achebe* (University of Mississippi Press, 1997) and *African Textualities: Texts, Pre-Texts and Contexts of African Literature* (Africa World Press, 1997). For twenty years he edited *Research in African Literatures*, a quarterly journal founded by him in 1970.

Kristina Stanley is a doctoral candidate at the University of Illinois, Urbana–Champaign, where she is writing on "Identity and Recognition in Fugard's Post-Apartheid Theatre." She has also directed several of Fugard's plays, including *The Island, Statements After An Arrest Under the Immorality Act, The Road to Mecca*, and the US premiere of *Dimetos*.

Ian Steadman was the Skye Professor of Dramatic Art at the University of the Witwatersrand. His work on South African Theatre has appeared in such journals as *Research in African Literatures, Journal of Southern African Studies*, and *Theatre Sur-*

vey. He was founding co-editor, with Temple Hauptfleisch, of the *South African Theatre Journal.* He is also a professional actor and director, and is currently Director of the Witwatersrand University Foundation.

Dennis Walder is Head of the Department of Literature and director of the Post-Colonial Literatures Research Group at the Open University, UK. He has published numerous articles and books on nineteenth- and twentieth-century literature. Author of the first book-length study of Athol Fugard (1984), he has also edited three volumes of Fugard's plays for Oxford University Press. His latest book is *Post-Colonial Literatures in English* (Basil Blackwell, 1998).

Toby Silverman Zinman teaches at the University of the Arts in Philadelphia, where she is both Professor of English and Dramaturg for the School of Theatre. She writes and lectures widely on contemporary drama, and by night she is the theatre critic for Philadelphia's *City Paper*, a reviewer for *Variety*, and a feature writer for *American Theatre* magazine.

Index

SELECTED TITLE INDEX

—— ജ ය ——